Regulatory Breakdown

Regulatory Breakdown

The Crisis of Confidence in U.S. Regulation

Edited by
Cary Coglianese

PENN

UNIVERSITY OF PENNSYLVANIA PRESS

PHILADELPHIA

Published by
University of Pennsylvania Press
Philadelphia, Pennsylvania 19104-4112

Printed in the United States of America on acid-free paper
10 9 8 7 6 5 4 3 2 1

Library of Congress Cataloging-in-Publication Data
Regulatory breakdown : the crisis of confidence in U.S. regulation / edited by Cary Coglianese.
        p. cm.
    ISBN 978-0-8122-4460-1 (hardcover : alk. paper)
    Includes bibliographical references and index.
    1. Trade regulation—United States—Evaluation.   2. Trade regulation—Political aspects—United States.   3. Consumer protection—Political aspects—United States.   4. Consumer protection—Law and legislation—United States.
5. Independent regulatory commissions—United States—Evaluation.
I. Coglianese, Cary.
KF1600 .R437   2012
343.7308   2012013168

Contents

Preface

Has the United States suffered a regulatory breakdown? The answer to this question would appear to be an obvious "yes." Times have been especially tough over the past several years, and virtually every account of the nation's woes places considerable blame on regulation. One might even say that criticism of regulation has become one of the rare commonalities between Democrats and Republicans—although their respective critiques differ profoundly. For those on the left, the United States never would have suffered calamities such as the financial crisis or the Gulf Coast oil spill had regulatory standards been more stringent or had regulators kept from falling asleep at the switch. For those on the political right, the country never would have suffered such deep and sustained economic problems had burdensome regulations—in particular, uncertainty over new regulations—not stifled the business risk-taking needed to jumpstart economic growth. Whichever account is correct—and perhaps both have merit—U.S. regulation clearly suffers a deep crisis of confidence. Government has become less trusted and politics more polarized, with debates over regulatory policy readily devolving into highly charged ideological disputes.

In such a heated political climate, academic research on regulation can make a valuable contribution. If policymakers hope to fix what ails the U.S. system of regulation, they need to do more than just act on hunches or respond to hasty conclusions. They need to understand problems as fully as possible and discover the causes that underlie those problems. Regulatory failures, after all, can arise for a variety of reasons, with triggering factors occurring at one or more stages of the regulatory process. Failures may occur because problematic activities or behaviors have remained unregulated when they should have been regulated. Or they may occur because relevant activity was regulated but with the wrong kind of rules. The process of creating the rules might well have broken down through ignorance, ideology, delay, or corruption. Another possibility is that the rules and the processes that generated them may have been appropriate but the monitoring and enforcement of those rules may have been insufficient—or, alternatively, much too overbearing. What we need is further research and careful analysis to disentangle the possible causes of regulatory failure, help identify appropriate policy responses, and assess whether reforms actually work.

The chapters assembled in this book provide much-needed scholarly perspective on recent controversies over regulation in the United States. Written by some of the nation's foremost experts in law, economics, political science, and public policy, the chapters dig beneath the surface-level diagnoses that have tended to dominate policy deliberations. In Chapter 1, Chris Carrigan and I explain how psychological and political factors have contributed to the current crisis of confidence over regulation, as politicians and the public naturally seek something to blame when calamities occur. We caution against leaping to the conclusion that regulation has failed whenever disaster occurs. Regulation manages risk; it cannot purport to eliminate it altogether, unless of course a risky business activity is banned outright. Accordingly, when a disaster occurs it may not necessarily reflect the failure of regulation as much as the tragic but rare and inevitable consequence of a regulatory policy that responds to and makes tradeoffs in society's competing values.

Effective risk regulation is not a one-size-fits-all proposition, as W. Kip Viscusi and Richard Zeckhauser remind us in Chapter 2. Disasters arise out of complex social interactions that have varying causes, victims, losses, and compensation challenges. Regulatory policies directed at different types of catastrophes must also necessarily be varied and at times complex. Invoking a range of examples in their chapter, Viscusi and Zeckhauser offer an accessible but rigorous framework for identifying successful regulatory responses to the problem of catastrophic risk. They urge the adoption of a portfolio approach that searches for an optimal deployment of market and tax incentives, ex post liability, and preventive regulation. For high-stakes risks such as those associated with nuclear power generation or deepwater oil drilling, they favor holding all firms engaged in risky operations strictly liable for damages after a catastrophe arises. They also believe firms should be required to demonstrate substantial financial resources—assets plus insurance—to cover most levels of potential harms. Firms should also face an up-front tax, before any accident occurs, for the expected excess costs of extreme catastrophes, that is, harms that would exceed their ability to pay. Such a tax would provide firms an immediate and continuous incentive to operate safely.

Viscusi and Zeckhauser's chapter provides a broad theoretical framework not only for identifying successful regulatory solutions but also for situating the next three chapters of the book, each of which zeroes in on a specific regulatory crisis: the Gulf Coast oil spill, the mortgage meltdown, and the financial crisis. In Chapter 3, Lori Bennear carefully analyzes the environmental and safety risks from offshore drilling in the wake of the Gulf Coast spill, showing how the current regulatory approach fails to address human factors that cut across the technological redundancies mandated by current rules. Bennear compares the regulatory status quo with two alternative strategies, one that requires firms to develop detailed management systems and the other that would require drilling firms to pay "safety deposits" that would provide meaningful, new incentives for firms to implement effective risk management.

In Chapter 4, Adam Levitin and Susan Wachter place the recent home mortgage crisis in historical context, arguing that the latest crisis emerged as a result of the unsynchronized development of the housing finance market and the regulatory structure overseeing that market. After tracing market and regulatory conditions from before the Great Depression to the present day, Levitin and Wachter suggest that successful regulation of housing finance requires either strong federal institutions that dominate the market or robust regulation of private market actors. Following the Great Depression, the United States built a mortgage market based on dominant governmental institutions, displacing the need for conventional forms of regulation. Yet as this public model broke down in the latter part of the last century, with the widespread emergence of private securitization in the secondary markets, the conventional regulatory model failed to return to take the place of the institutions.

Roberta Romano, in Chapter 5, looks closely at the recent financial crisis and the principal regulatory response to it, the Dodd-Frank Act. Romano explains that Congress's sense of a need to "do something" in the wake of a financial crisis has, both recently and in the past, resulted in legislation that increases costs and uncertainty for business without necessarily generating corresponding tangible benefits for the overall economy. In situations of crisis-driven legislation, she proposes that Congress incorporate into its statutes sunset provisions that would automatically force the evaluation and reconsideration of legislation after the crises subside. She also recommends legislative provisions that would give the agencies implementing such legislation the authority to grant waivers and introduce elements of flexibility and experimentation.

Romano's chapter shows how political factors can lead economic and natural crises to become regulatory ones, not only by contributing to the perception that regulation must have failed when disaster occurs but also by prompting the hasty adoption of "solutions" that later can result in other problems. In Chapter 6, Matthew Baum examines another major political force—ideology—and considers how the media reinforce the extreme ideological polarization that surrounds regulatory policy debates in Washington, D.C. Focusing on media coverage of the healthcare reform debate, Baum argues that the nation's ideological divide over regulatory issues derives in part from the breakdown of a shared informational environment that once existed in American mass media. The media balkanization revealed by Baum's data, a predicament characterized by Republicans and Democrats relying on different news sources that tend to reinforce their ideological predispositions, makes it more difficult to achieve agreement over both regulatory diagnoses and policy prescriptions.

Jonathan Baron and his coauthors, in Chapter 7, consider a further political factor affecting government's ability to craft successful regulatory policy, namely, the preferences of the public. Reporting results from four experimental surveys, Baron and his collaborators show that citizens generally do not appreciate the advantages that economists have attributed to various market-based regulatory innovations. The public instead tends to view regulatory policy in simple, moralistic terms. If something is deemed to be bad, it should be banned. Yet if effective regulatory policy requires adopting complex solutions that are adapted to complex problems, as Viscusi and Zeckhauser posit in Chapter 2, then democratically elected decision makers will face public pressure to eschew the very kinds of policies that are most likely to succeed. Perhaps regulatory failure is at least partly a price paid for democratic responsiveness.

Chapters 8 and 9 consider a further possible factor affecting regulatory performance, namely, the legal procedures imposed upon regulators. Many observers have claimed that the steady accretion of procedural hoops in the regulatory process prevents officials from addressing problems quickly and responding to potential threats before they arise. Jason Webb Yackee and Susan Webb Yackee consider this popular diagnosis of regulatory breakdown in Chapter 8—and they find the evidence wanting. Drawing on an empirical analysis of rulemaking by all federal agencies since 1983, they see no indication that regulatory agencies are systematically hampered by the procedures that have been placed upon them.

Susan Moffitt, in Chapter 9, considers whether the procedures governing the Food and Drug Administration help or hinder the agency's mission of improving the safety of pharmaceuticals. Moffitt suggests that drugs do suffer fewer safety problems if they have been adopted following consultation with an expert advisory committee, especially under procedures that screen committee members for conflicts of interest. However, she also finds that statutory deadlines for drug reviews make it less likely that agency officials will consult an advisory committee for expert advice. Analyses such as Moffitt's in Chapter 9 and Yackee and Yackee's in Chapter 8 reveal that procedures, much like other potential causes of regulatory failure, play a more nuanced role in explaining regulatory performance than conventionally assumed.

One of the distinctive features of the U.S. regulatory system is the way it overlays and interacts with a common law system based on judicial resolution of private litigation. Litigation brought by private actors continues to coexist with the work of federal regulatory agencies—at times complementing and at times undercutting regulatory policy. William Bratton and Michael Wachter, in Chapter 10, focus on a peculiar feature of U.S. securities regulation that authorizes enforcement of antifraud provisions by private actors through class action lawsuits. Bratton and Wachter show that this system of private enforcement is itself widely judged to have broken down, becoming little more than an insider game that mainly advantages plaintiffs' lawyers at the expense of shareholders without delivering much in the way of broader benefits. The better approach, they argue, would be to eliminate the traditional private enforcement route and instead vest responsibility for antifraud enforcement fully with the Securities and Exchange Commission, greatly expanding its enforcement budget.

Eric Helland and Jonathan Klick, in Chapter 11, entertain the possibility that private litigation helps check the dangers of regulatory capture, a source of perennial concern about the corruption of purpose in regulation. Using data they collected on both state insurance regulation and class action lawsuits over insurance, Helland and Klick fail to find support for a reliance on litigation as a check on regulatory capture. The states with insurance agencies least susceptible to capture—those with elected rather than appointed officials—also tend to have the most class action litigation. Helland and Klick's analysis suggests that regulation and litigation, rather than working in a coordinated fashion, actually operate as two independent systems in the United States, greatly complicating any effort to ensure that their combined impacts achieve optimal outcomes for society.

The overarching questions linking the chapters in this volume— namely, whether the regulatory system has systematically broken down and, if so, how to fix it—are premised on the existence of regulations on the books that at least ostensibly aim to solve major societal problems. Certainly the U.S. government has plenty of such regulations on its books, so most of the time the key issue is whether those rules are optimally designed and effectively enforced. Yet in the final chapter of this book, Theodore Ruger offers the fitting and important reminder that a regulatory system can fail through *inaction* as much as through ill-designed or ineffective action. Some of the most significant problems facing society, Ruger suggests, are those that remain unregulated. In the context of food and drug policy, the particular setting he emphasizes, the most pressing public health issues, such as obesity and the affordability of medicines, remain entirely outside the purview of the Food and Drug Administration's existing statutory authority.

Whether failure arises from action or inaction, making regulation work better stands as one of the most significant challenges of our time. The current crisis over the U.S. regulatory system draws into stark relief the stakes involved and the important demands that society places upon regulation. Perhaps in some cases society's demands are unrealistic, such as when the public expects regulation to be able to accommodate both unfettered economic risk taking and at the same time to provide absolute safety from harm. But certainly it is not unrealistic to ask that regulation today work better than it did yesterday and to hope that regulation tomorrow will respond to new problems more effectively than it does to those of today.

Achieving even realistic improvements in regulatory problems still presents major challenges and requires vast information and deep understanding. Regulation is a human institution, built on ideas and implemented within complex webs of institutions and individuals. To regulate well, policymakers must come to grips with the varied and complex technological, economic, and social realms within which regulation struggles to make a difference. Yet our knowledge about how regulation operates remains woefully undersupplied relative both to the stakes and to other fields of study. More academic research like that assembled within the pages of this volume is greatly needed, for without careful analysis and empirical inquiry policymakers have nothing other than instincts and ideologies to inform their judgments. Of course, we cannot expect to replace instinct and ideology entirely. Certainly no single academic study—nor even a single book with work by excellent scholars—can be expected to bridge the political divide in the United States. But greater research can help, especially when—as occurs more often than we might admit—what appear to be ideological disputes are actually disputes over empirical claims rather than genuine moral differences.

When a car stalls on the freeway, the driver and passengers can get out and debate all they want about what broke and how to fix it. Yet the only way to find out with any certainty what went wrong is for knowledgeable people to look under the hood and get their hands dirty. The same is true when we think regulation has broken down.

Cary Coglianese

Chapter 1

Oversight in Hindsight
Assessing the U.S. Regulatory System in the Wake of Calamity

Christopher Carrigan and Cary Coglianese

The first decade of the twenty-first century concluded, and the second decade began, with the United States having experienced one of the worst economic upheavals in its history as well as one of the worst environmental disasters in its history. These calamities, combined with a series of other major industrial accidents as well as a deep recession and sluggish economic recovery, have cast grave doubts over the adequacy of the nation's regulatory system. In the wake of each calamity, politicians and members of the public have attributed much of the blame to a general breakdown in the U.S. regulatory system.[1] The various investigative reports that followed the century's early disasters, for example, only reinforced this view of systemic regulatory failure:

- In response to the subprime mortgage crisis that started in late 2007, the Financial Crisis Inquiry Commission's majority report accused federal regulators of "pervasive permissiveness." The report's authors argued that "little meaningful action was taken to quell . . . threats in a timely manner," singling out "the Federal Reserve's pivotal failure to stem the flow of toxic mortgages . . . by setting prudent mortgage-lending standards" (National Commission on the Causes of the Financial and Economic Crisis in the United States 2011:xvii).[2]
- Six months after the 2010 explosion on the BP-leased *Deepwater Horizon* drilling rig, which killed eleven crew members and caused nearly five million barrels of oil to spill into the Gulf of Mexico, the federal investigating commission pointed to "decades of inadequate regulation"

as a critical cause (National Commission on the BP *Deepwater Horizon* Oil Spill and Offshore Drilling [hereafter abbreviated as the Oil Spill Commission] 2011:56). The Commission's report characterized the Minerals Management Service as "an agency systematically lacking the resources, technical training, or experience . . . to ensur[e] that offshore drilling is being conducted in a safe and responsible manner. For a regulatory agency to fall so short of its essential safety mission is inexcusable" (Oil Spill Commission 2011:57).

- After the worst mine disaster in the United States since 1970 killed twenty-nine miners, the Governor's Independent Investigation Panel concluded that the 2010 explosion at the Upper Big Branch Mine in West Virginia "is proof positive that the [Mine Safety and Health Administration] failed its duty as the watchdog for coal miners" (Governor's Independent Investigation Panel 2011:77).
- Following a 2010 explosion of a natural gas pipeline in California that killed eight people, injured several dozens more, and destroyed or damaged over one hundred homes, the National Transportation Safety Board determined that the energy company had "for years . . . exploited weaknesses in a lax system of oversight," one in which regulators had "placed a blind trust in the companies that they were charged with overseeing to the detriment of public safety" (National Transportation Safety Board 2011:135).

When so many diagnoses all share the common thread of regulatory failure, it is no surprise to see increasing appeals for regulatory change, some of which have already resulted in the adoption of new regulatory statutes as well as internal administrative reforms. Following the BP oil spill, for example, the Department of the Interior imposed a temporary moratorium on offshore drilling, closed its Minerals Management Service (MMS), and transferred regulatory authority to a new Bureau of Ocean Energy Management, Regulation, and Enforcement (U.S. Secretary of the Interior 2010). Responding to the financial crisis, Congress passed the Dodd-Frank Wall Street Reform and Consumer Protection Act of 2010, giving extensive new responsibilities to banking and other financial regulators, as well as creating a new agency with substantial regulatory authority, the Consumer Financial Protection Bureau (Dodd-Frank Act 2010). Adopted along a rather sharp party-line vote, the Dodd-Frank Act remains controversial, with the Republican-controlled House of Representatives in 2011 passing a bill to repeal the Act. Yet notwithstanding fierce partisan wrangling in Washington over both regulatory and nonregulatory issues, Republicans and Democrats have come together to enact other regulatory statutes in the wake of calamities. The nationwide recall of eggs stemming from an outbreak of *Salmonella* in August 2010 helped generate bipartisan support for passage of the Food Safety and Modernization Act (2011). By late 2011, both houses of Congress had unanimously approved new safety legislation responding to the 2010 natural gas pipeline explosion in California (Snow 2011).

Notwithstanding such moments of bipartisan support for new regulatory authority, the anemic pace of the economic recovery following the Great Recession has generally made regulation a matter of great political contestation. Regulatory reform has become one of the top talking points for Republican lawmakers and political candidates, who have repeatedly railed against "job-killing" regulations. By late 2011, the U.S. House of Representatives had, generally along party lines but with some Democrats joining in the majority, passed three major bills that would make changes to the procedures regulatory agencies must follow before adopting costly new regulations (Clark 2011; Kasperowicz 2011; Yang 2011). Even President Obama had come to assail regulation for "placing unreasonable burdens on business . . . that have stifled innovation and have had a chilling effect on growth and jobs," calling on his administration to conduct a thoroughgoing review of existing rules and eliminate those deemed unnecessary or counterproductive (Obama 2011).

Such discontent with the regulatory system has not been confined simply to political rhetoric and the corridors of power in Washington, D.C. Rather, it has manifested itself still more widely in popular opinion that takes a dim view of government (Nye et al. 1997; Stevenson and Wolfers 2011)—and of regulation in particular. Of respondents to a 2011 survey by the Pew Research Center, 59 percent agreed with the statement that "government regulation of business usually does more harm than good" (Pew Research Center 2011). A September 2011 Gallup poll revealed that 50 percent of Americans overall believe there is "too much" government regulation of business and industry (Newport 2011). As Figure 1.1 shows, this level of dissatisfaction with regulation is the highest ever reported, having increased from only 28 percent in 2002. According to the same polling data, in 2006 nearly the same proportion of Republicans and Democrats believed there was too much regulation (40 percent and 36 percent, respectively), whereas by 2011 the chasm between the parties had "widened substantially," with 84 percent of Republicans but only 22 percent of Democrats reporting a belief that there is too much government regulation (Newport 2011).

Obviously, strong political currents all point toward the conclusion that the U.S. regulatory system needs a major overhaul. Yet as a matter of scholarly inquiry, it seems to us a much more open, though still no less

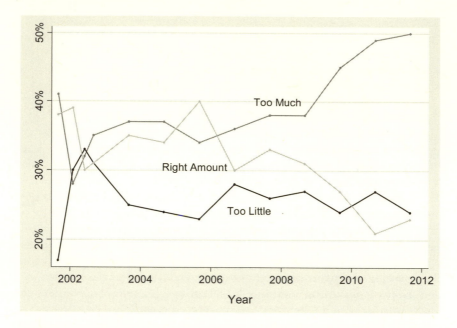

Figure 1.1. Public Attitudes on Government Regulation of Business (2001–11). *Source:* Newport (2011).

vital, question as to whether catastrophic events and a sluggish economy do actually signal a fundamental breakdown in the U.S. regulatory system. Is the apparent crisis of confidence in U.S. regulation really warranted?

Perhaps to some observers, the mere existence of disasters like a pipeline explosion or oil spill justifies a *res ipsa loquitur* conclusion that regulation has failed—that is, such situations speak for themselves. But do the recent disasters collectively, or indeed any of these disasters individually, really automatically justify a conclusion of regulatory breakdown? If individual calamities do speak for themselves as a sign of regulatory failure, through laxity, then perhaps the sluggish recovery of the U.S. economy following the Great Recession also speaks for itself as a sign of regulatory failure, through excessive stringency. Must those who see a regulatory breakdown from great industrial calamities also accept that regulations are to blame for anemic economic growth? And vice versa? If it is difficult, if not impossible, to see that the political left and the political right could both be correct at the same time—namely, that the United States has both too little regulatory oversight as well as too much—then perhaps thoughtful observers should not readily accept either side's view. Perhaps perceptions of regulatory failure are just that: perceptions, often viewed through partisan lenses.

We believe rigorous academic research needs to play a larger role in judgments about regulation, and regulatory failure, in the wake of major calamities, precisely to counteract and inform tendencies to leap to hasty conclusions. Determining causation is the aim of science. As such, a book like this one is premised on the view that serious academic research can helpfully illuminate—even if it can never completely dispel partisanship from—policy debates over regulatory reform in the wake of salient disasters.

Calamities, we suggest, bring with them strong tendencies for faulty assessments of both underlying causes and necessary reforms. These tendencies are due to a host of factors, including both psychological biases as well as nuances in the policy process itself. The pressure politicians feel to adopt change even without solid policy analysis behind their reforms means that solutions can end up being adopted that are either unrelated to the true cause of disasters or that actually work at cross-purposes to improving conditions. In addition, sometimes the underlying problem may not have to do with the day-to-day operations of the regulator or the regulated industry but may instead reflect inherent societal choices about tradeoffs.

Is it possible that the ultimate failure of the U.S. regulatory system is that the American public, through its elected representatives, asks regulators to oversee activities that are at once desired but also deadly? Is the problem actually not with the regulatory system itself but with a much-too-ready diagnosis of regulatory breakdown? Hindsight, it is said, is perfect vision. But it is also the case that, in the hindsight of a calamity, it is always possible to point to regulators and say that they failed.

As a way of framing the scholarly work assembled in this volume, in this chapter we raise broad, even perhaps unsettling, questions about the conventional wisdom that attributes the cause of calamity to a breakdown in the regulatory system. As much as anyone, we are saddened, even appalled, at the loss of life, the economic dislocation, the human anguish, and the ecological messes that have resulted from the disasters that have motivated this book. We are similarly sympathetic to the real and serious human consequences of job losses and sustained unemployment. Indeed, it is precisely out of concern for human welfare that we believe more serious, analytic attention needs to be paid to studying regulatory performance. Rather than supporting reflexive judgments and adopting symbolic responses that may do little more than make public officials and their constituents feel better, we hope that the work in this volume will contribute to and help motivate a reinvigorated effort to achieve a better understanding of social and economic ills and the ways, if any, that regulation might need to be improved in the wake of major calamities.

Inferring Regulatory Failure from Calamities

Psychological and behavioral economics research provides ample evidence to support the notion that people tend to focus more on worst-case outcomes and to believe that vivid events are more common than they really are (Tversky and Kahneman 1973). Moreover, researchers studying these phenomena—known as the "availability heuristic," along with other cognitive biases—also report that they can be exacerbated by the media, which for obvious reasons tend to focus on especially dramatic events (Shrum 2002). In an effort to make sense of tragedies, it is thus not surprising that, following a string of highly publicized disasters, journalists, policy advocates, and public officials can be heard making systematic denouncements of the U.S. regulatory infrastructure.

Although many citizens may have little understanding of regulatory policy, it does seem clear to them when the regulatory system is *not* working. The disconcerting images of birds covered in oil, of tar balls on the shoreline, and of a seemingly ever-expanding oil slick in the Gulf of Mexico in the wake of the 2010 BP oil spill made vivid a worst-case scenario that surely any good system of regulation should seek to prevent. As a result, it is not surprising that disasters such as the BP oil spill have stirred an intense desire to blame regulation and regulators. Even in cases when an unprecedented calamity occurs that truly surprises everyone—a "black swan" event (Taleb 2007)—the regulatory infrastructure seems to present the "obvious" source of the problem once the initial surprise wears off, regardless of whether the disastrous event could actually have been foreseen in advance.

In an effort to find actors to blame, politicians often make quick judgments. Even if they initially target the business firms involved in the disaster, soon thereafter they heap blame on the regulator charged with oversight. For example, in remarks made just ten days after the explosion at the Upper Big Branch mine, even after acknowledging that "there's still a lot that we don't know," President Obama identified not only Massey Energy, the mine operator, but also the overseeing regulator as a culprit: "For a long time, the mine safety agency was stacked with former mine executives and industry players" (Obama 2010a). Summing up, President Obama concluded that the disaster was "a failure, first and foremost, of management, but also a failure of oversight and a failure of laws . . . riddled with loopholes" (Obama 2010a).

The 2010 outbreak of *Salmonella* from contaminated eggs presents another case in point. Shortly after the government initiated the recall of half a billion eggs originating from Iowa producers, consumer advocates and news outlets began to question the pace of rulemaking at the Food and Drug Administration (FDA). In particular, they lamented delays in imposing a related rule that had been proposed several years before but was finalized only in July 2009 (FDA 2009). Critics claimed that had the new rules not "languished for more than a decade because of internal sniping in the federal bureaucracy and a general deregulatory atmosphere," the *Salmonella* outbreak would never have occurred (Martin 2010). Consumer advocates and others such as the U.S. Government Accountability Office (GAO) further criticized the structure of regulatory oversight of eggs, suggesting that the division of regulatory responsibilities between the Department of Health and Human Services and the Department of Agriculture triggered the regulatory torpor and fueled the resulting health crisis (GAO 2011; Martin 2010).

Placing blame on government regulators can have significant policy implications. In most areas of public policy, laws remain relatively stable for long periods of time, but proposals to change them emerge in reaction to crises or other salient events (Baumgartner and Jones 1993; Dodd 1994). Crises provide opportunities for policy entrepreneurs to place at center stage those solutions they have already been seeking to see adopted (Kingdon 1984:91). Even if those solutions were not developed to address the particular problem at hand, politicians often feel compelled to consider them—to "do something." Intense reactions by the public, after all, drive an intense desire by politicians to take action. Under such circumstances, taking any action targeted at the regulatory process, regardless of how well or poorly crafted, will be better politically than taking no action at all.

Political incentives point in the direction of quick legislative action that responds to calamities. Voters focus much less on considerations of how a law will be implemented than on the enactment of a new law itself (Mayhew 1974; Mazmanian and Sabatier 1983). Legislators can reap rewards from passing legislation regardless of whether doing so turns out to be realistic or effectual, and they can later reap rewards by lambasting regulatory officials in the executive branch for failing to live up to the aspirational (even if unrealistic) goals embodied in the initial legislation (Mayhew 1974). In short, the public's demand for action can be accommodated by representatives' enactment of window dressing as much as by the passage of well-founded, carefully analyzed reform.

Roberta Romano, in her chapter in this volume, explains the legislative response to financial crises in precisely these terms. Although it might take a highly trained and knowledgeable economist or legal scholar years to write a book explaining the causes of a financial crisis, Congress can propose, debate, and enact a nearly thousand-page bill in about half a year, as it did with the Dodd-Frank Act (2010). Such responsiveness is surely sometimes necessary, even laudatory. But it can also be just haste—perhaps for its own sake. As noted earlier, in responding to the BP oil spill, the Department of the Interior disbanded its offshore oil and gas regulator, MMS, less than one month after the *Deepwater Horizon* oil rig exploded. Explaining the Department's decision, President Obama declared: "For years, there has been a scandalously close relationship between oil companies and the agency that regulates them. That's why we've decided to separate the people who permit the drilling from those who regulate and ensure the safety of the drilling" (Obama 2010b). It did not seem to matter that the highly publicized scandals at MMS primarily centered on officials in the agency's separate revenue collection division located in an office roughly a thousand miles away from the agency inspectors who were responsible for monitoring safety on offshore platforms (Carrigan forthcoming).

To be sure, no one would disagree with the emotions expressed by Representative Tim Walberg (R-Mich.), who, following the fatal explosion at the Upper Branch mine in West Virginia, noted that he and others on his legislative committee were "anxious to act" and felt "a sense of urgency to move forward with mine safety reform" (U.S. House of Representatives 2011). But a "sense of urgency," however laudable and well intentioned, can also lead policymakers to act without undertaking sufficiently careful analysis or without giving adequate consideration to whether new laws can be effectively implemented.

In the wake of a calamity, the goal may seem perfectly clear, namely, to find a solution that will "prevent repetition of such a disaster" (Haines 2009). Yet without the rigor of independent analysis, policy decisions made in the moment of crisis can also readily succumb to the influences of political ideology. Reactions to calamity do vary according to the party affiliation of the beholder—and as Matthew Baum explains in his chapter in this volume, these partisan filters can be reinforced by the media's framing of calamitous events. The partisanship that Baum (this volume) finds in media coverage of the healthcare reform debate can be found in coverage of other regulatory issues, and it only mirrors if not bolsters how politicians and members of the public view calamities' causes and their solutions.

To see the divide, one need only compare editorials following the BP oil spill from the major newspapers for Washington, D.C. (*Washington Post* and *Washington Times*) and New York City (*New York Times* and *Wall Street Journal*). The editorials differed considerably in their views of the relative culpability of government in relation to the spill. The *Washing-*

ton Post and *New York Times* made reference to the scandals at MMS twice as often as their more conservative counterparts in the two months following the spill. The more liberal papers tended to tie MMS's problems to the Bush administration, such as by claiming that "the problem of regulator-industry coziness predated [Obama's] tenure" (*Washington Post* 2010) or asserting that the agency "was corrupted by industry in the Bush years" (*New York Times* 2010). In contrast, the more conservative *Washington Times* and *Wall Street Journal* repeatedly criticized the Obama administration's response to the spill after the fact.

Even when partisans agree on who is to blame for a catastrophe, they still usually differ dramatically in the remedies they support. Only about a week after the Massey Energy mine explosion, for example, editorials in both the *New York Times* and *Washington Post* recommended that Congress strengthen mine safety legislation. The *Wall Street Journal*, by contrast, simply favored better enforcement of existing laws (2010). Although statements issued by the left-of-center Center for Progressive Reform (CPR) and the right-of-center Cato Institute following the BP oil spill both accepted that MMS had been "captured" by the oil and gas industry, they differed markedly in the solutions that followed from this diagnosis. For Cato, regulatory capture provided another reason to distrust government reforms: "Policymakers never seem to worry about [capture] in their continual call to create new departments, agencies, commissions, boards, and other federal entities. . . . The government's recent advances into the health care and financial services industries after its prior failures in those areas will likely lead only to further failures and more economic distortions down the road" (Cato Institute 2010). In contrast, CPR argued that capture called for increased governmental effort, including tighter standards and increased "funding to permit reasonably competitive salaries and adequate training for agency staff" (CPR 2010:7).

Political leaders' own predispositions about the proper role of government will play a key role in decision making when they react hastily to calamities. Both their diagnoses and prescriptions will not only be subject to ordinary cognitive biases, such as the availability heuristic, but they will also more likely be grounded on ideological hunches rather than a careful, dispassionate consideration of the evidence.[3]

Regulation, Tradeoffs, and Low-Probability Events

The psychological impulses and political pressures that lead politicians to rush to judgment also tend to crowd out consideration of the tradeoffs inherent in almost all regulatory decisions. Regulatory goals are often competing ones, with the purpose being to manage risk rather than to eliminate it altogether. People want both to drive cars and to be safe; they want oil to fuel their cars and an environment free of oil spills; and they want the energy and materials made possible from mining and other industrial operations without injuries and fatalities from work-place accidents. But the complete elimination of all harms, including from low-probability catastrophic events, is not possible without stopping altogether the very activities that give rise to these harmful events. As a result, regulations may be effective at reducing risk, and thus may fully fulfill their public mandate, even if they do not completely remove the possibility of disaster. In a world governed by probabilities, harms will still occur whenever a regulator is asked to balance risks.

The very choice to regulate, rather than to ban, a specific type of economic activity implicitly rejects the goal of eliminating risk entirely. Everyone wishes that untoward risks could be eliminated altogether, and regulations do seek to prevent harms—whether from restaurants operating in an unsanitary manner, from nuclear plants ignoring safety protocols, or from any of a myriad of other hazardous conditions. How-ever, this does not imply that society seeks to get rid of restaurants, nu-clear reactors, or other fixtures of society and the economy.

On the contrary, some laws assume that regulation will leave the public exposed to some degree of residual risk. How else can one explain the recall authority Congress has granted to the Consumer Product Safety Commission, the Food and Drug Administration, and the National Highway Traffic Safety Administration (NHTSA), notwithstanding these agencies' corresponding authority and responsibility to adopt preventive regulatory standards? Such recall provisions are an implied acknowledgment that even regulated products will still pose some risk of harm—a risk that calls for a governmental response to be available to pull a dangerous product from the marketplace.

Sometimes legislation does more than just tacitly recognize risk; it builds it in by recognizing competing objectives of promoting industry while regulating it. For example, the Outer Continental Shelf Lands Act (1953), which forms the foundation for oil and gas policy and regulatory oversight in federal offshore waters, explicitly recognizes the tradeoff between environmental protection and the need for energy development. The law declares that offshore areas "should be made available for expeditious and orderly development, subject to environmental safeguards, in a manner which is consistent with the maintenance of competition and other national needs" (Outer Continental Shelf Lands Act 1953:§3). Such language may provide little clarity about exactly how to strike the balance between oil exploration and environmental concerns, but because the act still allows for some oil drilling it does not eliminate the possibility of disaster altogether.

The recognition of tradeoffs and residual risks is crucial when seeking to evaluate the regulatory system in the wake of calamities. When laws allow activities to go forward that have even a trivial probability of a catastrophic event occurring, it is hard to know what to make of the underlying system when such an event occurs. When *Salmonella* contamination breaks out under the FDA's watch, does it indicate a systemic failure by the FDA—or is it just the occasional occurrence that statistically will arise because of regulation's balancing of tradeoffs? Does an oil spill, even a massive one, necessarily mean that the regulator failed to oversee sufficiently—or just that the nation's environment has suffered one of the inevitable tragedies that can be expected from a congressional policy that seeks to balance oil exploration with environmental concerns?

We believe the answers to these questions are much harder to determine than most people think they are, and certainly harder than they seem in the immediate aftermath of a disaster. We do not mean to suggest that regulations and regulatory officials never have any responsibility for the disasters that occur under their watch. We firmly accept that officials in regulatory agencies, like employees anywhere, could always do better. But in hindsight it will almost always be possible to conclude that regulatory agencies could have prevented a disaster from occurring. No matter how things look in hindsight, the mere existence of an accident or disaster does not necessarily mean that the regulatory system has broken down or that regulators have failed to carry out their mandates. Although any regulatory agency might fail to achieve the proper balance between competing objectives, an accident or disaster in itself does not tell us whether that agency failed in its mission. Indeed, provided that such disasters occur infrequently, it may well be impossible to judge from their occasional occurrence whether the regulatory agency has struck the optimal balance in its risk management strategies. With any low-probability risk, we would not expect the hazardous event to occur anything but infrequently.

Perhaps to some readers it will be obvious that regulatory systems seldom aim to eliminate all harm. Yet this point is hardly obvious if judged by the rhetoric typically deployed by politicians in the wake of disasters. President Obama's remarks after the Upper Big Branch mine disaster underscored his desire to act "so we can help make sure a disaster like this never happens again" (Obama 2010a). In his 2012 State of the Union address, he defended the legislative reforms enacted following the financial crisis by saying that they will ensure "a crisis like that never happens again" (Obama 2012). Statements like these, which are made by many politicians in addition to President Obama, convey an admirable goal for a regulatory system in an ideal world. The reality is, though, that as long as mining and other industrial operations continue to take place, there will remain some probability, however small, that another disaster will occur. When that rare tragedy strikes again, the public and their policymakers may very well again claim that the regulatory system is broken. But doing so instinctively loses sight of the trade-offs created by inherently risky industrial operations. After the fact, nearly any disaster will appear to have been avoidable.

What is obvious after a disaster is not always obvious beforehand. Some disasters do arise because we fail to foresee them—sometimes notwithstanding the best efforts by researchers at think tanks, universities, public health groups, and government agencies. Should a product made with nanotechnology, for example, someday create a terrible public health crisis, it may be tempting to conclude, after the fact, that the regulatory system failed and that warning signs had been in place but went ignored (Bazerman and Watkins 2004; Taleb 2007). Yet at the present time, very little beyond abstract anxieties have emerged that would point to any specific problems or would indicate any obvious, best way to regulate nanotechnology (Coglianese 2010; Davies 2007).

Hazards from emerging technologies cannot be eliminated, or even necessarily managed properly, if they are hard to predict or even completely unknown. As Kip Viscusi and Richard Zeckhauser explain in their chapter in this book, statistical models based on normal distributions do not easily account for the thicker tails associated with a distribution that includes the low-probability, extreme events that exist in the world. Given the demonstrated difficulties people have in dealing with low-probability, extreme events (Kunreuther and Michel-Kerjan 2010), it should not be surprising that sometimes these events do still tragically occur.

In retrospect, BP's Oil Spill Response Plan—which identified worse-case scenarios for oil discharge into the Gulf of Mexico ranging from 28,033 to 250,000 barrels (Oil Spill Commission 2011:84)—was clearly out of line with the subsequent consequences of the actual spill. Although there may be very good reasons to fault BP for submitting and MMS for approving such a plan, the mere fact that the resulting oil spill dumped 4.9 million barrels rather than 250,000 barrels does not necessarily suggest that the company and its associated regulator were negligent. The difficulty in accounting for low-probability events is that they are just that—of low probability.

Improving Regulatory Performance Under Uncertainty

Given that some disasters may be unavoidable and even unpredictable, and given the incentives for adopting quick, symbolic policies in their wake, is there anything that can be done? Of course, the answer to this question is hardly straightforward and is in large part the reason this volume has been written—as one step toward improving the knowledge base needed to craft better regulatory institutions.

Even as more research proceeds, the work in this volume suggests some strategies to consider for limiting the potential for disasters. For example, one option might be to use safety management systems that place the onus on firms to demonstrate their ability to operate safely (Bennear this volume; Coglianese and Lazer 2003). Another possibility would be to recalibrate financial requirements, imposing strict liability for damages and using taxes to promote more optimal risk taking by individuals and firms (Viscusi and Zeckhauser this volume). These and the other ideas in this volume merit policymakers' thoughtful consideration.

One of the primary difficulties associated with studying regulatory failures is that we do not observe accidents that could have happened but did not. We see the disasters that were not prevented; we seldom see evidence of the disasters that were successfully prevented, unless obvious precursors exist so that "near-miss" data can be collected. Yet to make good policy reform decisions, policymakers need to consider more than just the disasters. Disasters can be blinding as much as they are illuminating, clouding judgment and, as described, increasing the impetus for swift, radical action.

As we have suggested, fixating on a disaster or even a series of disasters as measures of regulatory performance can make it very difficult to consider the possibility that the system is, in fact, not fundamentally broken. Alternative hypotheses do need to be explored. Before concluding that something is seriously awry with the regulatory system or the regulator, all the evidence should be considered. It is striking how quickly NHTSA came in for sharp rebuke in 2010 after consumers reported numerous cases of sudden acceleration in Toyota vehicles (Lichtblau and Vlasic 2010). If allegedly malfunctioning accelerators in a subset of Toyota vehicles supposedly signaled a breakdown of auto safety regulation, why did we not see similar problems with all of Toyota's models or with other manufacturers' vehicles? In a similar vein, if we do not see blowouts in the wells used by many of the firms engaged in deepwater drilling, perhaps we should not assume that the problem lies with a systematic lack of adequate regulatory oversight.

Analogously, examining the regulatory mechanisms employed in other similarly situated regulatory environments (or time periods) can also be helpful. If the proposed causes of a regulatory failure in one domain mirror the activities of regulators in another domain, where no similar disaster occurred, perhaps the causes do not so clearly rest with regulation. For example, the Obama administration has asserted that MMS failed in its offshore drilling oversight duties because the agency faced the conflicting responsibility of raising revenues from drilling fees (and lawfully pocketing the funds in its budget) as well as regulating those very same drilling platforms. But in addition to giving a close examination to the internal structure of the agency in question, anyone seeking to determine whether such a conflict really exists will also need to consider other regulatory domains where similar conditions are present.

Then again, relying on the absence of a failure in one domain to question a purported regulatory cause in another domain presents its own problems. Because of the low probabilities and inherent risk trade-offs, assuming failure because of a disaster, and assuming no failure because of no disaster, could well both be analytic and empirical errors. Even so, gathering additional data can only help in making more reasoned assessments in the wake of catastrophes.

In addition to examining other regulatory environments, evaluations of regulatory performance unrelated to the disaster but still within the policy domain of interest can also prove helpful to decision makers. Much can be learned from little failures as well as little successes. The recent implementation of broad governmental data gathering projects such as the Office of Management and Budget's Performance Assessment Rating Tool and the Office of Personal Management's Federal Employee Viewpoint Survey, along with other data sets made available via the Data.gov website, present some promising possibilities for use within regulatory program evaluations. Regulators themselves should be encouraged to collect more data on industry operations to assist in examining performance in a more fine-grained manner than just focusing on infrequent disasters.

Clearly, we should all remain wary when anyone trots out stock reasons for regulatory failure in the wake of any disaster, just as we should raise questions about whether regulations really inhibit economic recovery after a recession (Brooks 2011). We should be skeptical not for skepticism's sake but because acting on stock reactions could lead to other kinds of failures in the future. Rulemaking delay, for example, is sometimes thought to explain some types of regulatory failure (Mashaw and Harfst 1990; McGarity 1992); however, increasing rulemaking speed could contribute to still other failures (Magill 1995; Yackee and Yackee this volume). Especially if delay is not the real reason for a calamity, procedural responses to increase the speed of decision making might only encourage haste and increase the probability of future disasters from poorly considered regulation. For example, statutory deadlines have been adopted to increase the pace of rulemaking (Gersen and O'Connell 2008; Magill 1995), but research on such deadlines imposed on FDA drug reviews has suggested that mandated approval times actually increase the probability of subsequent safety problems (Carpenter et al. 2008; see also Moffitt this volume). Thus, an effort to solve the problem of delay by using deadlines may create another problem to replace it.

Similar care should be taken when considering allegations of, and responses to, regulatory capture. Cases like the Interstate Commerce Commission's close association with the railroads in the 1930s and 1940s provide good reason to believe that captured regulators are capable of implementing rules in ways that benefit regulated firms at the expense of the public (Huntington 1952). Yet there is also good reason to believe that some cooperation between the regulatory agency and the industry actually improves regulators' chances of eliciting data from regulated entities that can help improve overall regulatory performance (Coglianese et al. 2004).

In addition to taking a more critical approach to claims about regulation and the regulatory process, policymakers and members of the public would do well to consider ways of limiting the damage from the inherent biases and limitations of the policy process. Mechanisms exist to limit the impacts of potentially rash responses to catastrophes. For example, by imposing sunset provisions on resulting legislation, political actors can satisfy constituents with (symbolic) action while at the same limiting the role that inertia plays in entrenching uninformed laws forever (Romano this volume). Such sunset provisions may even dampen, we might hope, the tendency toward overreaction or at least promote greater effort to generate information that will be needed for thoughtful decision making when a law comes up for renewal.

Another key need is to devote more resources to retrospective evaluations of regulatory systems. For at least the past thirty years, U.S. regulators—operating under successive executive orders—have engaged in much prospective benefit-cost analysis of important rules to ensure that the benefits exceed the corresponding costs. Although the merits of such requirements continue to be a source of debate (Ackerman and Heinzerling 2004; Adler and Posner 2006), they have certainly added rigor to the decision-making climate surrounding proposed regulations. However, no similar, top-level requirements exist for analyzing the impacts of rules retrospectively (Coglianese and Bennear 2005; Greenstone 2009). Although academic studies can yield important evidence on the effects of regulations, too few retrospective analyses have been pursued or funded by government agencies relative to the volume of regulation that exists or the magnitude of the problems that existing regulation aims to solve. Increasing the quantity and rigor of retrospective evaluation will be helpful in overcoming poorly conceived policy shifts that can occur in response to regulatory disasters. By engaging in retrospective evaluation, the longer-term effects of the biases and limitations associated with policy reform in the wake of catastrophe can be better understood and, one hopes, significantly limited.

Conclusion

The calamities of the past few years that we have mentioned in this chapter—including the housing meltdown and subsequent financial collapse, the BP oil spill, the Upper Big Branch mine disaster, the pipeline explosion in California, the Toyota auto recall, and the *Salmonella* outbreak—have each brought with them increased, even intense, public and political interest in the role of regulation in the U.S. economy. Moreover, many of these catastrophes have been accompanied by dramatic changes in the underlying regulatory systems, from the creation of new agencies to the adoption of extensive new laws.

We have argued in this chapter that although such sweeping reforms are predictable, they may be neither necessary nor sound, at least not without a better empirical grounding in the true determinants of regulatory performance. In addition to pointing out biases and limitations, we have also suggested a number of mechanisms that can help overcome these problematic outcomes either during or after their implementation. Most important, we have attempted to show why devoting greater empirical and analytical attention to regulation—as this volume seeks to do—is a sensible part of an overall strategy for improving the performance of the U.S. regulatory system.

Notes

1. By "regulatory breakdown," we mean a significant and systemic failure by regulation or the regulatory process that results in a meaningful loss of public value, particularly when regulatory failings contribute to catastrophic harm in the form of major industrial accidents or massive financial or economic losses. In this sense, we mean something similar to what others have meant when they have used the language of regulatory breakdown. For example, Joskow (1974) and Mullin (1992) conceive of regulatory breakdown in terms of the disruption of equilibrium in the political, economic, and institutional environment within which a regulatory agency operates, whereas Frank and Lombness (1988) use the term to refer to the abandonment of effective regulatory enforcement. The majority members of the National Commission on the Causes of the Financial and Economic Crisis in the United States (2011) deplored a "systemic breakdown in accountability and ethics" that they concluded had undermined market integrity, and Davidson (2011) has written summarily about the "regulatory breakdown that contributed so clearly to the economic crisis."

2. Even the Commission's dissenting reports, which emphasized different causal accounts of the crisis, acknowledged that "ineffective regulation and supervision" helped explain certain "irresponsible" financial practices (2011:414), that

"the SEC's supervisory process was weak" (446), and that federal housing policy was "the sine qua non of the financial crisis" (444).

3. We recognize that claims about hasty or ill-informed policy decision making can be influenced by ideology, too. Our own belief is that decision makers across the entire ideological spectrum succumb too readily to reflexive judgments, and we have no reason to believe that Democratic or Republican legislators and administrators are more (or less) prone to hasty decisions.

References

Ackerman, Frank, and Lisa Heinzerling (2004) *Priceless: On Knowing the Price of Everything and the Value of Nothing*. New York: New Press.

Adler, Matthew D., and Eric A. Posner (2006) *New Foundations of Cost-Benefit Analysis*. Cambridge, Mass.: Harvard University Press.

Baumgartner, Frank R., and Bryan D. Jones (1993) *Agendas and Instability in American Politics*. Chicago: University of Chicago Press.

Bazerman, Max H., and Michael Watkins (2004) *Predictable Surprises: The Disasters You Should Have Seen Coming, and How to Prevent Them*. Boston: Harvard Business School Press.

Brooks, David (2011) "The Wonky Liberal." *New York Times*, December 6, A29.

Carpenter, Daniel et al. (2008) "Drug-Review Deadlines and Safety Problems." *New England Journal of Medicine* 358: 1354–61.

Carrigan, Christopher (forthcoming) "Minerals Management Service and *Deepwater Horizon*: What Role Should Capture Play?" In D. Carpenter, S. Croley, and D. Moss, eds., *Preventing Capture: Special Interest Influence in Regulation and How to Limit It*. Cambridge, Mass.: Tobin Project.

Cato Institute (2010) "MMS 'Captured' by Industry." Downsizing the Federal Government, http://www.downsizinggovernment.org/mms-%E2%80%98 captured%E2%80%99-industry, accessed October 28, 2011.

Center for Progressive Reform (2010) "Regulatory Blowout: How Regulatory Failures Made the BP Disaster Possible, and How the System Can Be Fixed to Avoid a Recurrence." Center for Progressive Reform White Paper 1007. Washington, D.C., October 10.

Clark, Charles S. (2011) "House-Passed Regulatory Reforms Face Uphill Battle." *Government Executive*, December 2. http://www.govexec.com/story_page .cfm?articleid=49466andoref=todaysnews.

Coglianese, Cary (2010) "Engaging Business in the Regulation of Nanotechnology." In C. J. Bosso, ed., *Governing Uncertainty: Environmental Regulation in the Age of Nanotechnology: Confronting Conditions of Uncertainty*. Washington, D.C.: Resources for the Future.

Coglianese, Cary, and Lori Snyder Bennear (2005) "Program Evaluation of Environmental Policies: Toward Evidence-Based Decision Making." In G. D. Brewer and P. C. Stern, eds., *Social and Behavioral Science Research Priorities for Environmental Decision Making*. Washington, D.C.: National Academies Press.

Coglianese, Cary, and David Lazer (2003) "Management-Based Regulation: Prescribing Private Management to Achieve Public Goals." *Law and Society Review* 37: 691–730.

Coglianese, Cary et al. (2004) "Seeking Truth for Power: Informational Strategy and Regulatory Policymaking." *Minnesota Law Review* 89: 277–341.

Davidson, Nestor M. (2011) "Property's Morale." *Michigan Law Review* 110: 437–88.

Davies, J. Clarence (2007) "EPA and Nanotechnology: Oversight for the 21st Century." Project on Emerging Nanotechnologies, http://www.nanotech project.org/publications/archive/epa_nanotechnology_oversight_for_21st/.

Dodd, Lawrence C. (1994) "Political Learning and Political Change: Understanding Development Across Time." In L. Dodd and C. Jillson, eds., *The Dynamics of American Politics: Approaches and Interpretations.* Boulder, Colo.: Westview Press.

Food and Drug Administration (2009) "Prevention of Salmonella Enteritidis in Shell Eggs During Production, Storage, and Transportation." *Federal Register* 74: 33030–101.

Frank, Nancy, and Michael Lombness (1988) "Gaining Regulatory Compliance: Law Enforcement and Power in an Interactionist Perspective." *Administration and Society* 20: 71–91.

Gersen, Jacob E., and Anne Joseph O'Connell (2008) "Deadlines in Administrative Law." *University of Pennsylvania Law Review* 156: 923–90.

Governor's Independent Investigation Panel (2011) *Upper Big Branch: The April 5, 2010, Explosion: A Failure of Basic Coal Mine Safety Practices.* Report to the Governor. Charleston, W.V.: Governor's Independent Investigation Panel.

Greenstone, Michael (2009) "Toward a Culture of Persistent Regulatory Experimentation and Evaluation." In D. Moss and J. Cisternino, eds., *New Perspectives on Regulation.* Cambridge, Mass.: Tobin Project.

Haines, Fiona (2009) "Regulatory Failures and Regulatory Solutions: A Characteristic Analysis of the Aftermath of Disaster." *Law and Social Inquiry* 34: 31–60.

Huntington, Samuel (1952) "The Marasmus of the ICC: The Commission, the Railroads, and the Public Interest." *Yale Law Journal* 61: 467–509.

Joskow, Paul L. (1974) "Inflation and Environmental Concern: Structural Change in the Process of Public Utility Price Regulation." *Journal of Law and Economics* 17: 291–327.

Kasperowicz, Pete (2011) "House Approves Latest Bill Reining in Federal Regulations." *The Hill,* December 2 (Floor Action Blog). http://thehill.com/blogs /floor-action/house/196883-house-approves-latest-bill-reining-in-federal -regulations.

Kingdon, John W. (1984) *Agendas, Alternatives, and Public Policies.* New York: Longman.

Kunreuther, Howard C., and Erwann O. Michel-Kerjan (2010) "Overcoming Myopia: Learning from the BP Oil Spill and Other Catastrophes." *Milken Institute Review* (Fourth Quarter): 48–57.

Lichtblau, Eric, and Bill Vlasic (2010) "Safety Agency Scrutinized as Toyota Recall Grows." *New York Times,* February 9, B1.

Magill, M. Elizabeth (1995) "Congressional Control over Agency Rulemaking: The Nutrition Labeling and Education Act's Hammer Provision." *Food and Drug Law Journal* 50: 149–90.

Martin, Andrew (2010) "Egg Recall Exposes Flaws in Nation's Food Safety System." *The New York Times,* August 24, B1.

Mashaw, Jerry L., and David L. Harfst (1990) *The Struggle for Auto Safety.* Cambridge, Mass.: Harvard University Press.

Mayhew, David R. (1974) *Congress: The Electoral Connection.* New Haven, Conn.: Yale University Press.

Mazmanian, Daniel A., and Paul A. Sabatier (1983) *Implementation and Public Policy.* Glenview, Ill.: Scott, Foresman.

McGarity, Thomas O. (1992) "Some Thoughts on 'Deossifying' the Rulemaking Process." *Duke Law Journal* 41: 1385–1462.

Mullin, Wallace Patrick (1992) "Causes and Consequences of Regulatory Breakdown: An Empirical Analysis." Ph.D. dissertation, Department of Economics, Massachusetts Institute of Technology.

National Commission on the BP *Deepwater Horizon* Oil Spill and Offshore Drilling (2011) *Deep Water: The Gulf Oil Disaster and the Future of Offshore Drilling: Report to the President.* http://www.oilspillcommission.gov/.

National Commission on the Causes of the Financial and Economic Crisis in the United States (2011) *The Financial Crisis Inquiry Report.* Washington, D.C.: GPO.

National Transportation Safety Board (2011) *Pipeline Accident Report: Pacific Gas and Electric Company Natural Gas Transmission Pipeline Rupture and Fire, San Bruno, California, September 9, 2010.* http://www.ntsb.gov/doclib/reports/2011/PAR1101.pdf.

New York Times (2010) "Industry Doesn't Step Up." Editorial, May 12, A24.

Newport, Frank (2011) "Despite Negativity, Americans Mixed on Ideal Role of Gov't." Gallup, http://www.gallup.com/poll/149741/despite-negativity-americans-mixed-ideal-role-gov.aspx.

Nye, Joseph et al., eds. (1997) *Why People Don't Trust Government.* Cambridge, Mass.: Harvard University Press.

Obama, Barack (2010a) *Remarks by the President on Mine Safety,* http://www.white house.gov/the-press-office/remarks-president-mine-safety.

———— (2010b) *Remarks by the President on the Gulf Oil Spill,* http://www.white house.gov/the-press-office/remarks-president-gulf-oil-spill.

———— (2011) "Toward a 21st-Century Regulatory System." *Wall Street Journal,* January 18, A17.

———— (2012) *Remarks by the President in State of the Union Address,* http://www.whitehouse.gov/the-press-office/2012/01/24/remarks-president-state-union-address.

Pew Research Center (2011) *The Generation Gap and the 2012 Election.* http://www.people-press.org/files/legacy-pdf/11-3-11%20Generations%20Release.pdf.

Shrum, L. J. (2002) "Media Consumption and Perceptions of Social Reality: Effects and Underlying Processes." In J. Bryant and D. Zillman, eds., *Media Effects: Advances in Theory and Research.* Mahwah, N.J.: Erlbaum.

Snow, Nick (2011) "Senate Quickly Follows House, Passes Pipeline Safety Bill." *Oil and Gas Journal,* December 15. http://www.ogj.com/articles/2011/12/senate-quickly-follows-house-passes-pipeline-safety-bill.html.

Stevenson, Betsey, and Justin Wolfers (2011) "Trust in Public Institutions over the Business Cycle." NBER Working Paper 16891 (March 8). Cambridge, Mass.: National Bureau of Economic Research.

Taleb, Nassim (2007) *The Black Swan: The Impact of the Highly Improbable.* New York: Random House.

Tversky, Amos, and Daniel Kahneman (1973) "Availability: A Heuristic for Judging Frequency and Probability." *Cognitive Psychology* 5: 207–32.

U.S. Government Accountability Office (2011) *Federal Food Safety Oversight: Food Safety Working Group Is a Positive First Step but Governmentwide Planning Is Needed to Address Fragmentation.* Washington, D.C.: GAO.

U.S. House of Representatives, Committee on Education and the Workforce (2011) *Walberg Statement: Hearing on Examining Recent Regulatory and Enforce-*

ment Actions of the Mine Safety and Health Administration. http://edworkforce
.house.gov/News/DocumentSingle.aspx?DocumentID=227132.

U.S. Secretary of the Interior (2010) *Establishment of the Bureau of Ocean Energy
Management, the Bureau of Safety and Environmental Enforcement, and the Office of
Natural Resources Revenue.* Order 3299. Washington, D.C.: Department of the
Interior.

Wall Street Journal (2010) "The Upper Big Branch Disaster." Editorial, April 10,
A12.

Washington Post (2010) "Oil Spill Answers; Mr. Obama Takes Responsibility for
the Response—and Points to the Need for Energy Changes." Editorial, May
28, A24.

Yang, Jia Lynn (2011) "GOP Takes Aim at Process of Crafting Regulations."
Washington Post, November 30.

Statutes Cited

Dodd-Frank Wall Street Reform and Consumer Protection Act of 2010, Pub.
Law No. 111-203.

Food Safety Modernization Act of 2011, Pub. Law No. 111-353.

Outer Continental Shelf Lands Act of 1953, 43 U.S.C. §§1331–56.

Chapter 2
Addressing Catastrophic Risks
Disparate Anatomies Require Tailored Therapies

W. Kip Viscusi and Richard Zeckhauser

Catastrophic risks are hazards that inflict substantial loss of life on large populations or cause tremendous property damage. Fortunately, catastrophic risks tend to involve rare events. Unfortunately, their distributions tend to be fat-tailed, implying that when catastrophes do occur there may be extreme outliers. These two factors imply that the occurrence and consequences of catastrophes will be difficult to predict. Eliminating catastrophes is not possible and in many cases should not be attempted. Moreover, even where some sources of catastrophe could be eliminated, by means such as banning deepwater drilling, it will often be undesirable to do so. The objective should be to communicate risk levels adequately; allow risk-related bargains to be struck; and impose liability, regulation, and risk-based taxes on a strategic basis in order to tamp risks down to efficient levels. When compensation is not likely, compensable losses should be covered by insurance.

Although generic issues about the roles of different institutions in controlling risks have a long history in the literatures of law and economics, and in that of general jurisprudence as well, we know of no comprehensive assessment of the ways that different institutions address the diverse challenges posed by catastrophic risks.[1] Those who prescribe policies for dealing with catastrophic risks often favor particular instruments. Some embrace market solutions, with an appropriate nod to liability arrangements and the Coase theorem. Others, at the opposite end of the political spectrum, posit that regulation and other government prescriptions can work effectively. Some champion insurance: risks that are spread, they observe, impose lower utility losses. Still others focus on providing information, primarily to allow people to keep themselves out of harm's way.

Our analysis recognizes the disparate anatomies of various catastrophes and the limitations of relying only on any single-policy approach, given the diversity of threats and potential responses. The many fearsome possibilities that make up the spectrum of catastrophes differ substantially from one another. A broad classification would look at the causes of catastrophes and at those that suffer from them. Appropriate policy instruments for different catastrophe types will differ substantially in both objectives and modes of operation. Some policy instruments will seek to prevent the catastrophes entirely, some to reduce their likelihood, others to minimize their consequences, and still others to spread and thus dissipate the impact of their costs.

Three principal considerations emerge from the analysis presented in this chapter. First, catastrophes—replete with disparate anatomies— require therapies that differ across and sometimes within categories. That is, oil spills differ dramatically from hurricanes; within the categories of oil spills and of hurricanes, there are additional and significant differences, and these differences also call for distinct policy measures. Second, given that catastrophes have complex social dimensions—such as what entities cause them, who or what suffers from them, the nature of the losses, the role of information provision, and the compensability of the losses—a portfolio approach is required for effective control and response. Thus market processes, regulation, litigation, risk-based taxation, insurance, and information provision may all be part of the appropriate strategy for addressing a particular type of catastrophe. Third, the existing mix of policy instruments should be changed. We propose a liability system that bolsters the financial incentives to control risks and shifts much of the responsibility for safety from government regulators to the parties generating the risk.

The Causes of Catastrophes

Catastrophes can be caused or amplified both by humans and by nonhuman agents; the latter we call "nature." Even with catastrophes of natural origin, nature working alone rarely imposes losses so great as to make the front pages of newspapers. Virtually all significant natural catastrophes involve some human actions that amplify the risks of the natural hazards. That is, nature is abetted by humans—for example, by humans making choices about where to live or how to farm—in generating catastrophes out of nature's occasional but inevitable extreme expressions. Human behavior often leads to increased vulnerability to natural hazards. This is precisely what happened when an array of local and national American actors channeled the Mississippi River and thereby removed existing protections against storms such as Hurricane Katrina or when Japanese entities designed the Fukushima Daiichi Nuclear Power Plant and perched it precariously in an earthquake zone. More generally, people all over the world have flocked to ocean coasts, where they have greater exposure to storms and ultimately to any sea level rise accompanying global warming.

Nature usually needs a partner to wreak extreme damage on society. Hurricane Katrina decimated New Orleans because human action had wiped out protections afforded by the Mississippi River's delta. When a massive earthquake strikes Istanbul, as it is predicted to do, a great city will suffer extreme losses of life and property because of its location and lax building standards (Revkin 2010).[2]

Humans, however, can create catastrophes completely (or almost completely) on their own. So it was with the one monumental nuclear catastrophe experienced to date, at Chernobyl in 1986. Humans also get all the blame for the financial meltdown of 2008 and 2009 and the extreme recession that has followed.

Human-abetted or human-induced catastrophes come in many forms. Some are the products of decisions by multitudes of individuals—among these are most financial crises, most current species extinctions, and the consequences of our accumulation of greenhouse gases. But in some cases, blame can be assigned to one or a few responsible parties, as with the BP *Deepwater Horizon* oil spill in 2010. Although BP is a corporation employing tens of thousands of individuals, it has a unified structure. Thus, it had the potential to act in a unified manner, unlike the billions of individuals who contribute to global warming. And although Halliburton, Cameron International Corp., and Transocean Ltd. have been implicated in the catastrophe, BP was in charge and could have insisted on and paid for more prudent behavior by the others. BP has filed lawsuits against these three firms to recoup some of the damages it has paid or will pay.

In other instances, the human actions generating catastrophes may involve multitudes of individuals across many nations. So it has been with the depletion of the ozone layer. Billions of consumers may have sprayed chlorofluorocarbons, but the concerted action of just a few producers changed what could have been a worldwide catastrophe into a situation where relatively modest losses were incurred. Some finger-pointing analysts, or catastrophe analysts in love with the story of the butterfly flapping its wings in the Amazon, see giant cascades of events having been preventable if merely a few parties had behaved better. For example,

John Taylor (2010) gives the U.S. Federal Reserve and its lax money policies the overwhelming blame for creating the global financial meltdown. Other critics assign disproportionate blame to a few rogue private players. We find more compelling those analyses that identify dozens of parties who behaved poorly or simply failed to do their jobs (Zeckhauser 2011).

In addressing causality, we distinguish between situations where one or a few persons or groups could have prevented a catastrophe, as opposed to those where only the actions of a multitude—numbers stretching from dozens to billions—could have made a difference. If a few parties could have controlled the actions of the multitude, we assign responsibility to those few. We thus classify catastrophes according to whether there are few causal agents or many. To be clear, sometimes these "causal agents" are in effect "firefighters" who did not do their jobs effectively and let a conflagration start or spread. While many would not accuse regulators of creating the excesses, misrepresentations, and foolhardiness that produced the financial catastrophe of 2008–9, some critics would argue that if just a few regulatory agencies had done their jobs effectively, the crisis could have been avoided. Yet it remains unclear whether it would have been feasible for the regulators to have been as effective as these critics specify after the fact. Following most catastrophes, particularly those where humans were major contributors, hindsight readily identifies the warning signs that were not heeded.

The Victims of Catastrophes

The catastrophes that concern us here are only those that cause suffering to many. Personal catastrophes, such as having lightning mangle one's house (as happened to one of this chapter's authors the night before the conference for this volume), may impose substantial costs on a household but hardly impose significant costs at a societal level. They involve different issues from the broad catastrophes that we study. They are not the types of catastrophes that concern us here—catastrophes that involve major losses to significant numbers of people.

One basic difference among catastrophes affecting significant numbers of people is whether the causers and the sufferers are the same or distinct. Some, but not all, catastrophes result from human actions in a group bringing harm onto itself. If those generating the catastrophe and those suffering the harm are predominantly the same, we have the risk-related variant of a *commons problem*. We refer to this as a *commons catastrophe*. The preeminent example of a potential commons catastrophe today is climate change; most humans are spewing greenhouse gases, and the potential losses will affect all of us—some of us directly and all of us because of our common concern for future generations.

We make an important distinction between two types of commons problems: those that are balanced, where all participants are in roughly symmetric positions; and those that are unbalanced, where the parties are significantly unequal in size or otherwise asymmetrically situated and therefore impose and suffer different risks. Climate change is an unbalanced commons problem because some nations and individuals are responsible for far more greenhouse emissions than others, some nations and individuals are suffering disproportionately now, and future generations will potentially suffer much more than those living now.

There are many potential catastrophes where the potential sufferers play little or no role in creating the conditions for catastrophe, as was the case with the BP oil spill. We label such a situation in which injurers are imposing losses on others as an *external catastrophe*. The appropriate policy instruments for dealing with commons and external catastrophes are often far different. Note that commons problems inevitably involve externalities, but we do not refer to them as external catastrophes because the group is inflicting harm onto itself rather than on others who are not part of the group.

The Policy Portfolio: Therapies and Criteria for Catastrophic Risk Policies

Although catastrophes will always be with us, some can be avoided, most can be minimized, and virtually all can have their risks spread more effectively. To these ends, society has developed a range of policy instruments for addressing various circumstances. Our basic assertion is that the accurate classification of the anatomy of a catastrophe helps enormously in identifying what policy instruments should be employed in dealing with it. Three social institutions receive our major attention: markets and Coasean bargains, civil liability, and governmental regulations and taxation. Within these broad categories, there are specific policy instruments, such as insurance and risk communication. Additionally, each of these instruments comes in a variety of forms. Thus, for example, insurance can be provided by the government or by the private sector, or the private sector can provide it with the government offering reinsurance. Often these instruments should be used in tandem.

Our overall conclusion is that there is no single institution and no single set of policies across institutions that will always be the most effective choice, even within a single type of catastrophe. Given this, the task should be to design and coordinate portfolios of policies that will address the catastrophic risks under study. These policies have three principal objectives: (1) providing an efficient level of risks and protection from catastrophic risks; (2) providing an efficient level of compensation for harm, hence optimal liability payments and insurance; and (3) providing an adequate level of risk communication so that people and institutions can protect and insure themselves appropriately.

Consider first the task of achieving efficient risk levels. Efficient policies set risk levels where the costs of further risk reduction just equal the benefits such reduction would provide—that is, where marginal costs equal marginal benefits. In the case of risks caused by nature, nature's trajectories cannot be readily altered, except perhaps in the long term, such as through carbon taxes if climate change is the driver. The principal task in efficiently ameliorating nature-induced risks is to invest in avoiding them and to engage in protective actions such as flood control projects, hurricane warning systems, and structural requirements in earthquake-prone areas. Catastrophic risks caused predominantly by human behavior offer opportunities both to reduce the risk and to reduce the exposure to the risk by, for example, having effective regulation that enhances nuclear safety. For both risk prevention and risk protection, the efficient level of risk reduction should strike an appropriate balance between benefits and costs. The challenge with catastrophic risks is that the probabilities associated with various levels of damage are very difficult to assess. Because the probabilities are small, society will have little or no experience with any particular category of catastrophic risk. Moreover, many risks arise from previously unseen conditions such as with climate change, or from innovative technologies such as deepwater drilling.

Similarly, the standard principles for optimal levels of insurance also carry over to coverage for catastrophic risk. People who are risk-averse, as most of us are, would prefer full insurance coverage of financial or otherwise compensable losses (e.g., loss of earnings) if insurance is offered at actuarially fair or close to actuarially fair rates. Such insurance will make the victim whole after the catastrophe and is efficient despite its costs. Matters, however, are quite different for nonmonetary losses, such as bodily injury or loss of life. The optimal insurance amounts in such cases are similar to the values for economic loss in tort liability for wrongful death and personal injury. Lost earnings, medical costs, rehabilitation expenses, and other financial losses are valued compensation components. However, generally it would not be optimal and often would not even be possible to obtain insurance that makes the individual whole for such outcomes from disasters. For example, no amount of money can compensate an individual for being killed. The efficiency goal of insurance is to equate the marginal utility of money across various states of the world.[3] Compensating for injuries and deaths is quite different from paying for compensable losses because the former losses are nonmonetary and cannot be replaced with money.

Whole compensation equates utility across states; it does not equate marginal utility. In a first-best world, an individual's own health, life, and disability insurance would provide appropriate compensation. In the second-best world in which we reside, insurance is underpurchased—in part because of behavioral mistakes and in part because of the lack of roughly actuarially fair insurance. In this world, compensation for lost income and other financial consequences makes sense and is a desirable component of a policy portfolio. But compensation for the welfare loss associated with suffering chronic pain does not.[4] These principles are borne out in patterns of private insurance purchase. People buy insurance for financial losses but not for grief or pain and suffering.

Likewise it would not be desirable to provide financial compensation to the citizenry to restore their welfare after the destruction of rare archaeological sites by floods, or to cover them for the loss of 1.6 million acres of forest in Yellowstone National Park from fire in 1988,[5] or to compensate them for the extensive wildlife deaths after the *Exxon Valdez* spill. Such losses are not equivalent to monetary harms, and money is not a capable substitute.

That such nonmonetary losses cannot or should not be fully compensated in no way diminishes their importance. For example, even though money will do nothing to restore your welfare if you are killed by a disaster, preventing each expected death has an economic value on the order of $9 million, as judged by decisions in other domains (Viscusi 2011). As a result, for nonmonetary harms for which money cannot effectively restore one's welfare, the emphasis should be on preventing those harms from occurring, usually by deterring the party or parties that create the risk. Simply transferring money to those who have suffered a loss would be an inadequate response, as it could not restore the victim's welfare. It would also be an inappropriate response because it would exceed the insurance amount the person would have chosen if free to do so.

If private risk decisions with respect to self-protection and insurance are to be efficient, people must have a reasonable understanding of the risk involved. Information provision through risk-communication efforts can play a key role in fostering such understanding. Market prices for insurance often convey appropriate information, but not always. For example, although insurance prices in a locale may provide some information about the level of the risk, they will not indicate whether there is a current crisis or whether the risk level has changed from the historic level used to set insurance rates.[6] The risk-communication task is often complicated by the fact that even the government or private party most knowledgeable about the risk may not fully understand it. Even in situations where we have a substantial scientific basis for making risk judgments, as with hurricane warning systems, the magnitude of the risk may not be widely known until the emergency has passed.

If the government offers shrill warnings that lead people to evacuate needlessly when the damage turns out to be modest, it runs the risk of people dismissing the warnings in the future. Maintaining the credibility of the warnings effort is an essential but complex task when dealing with ambiguous risks that are rare or evolving occurrences. Telling people on a barrier island to evacuate because a disastrous hurricane risk is 5 percent likely, as would seem prudent, will have them evacuating ten times on average before a disastrous hurricane hits. Over time, residents may level charges of excessive wolf-crying and become complacent when future warnings are received.

Because of the scale of the harms produced and the multiplicity of causes of catastrophic events, societal efforts to foster efficient risk and insurance responses to catastrophic risks will require that multiple social institutions be involved and coordinated. Below, we consider in illustrative contexts these different institutional mechanisms and the particular roles that they might play. Identifying the respective roles that might be served by different institutions is a useful starting point for conceptualizing the appropriate policy design. However, in some countries—such as the United States—these institutions are not subject to centralized control. There is not, for example, a single administrator who can dictate the roles of market forces, common law doctrine, and regulatory policies. Nor would we propose such. Despite the virtue of unity for dealing with catastrophes, most government agencies concerned with catastrophes have many other roles to play, roles that should be kept separate. Further increasing the challenge, in the case of catastrophes with an international dimension, such as climate change, even coordinated actions by a single country will be far from sufficient because of the global dimensions of the problems.

Our proposed framework distinguishes three broad sets of social institutions: the market and Coasean bargains; civil liability; and government regulation through rulemaking, legislation, and taxation. Within each of these three sets, different mechanisms—such as insurance and information—can play a role with respect to catastrophic risks. Effective policymaking consequently requires that different institutions be engaged and that choices be made within each of them regarding the most appropriate forms of intervention. The optimal policy mix will differ substantially as the efficacy of the institutions varies according to the source of the risk and whether the catastrophe is self-imposed, commons, or external. For example, the annual occurrence of 400,000 smoking-attributable American deaths from a series of individual risk-taking behaviors is a self-imposed loss to a large number of smokers. However, it would not be categorized as a catastrophe, as this loss is the aggregation of a series of isolated risks. In contrast, 400,000 people being killed by a natural disaster would be categorized as a monumental catastrophe.

The Scale of Catastrophic Risks

What are the characteristics of catastrophic risks, and how do those characteristics affect the ability of the market, political processes, and other institutions to deal with them? The scale of catastrophic risks greatly affects the ability of conventional decentralized institutions to address them. Figure 2.1 indicates the number of fatalities per year and the associated cumulative number of events involving different levels of fatalities for earthquakes, floods, tornadoes, and hurricanes. Each of the scales in the diagram is logarithmic; thus the figure represents what are called "power laws." A variable $p(x)$ has a power law distribution if it can be characterized as $p(x) = cx^d$, where c and d are constants, so that $\log p(x) = \log c + d \log x$. Thus, moving from 10 fatalities to 100 fatalities on the horizontal axis doubles the distance along the horizontal axis but increases the number of fatalities by a factor of 10. After transforming the scale in this manner, the pattern of catastrophes appears well behaved. Note, however, that this happens only after the scale has, in effect, been compressed more strongly for higher values, thus allowing substantial outliers to be visible. Scientists have used power functions to characterize the distribution of catastrophic events because familiar well-behaved distributions, such as the normal distribution, do not come close to characterizing the pattern of catastrophic risks. Catastrophes have too many extreme outliers. For example, a normal distribution, or even a lognormal distribution, would not fully capture the potential for

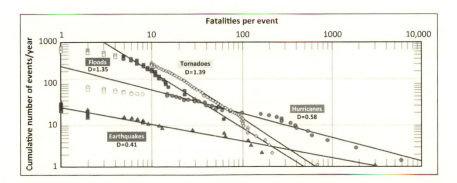

Figure 2.1. Fat Tails for Catastrophic Events. *Source:* U.S. Geological Survey (2003).

truly extreme catastrophic outcomes that differ markedly from less severe catastrophes. The distributions for such catastrophic risks are called "fat-tailed," reflecting the fact that extreme outliers are much more likely than they are with well-known distributions, such as the normal or log-normal. Such extreme outliers cause inordinately severe harm and account for a substantial percentage of expected losses from catastrophes.

One encounters outliers for a variety of catastrophic risks. The Japanese earthquake in 2011—merely one of the four largest earthquakes since 1990[7]—merits outlier status because of the extreme damage it caused to the Japanese economy. The BP *Deepwater Horizon* oil spill in 2010, which is the largest oil spill to date in North American waters, dumped 4.9 million barrels of oil into the Gulf of Mexico (Oil Spill Commission 2011:55, 167).[8] The *Exxon Valdez* oil spill, which riveted the nation in 1989, was the second largest oil spill in U.S. waters (King 2010). That spill dumped an estimated 257,000 barrels of oil into Prince William Sound, but it provided little clue that there might be a BP disaster that would involve much more spillage: the BP *Deepwater Horizon* disaster dumped nearly twenty times as much oil, though fortunately warm water tamed its consequences.[9] The only greater spill anywhere in North America happened over a century ago, in 1910, when nine million barrels of oil were spilled by the Lakeview Gusher in California (Harvey 2010; KPMG Global Energy Institute 2011). However, that spill did little damage because the affected area was inland and barren. The 9/11 terrorist attack took almost three thousand lives, far more than the worst previous terrorism loss on American soil, the 168 deaths from the Oklahoma City bombing (U.S. Department of Homeland Security 1995). As these examples show, the potential for extreme outliers consequently involves a scale that may pose insurmountable challenges to conventional institutional responses, such as private insurance arrangements. Moreover, the scale associated with catastrophes is difficult to predict because such harms are unprecedented.

Insurance companies base their rates on the history of premiums and losses for a particular line of insurance. Doing so in a meaningful way requires that there be sufficient data with which to assess the riskiness of particular policies. The government often assists in providing risk assessments, particularly with respect to weather patterns and natural hazards. For a firm to remain solvent, the premiums plus the returns earned on the policies must be sufficient to cover the firm's losses when they occur, plus its capital costs and administrative expenses. Random modest losses that are not anticipated cause little difficulty. However, if there are catastrophic events generating a scale of damages that is unprecedented, as is the case with many record-setting catastrophic events, it will be difficult to provide appropriate and viable insurance coverage.

These catastrophic events could involve a single concentrated loss or a multitude of highly correlated losses. The home mortgage financing crisis was not the result of a single bad mortgage but rather was caused by many hundreds of thousands of mortgages that fell into default in a single year. Banks' portfolios included very large numbers of mortgages, but these numbers did not provide diversification since all mortgages were vulnerable to the common risk of plummeting housing prices.

Despite the bailouts, the recent financial meltdown showed the tremendous spillover effects that catastrophes often generate. Three years later, most of the developed world's economy was still reeling from this financial collapse. Similarly, the harm to Japan from the earthquake and its dual accompaniments of a tsunami and the Fukushima Daiichi nuclear crisis reverberated throughout the Japanese economy, which in turn affected Japan's trading partners.

At a most fundamental level, the scale and associated probabilities of catastrophic events are poorly understood because small probabilities are often coupled with comparatively little relative experience with the risk. To the extent that the risks result from human actions, those responsible for generating the risks may not fully understand either the levels of the risks or how these might be altered by precautionary behavior on the part of potential sufferers. For risks that result from nature, the only possible effective responses are precautionary actions and the provision of insurance. Offering insurance to homeowners for potential damage from fires—excluding massive fires from single events, such as an earthquake or terrorist attack—will generate a portfolio of independent risks, thus making risk pooling feasible.[10] However, for catastrophic risks that kill hundreds of thousands, as did the Tangshan, China earthquake in 1976, or produce vast damage, as did the 1906 San Francisco earthquake, which when combined with the resulting fires caused extensive damage throughout the city, the risks are strongly dependent.[11] For correlated risks affecting very large groups, the scale of the harm and the interdependence of the risks often undermine the potential role of insurance.[12]

The difficulties posed by low-probability severe-loss events affect all catastrophic risks, whether they are generated by human action, by nature, or by the two jointly. Where human action precipitates the event, dimly understood risks lend themselves neither to fostering adequate risk controls by the injurer nor to self-protective actions by the potential victims. Whatever the cause of a harm, insurance approaches through market forces will be impeded by the substantial scale, the inability to predict the distribution of potential harm, or both.

The limits of markets in dealing with catastrophic risks caused by nature are exemplified by considering a doomsday-rock scenario, whereby a large asteroid threatens to collide with the Earth and wipe out much, if not all, of its population.[13] Averting such a disaster is not feasible given available technologies, though humans could attempt to develop weapons to blow the rock off course if a real threat were anticipated with sufficient lead time. If efforts to divert the on-course rock were unsuccessful, potential insurance responses would, at best, be woefully inadequate and probably irrelevant. Many less draconian catastrophes present the same difficulties as the doomsday-rock scenario, albeit on a smaller scale. For example, no insurance arrangements could have protected widely against the 2008 financial meltdown.

Risk assessment and risk communication could help address the political challenges of dealing with catastrophes. Unfortunately, it is often difficult to determine when preventive measures did avert a catastrophe and, therefore, when to give due political credit. Because disastrous outcomes are unlikely to occur during any particular politician's watch, the natural political response is to do little to avoid or ameliorate low-probability risks, even though such measures would be quite worthwhile on an expected-value basis. Nonetheless, providing good risk assessments would help the public understand current risk levels. Equally important, it would help voters assess the contributions of government policies in reducing risks. Although policies are sometimes undertaken for symbolic reasons and have no demonstrable effects, concrete evidence of policy impact often helps bolster public support. In the political realm, accomplishments that cannot be measured are often those that are not pursued. If antiterrorism measures reduced the risk of another 9/11-type attack from 10 percent to 5 percent in the decade following 2001, that was a major accomplishment. But with present technologies, reporting systems, and media practices, no one would know the magnitude of the accomplishment or even whether there had been any accomplishment.

External Harms

If risks are self-imposed, people have an incentive for self-protection— at least to the extent that they understand those risks and the risks respond to ways people might change their behavior. If human action imposes external harms, then self-interested behavior alone will lead to inadequate control of the risk. In the case of risks generated through market contexts, such as the manufacture of a prescription drug that could cause thousands of birth defects, there will be market incentives to produce safer products if consumers are cognizant of the risks. But if the prospect of harm is not recognized, the potential losses to the firm will be limited by the firm's available financial resources. In the case of externalities not in a market context—sometimes referred to in the law and economics literature as "harm to strangers"—the market will exert little or no incentive to exercise caution. This is equivalent to the classic problem of excess pollution when the source cannot be traced.

In theory, externalities caused by human action can be addressed by applying the Coase theorem (Coase 1960). The many well-known limitations of voluntary agreements to control risks affecting broad population groups—most notably high transaction costs for reaching an efficient agreement—apply to catastrophic risks. But with catastrophic risks, the challenges facing potential application of the Coase theorem are magnified. Consider the case in which the injurer has the property rights to engage in the risky activity. The potential injured parties collectively may suffer enormous damage from a catastrophe; but not being aware of the risk levels and the potential harms, they will have little basis on which to propose such Coasean bargains, much less to organize themselves effectively to avoid free-rider problems. However, if the risks are reasonably well understood and the potential victims own the property rights, then it is likely that the risky activity can be shut down through, for example, an injunction, as the injurer will not have adequate resources to compensate the victims for the expected losses.

Internal Harms

It would seem that if parties are imposing risks on themselves only, effective policy would not be a major challenge. That is true if the predominant costs incurred by each party are caused by its own actions, if good and intelligible information is provided on risks, and if parties respond rationally. Alas, the second and third conditions are rarely satisfied for catastrophic risks. The field of behavioral decision has amply demonstrated that humans are poor at dealing with low-probability events (Berger et al. 2011).

We label as a "commons catastrophe" the loss that results when people impose harm on their shared resource. Although commons problems represent merely a subset of externalities, they are an important subset. The commons name is borrowed from Garrett Hardin's (1968) essay, "The Tragedy of the Commons," examining the process by which farmers raising sheep on a village commons, which was available to the community for free, led the commons to be severely overgrazed. To achieve an efficient outcome in such a situation, some regulatory regime, in the broadest sense of that term, must be created.

We distinguish between *balanced* and *unbalanced* commons. In a balanced commons, symmetric agents impose risks on each other. Given their balance, the prospects for a successful regulatory regime brighten considerably. The sheep farmers would surely note the overgrazed commons and their scrawny sheep with their lusterless wool. They would be likely to get together and formulate a scheme of taxation or a regulation limiting the number of sheep per farmer. None would expect to be allowed to graze six sheep to the neighbor's four. Given the symmetry among the parties, the achievable outcomes would inevitably be symmetric as well. The tragedy of this commons would become merely an episode of minor loss, as the farmers worked out appropriate impositions on each to the benefit of all, thereby demonstrating the compatibility of a balanced commons with Coase theorem success.

A similar outcome could be expected when symmetric agents create a hazard by using the commons as a dump. For example, equal-sized metal plating firms could be dumping toxic wastes into their joint "backyard." They might mutually agree to limit or eliminate such dumping, accepting equal restraints on their access to the commons.

In an unbalanced commons, asymmetric agents, perhaps some large and others small, might find a compromise much more elusive. The potential gains from an efficient regulatory regime would be no less, but each agent would have a logical argument in favor of a preferred distribution of impositions. Many would believe the normative strength of their own proposals. This, of course, is the situation the world confronts with global warming.[14] The two biggest emitters of greenhouse gases, China and the United States, see the world very differently. China argues that it is poor, that most gases dumped to date have come from highly developed countries, and that those countries bore no restrictions on their emissions while they were passing through China's current state of development. The United States, by contrast, argues that emissions should be tied to amounts produced at some prior date, that China should refrain from building many new coal-fired power plants that threaten the world's climate, that China is prospering even as the United States struggles, and that China should certainly bear a significant share of the burden of reducing gases, and so on. Given this stark clash of policy views, optimism for reaching an effective agreement is hardly merited. On the brighter side, if the major players in this unbalanced commons situation can reach an agreement, the prospects of other nations following are favorable.

To see the challenge of the unbalanced commons, consider two dissimilar chemical companies, A and B, that are the sole residents around a small lake, each reliant on its water as an input for its production and as an outlet for its filtered effluent. Company A, the larger firm, has been there for decades. Company B, the smaller but much faster growing firm, is a new arrival. Both firms are adhering to Environmental Protection

Agency (EPA) effluent regulations, but those are insufficiently strict. The toxic buildup in the lake water from both companies' discharges has raised production costs for both companies significantly.

There is a bigger concern for these agents than escalating production costs. The lake may pass a point of no return, a risk that would shutter both the plants. Unfortunately, the science on dealing with such toxic accumulations is unclear. The firms may not know whether they are approaching the "point of no return."

Company A proposes that the total toxic content of effluents be reduced 20 percent below 2011 levels and held there. Faster-growing Company B points out that much of the toxic buildup in the lake is the result of A's dumping over decades, including dumping at high levels in the old days when EPA restrictions were much laxer. It proposes that until its cumulative contribution to the buildup reaches the cumulative contribution of A, that A cut back by 40 percent from its 2011 levels, with no cutbacks imposed on B. Once cumulative contributions are equal, B expects that its output will be greater than that of A. It proposes that then both firms adhere to a per-unit-of-output standard, one that would have to be tightened over time so as to hold the toxic level in the lake steady.

The prospects for reaching voluntary agreement in this situation are poor. Both firms have a negotiating position that can be supported with good arguments and moral claims. Moreover, they are not close to agreement. An unbalanced commons is likely to be a heavily overburdened commons. If a commons catastrophe is a possibility, its risk is likely to rise with little restraint until the commons is on the verge of collapse. To return to our prior metaphor, if the doomsday rock were five years away, given the world's impending demise, the nations of the world would likely pitch in wholeheartedly to mount a diversion effort, quite unlike their behavior for the control of greenhouse gases, where the danger is both less and more distant. But if the doomsday rock would not hit for another fifty years, we could expect fierce debate on who should pay what, with valuable time wasted before agreement was reached, possibly too late.

Our principal argument about commons catastrophes brings both good and bad news. The good news, contrary to much that has been written about commons problems (which are usually presented with symmetric players), is that solutions to the balanced commons are readily available and plausibly achievable. The bad news is that most of the world's salient commons problems, many of which bring risks of commons catastrophes, have players in quite asymmetric positions. These problems are much harder to solve than those that are usually presented in scholarly articles and textbooks. Climate change is a salient case. With major agents as dissimilarly situated as the United States and China, the task of dealing effectively with this commons problem is almost insoluble.

To be sure, if the commons were privatized, that is, if a single party owned the lake where the two chemical companies reside, dumping would be controlled to maintain the lake's quality. A reasonable outcome would be achieved regarding an unbalanced commons. Unfortunately, most unbalanced commons are not owned in this manner—the earth's atmosphere being the best example. In theory, many other unbalanced commons, including local air quality and lakes, are under the control of a government that could act like a private owner. Any poor outcomes then would be the result of inappropriate regulatory policies, stemming in turn from such factors as information shortcomings, inflexible options, and political distortions. Such factors would probably be much more indicative of an unbalanced commons, since agents in a balanced commons would gladly assist the government in developing regulations.

Our ability and the methods to fix all such political economy concerns are beyond the scope of this chapter.[15] We now turn, however, to an analysis of a variety of mechanisms, each of which can help in dealing with catastrophic risks in some contexts.

Tort Liability

When human activity imposes external risks, liability for torts can be an effective mechanism for controlling those risks and providing compensation to the injured. Tort liability generally deals with physical and monetary harms such as auto accidents, medical malpractice injuries, and product risks. These harms rarely involve a "commons" situation. When nature creates the risk, liability is not a factor, since nature cannot be sued nor otherwise incentivized. Therefore, we examine here only human-created external harms when examining the tort system's role in fostering safety incentives and providing compensation. If all losses are financial or, more generally, compensable, then liability rules that require the injurer to make any injured party whole produce both efficient outcomes and optimal insurance. In addition, for many contexts, tort liability establishes requirements that the potential injurer provide adequate information, thereby enabling those at risk either to avoid the hazard or to take precautions against it. However, because tort liability is generally limited to foreseeable harms, catastrophic events may be so rare that they could not be anticipated.

However, if the losses involve harms for which money is not a viable substitute, such as the loss of a scenic view or the loss of life or limb, it will often not be feasible to make the injured party whole. To adequately deter risk-imposing actions, institutions beyond the market and its partner liability arrangements, such as government regulations, will be required. Liability rules have other shortcomings, such as difficulty parsing the causal influences in situations involving multiple contributing parties. As part of our two-tier liability proposal below, we suggest that joint and several liability not be applied and that a single party be subject to strict liability for all catastrophic risk damages. The expectation is that the responsible firm will contract with other participants on a contingent basis for their share of the liability.

The shortcomings of the current tort liability system are well known. Catastrophic risks, which can involve large-scale losses, present severe additional challenges to the tort system. Legal limits restrict the amount of liability to a firm's financial resources; this prevents the liability system from providing either adequate safety incentives or sufficient compensation for catastrophic risks. This is not to say that liability rules are irrelevant. Rather, they are insufficient. The potential benefit of liability rules in controlling risks lies in forcing external harms to be internalized by the injurer. However, to be truly effective for catastrophic risks, society must address the fact that liability has no effect beyond a certain scale of loss. If such beyond-scale losses are significant in expectation, as they usually are with the fat tails of catastrophic risks, then risk imposers lack the incentive to be sufficiently cautious.

A Two-Tier Liability Solution

To overcome these limits of liability in addressing catastrophic risks posed by human action, we have proposed a two-tier liability system.[16] Although we developed this proposal in the context of oil firms such as BP undertaking deepwater drilling, the structure applies broadly to a wide range of human activities posing catastrophic risks. Our proposal is targeted at the demonstrably high stakes situations of deepwater drilling and nuclear power but can be readily extended to a broad array of contexts, including many where the stakes are far lower. Use of the two-tier liability approach is best suited to potential catastrophic risk situations in which there is a single party that can be identified as being in control of the risky activity. Adopting our proposal anywhere would require legislation to replace the current legal regimes, and there would need to be a change in regulatory functions as well.

The first tier of our proposal makes a firm that is engaged in potentially risky activities subject to strict liability for all damages. Moreover, the firm must provide evidence that it has the financial resources, including insurance, commensurate to meet potential harms in most circumstances. The second tier of the proposal is that a firm should be taxed for the expected value of harms it imposes beyond its demonstrated financial capabilities. This ensures that the firm will internalize the full costs of the catastrophic risks it is creating through its behavior. In addition to serving as a safety-incentive mechanism, this tax can be used to establish a compensation fund that, across firms, will cover losses beyond the established resources of the perpetrators.

Before detailing these principal tiers of the proposal, it is useful to summarize all the proposal's various main features. Our overall objective is to create a set of economic incentive mechanisms to generate efficient levels of risk taking even in situations in which adverse outcomes may be catastrophic. The policy emphasis would shift from the current regulation-oriented approach to a decentralized financial incentive system. Experience with past catastrophes—such as the *Valdez* and BP spills and the Fukushima disaster—points to the inadequacy of using regulation as the primary control mechanism. Government regulators, at least in the United States, are woefully underpaid relative to the market and hence are likely to be underskilled. Furthermore, political pressures or conditions of regulatory capture often lead them to be undervigilant. Finally, regulators usually have much less information than the parties imposing the risks; therefore, they are not the most effective decision makers for controlling those risks.

To establish financial incentives, we propose a financially meaningful structure in which full responsibility is placed on the lead firm in the risky activity. As just mentioned, this firm is better situated than government regulators to have the requisite technical expertise and ability to monitor contractor and worker behavior to ensure that it meets appropriate standards of care.

Our proposal will make the responsible party for the risky behavior subject to strict liability. There will be no joint and several liability. Instead, the lead firm can contract with other firms involved in the risky operation to share in liability on a contingent basis. To provide appropriate incentives, any existing damages caps will be eliminated, and the lead firm must demonstrate adequate financial capacity, either through its assets or insurance, to cover most levels of catastrophic loss. Damage payments will be limited to compensatory damages, as there is no deterrence rationale for punitive damages when the probability of detection is 1.0, as it is with the types of catastrophic situations we are discussing. The second tier of the liability structure establishes a risk tax for expected losses in excess of the firm's demonstrated resources. Regulators will continue in their traditional role in terms of safety inspections, but the policy approach would recognize regulators' likely inability to ensure safe operations. There would be a shift in regulators' main responsibility to setting the financial requirements for firms engaged in the risky activity and establishing the amount of the risk tax.

Implementation of the first liability tier of this proposal requires that a minimum level of financial resources be set, presumably in light of the scale of potential catastrophic harms. Of course, it is not possible to predict the worst-case scenarios, given the fat-tailed nature of catastrophic risks. But a convenient starting point might be the worst harm that has been experienced to date in that activity. Thus, for deepwater drilling in the Gulf, firms might be required to demonstrate a level of financial resources and insurance that is adequate to cover losses of the magnitude of the fund that BP set up after its spill, which was $20 billion (Oil Spill Commission 2011:185). A high financial threshold will restrict operations to firms with resources sufficient to cover major losses, thereby restricting competition and possibly turning away the most efficient producers. But the alternative of opening up operations to firms with limited financial resources will dilute safety incentives and create an influx of small firms that have little financial stake in potentially high payoff–catastrophic loss ventures. The threshold should be set neither too high nor too low, so as to balance these two sources of disadvantage.

Ensuring adequate financial resources at a very high level does not guarantee that there would be sufficient resources to compensate for all possible losses. In addition to financial losses that might not be compensated, there could be irremediable harms, including losses of life and of natural resources. However, by providing much stronger safety incentives than those the tort liability system can currently impose alone, this proposal would increase the degree to which the potential injurers internalize the costs imposed by their activities for losses both below and above their financial resources.

A complementary component of our proposal is that one firm should be identified as the responsible party for the two-tier liability regime. In the case of deepwater drilling, this party would be the operator. The principal impetus for making the responsible firm, rather than government regulators, the linchpin of the proposal is that the firm is more likely to have technical expertise and private knowledge about the risky activity. There are few enough situations where catastrophic risks are created that identifying such parties in advance should not be burdensome. The responsible firm then can make arrangements with its contractors to monitor their activities and to share possible financial responsibility with these firms.

In the case of the BP oil spill, BP purchased the rights to drill in that location and for legal purposes became the operator of the well (Oil Spill Commission 2011:92). BP then hired Transocean to be its drilling contractor, which in turn hired Smit Salvage Americas to salvage the rig (Oil Spill Commission 2011:130). BP also hired Halliburton to cement the production casing into place at the bottom of the well, and a

Halliburton subsidiary (Sperry Sun) did the "mud logging," that is, the examination of the rock or sediment dislodged during drilling (Oil Spill Commission 2011:3, 100, 224). BP also hired other contractors for specialized jobs, such as "mud engineers from I-I SWACO (a subsidiary of Schlumberger, a major international oilfield services provider), remotely operated vehicle technicians from Oceaneering, [and] tank cleaners from the OCS Group" (Oil Spill Commission 2011:3). Under our proposal, BP would have full liability but could make arrangements with its many contractors to be reimbursed for part of its liability costs, depending on the nature of the damage, the role of the contractor in relation to the harm, and whatever other provisions are mutually agreed upon. Similarly, contractors such as Transocean and Halliburton could make independent arrangements with any subcontractors that they employ. But regardless of these arrangements and whether their subcontractors can pay for the damages, they will nevertheless be liable for any damages specified in the agreement that they have with BP.

Legislation and Taxation

Our two-tier liability proposal for addressing external catastrophic risks caused by human actions requires government action. In the case of oil spills resulting from deepwater drilling, there already is an initial tier that is administered on a case-by-case basis. The threshold financial resources amount for offshore drilling can currently be set at a level ranging from $35 million to $150 million, but the amount is set more typically in the $10 million to $35 million range (Oil Spill Commission 2011:283). Liability for oil spills is capped at a level of $75 million except when firms are shown to have been grossly negligent or otherwise reckless (Oil Pollution Act 1990:§ 2704(a)(3)).[17] Similarly, operators of nuclear reactors are required to obtain private insurance of only $375 million (Price-Anderson Act 1957:§ 2210(s)).[18] All these levels are ridiculously low relative to the magnitudes of possible losses from accidents. Our proposal would remove all caps and would impose much more substantial financial requirements on the responsible firm.

The second tier of our liability proposal would involve government taxation of the residual risk. The level of this tax should be set to reflect the risk level of the particular firm's activities. It should be set to equal the expected cost of damages beyond the firm's demonstrated financial resources. This is the level just sufficient to provide appropriate safety incentives to the firm. There are similar kinds of fee systems in place at present. However, those fee systems are not the safety incentive tax that we propose but instead are more modest fees designed to establish victim-compensation funds. The tax would serve a second purpose. It should be sufficient in expectation to pay for the cost of accidents beyond the responsible firm's ability to pay.

The appropriate tax level for any project, such as a deepwater well, would depend on the risk involved, which would involve difficult assessments of the likelihood and size of possible accidents. The government may be poorly equipped to make such an assessment. One possible approach would involve knowledgeable private parties, such as other oil firms or insurance companies. They would bid to assume a sliver, say 5 percent, of the damages above the responsible firm's total of demonstrated resources plus insurance. This would establish the appropriate tax rate, which in this case would be twenty times the low bid for assuming the 5 percent sliver of responsibility. The sliver amount plus the tax collected for the remaining 95 percent of excess risk would simultaneously provide efficient incentives for safety as well as funds that in expectation would cover losses beyond the responsible firm's ability to pay.

Safety Regulation

Our proposal does not, it should be stressed, rely substantially on government regulation, which is the usual mechanism for fostering safety incentives involving major risks. We do not propose that regulation be abandoned. For example, there should continue to be regulation of nuclear safety and other highly dangerous activities. The assessments by these regulators also can play a role in evaluating the riskiness of the firm's activities. However, as the BP *Deepwater Horizon* oil spill demonstrated, the idea of relying on regulation as the principal instrument for ensuring safety fails for two principal reasons.[19] First, there is substantial inequality of information. The firm undertaking the risky behavior has significant private knowledge of the risks and precautions, and this knowledge is not generally available to regulators. Second, the activities involved often are highly technical and require specialized expertise that government officials with broad regulatory responsibilities may not possess. Corporate engineers who have substantial relevant expertise often can earn salaries well above the government pay scale, suggesting that the government will continue to be unable to secure sufficient talent to deal with many classes of risks (Donahue 2008).[20]

For risks generated by nature, regulation can play a much more constructive role than any liability system to achieve proper safety, since nature is not deterred by potential financial penalties. Although it is not feasible to regulate nature, it is possible to regulate the human behaviors that could amplify the losses inflicted by nature. A relatively unobtrusive form of regulatory intervention is the provision of information. Sirens and media announcements alerting citizens to an approaching tornado can enable people to take shelter, and weather warnings can limit the harms caused by major hurricanes. In some instances, this informational intervention can be bolstered with either recommendations or require-ments that an area be evacuated, as in the cases of Hurricanes Katrina and Irene. More generally, the government can require that houses meet building codes pertinent to the risks in the region or that no resi-dential or commercial construction occur on a fault line or in a flood-prone area.

The Government Role with Respect to Insurance

The government also has actively imposed requirements for purchasing insurance and providing government-subsidized insurance for disas-ters, most notably for floods. One rationale for the government provi-sion of catastrophic-risk insurance, or reinsurance beyond normal coverage, is that the scale of the losses is so great that private markets are not up to the task. But perhaps an even stronger rationale is that, after a catastrophe, there will be huge numbers of people who have suf-fered major harm or firms whose collapse would cause major suffering in the economy. The pressures for the government to mitigate these harms with post-disaster relief are generally strong and at times irresist-ible. By requiring that people or firms buy insurance when exposed to catastrophic risks, the government in effect provides for some of the funding that will ultimately be needed after disaster strikes.

That government-mandated insurance can serve constructive roles does not imply that current insurance arrangements are ideal. Most gov-ernment mandates for insurance tend to be accompanied by heavy gov-ernment subsidies, as we see in such areas as flood insurance, pension insurance, or terrorism reinsurance for real estate.[21] Unfortunately, a government-subsidized catastrophic-risk insurance program would ad-versely affect behavior. People and corporations would have an unin-tended inducement to build in flood- or hurricane-prone areas or in high-risk terrorism locales since they would be undercharged for their expected risks. The classic problem of insurance is that of moral haz-ard, in which the insured feel less need to exercise sufficient care. If natural disasters or terrorism were the source of losses, the covered party would not control the risk, as they would be caused by nature or terrorists. However, the extent of the harm caused by such disasters is very strongly related to the siting of construction and to the efforts that are made to protect it. Should catastrophe insurance be subsidized, peo-ple would relocate inappropriately and would make insufficient efforts to protect themselves or reduce their losses. To the extent that people anticipate a government bailout after a disaster effected by humans and consequently do not take protective actions, the problems are similar, although probably less severe, since there is less assurance of a bailout than there would be of compensation from a subsidized disaster-insurance program, whether run by the government or by private companies.

Allocating Institutional Responsibilities

We have described the anatomy of catastrophic losses, focusing not only on the identity and incentives of those who impose the risk but also on the relationship of the risk imposers to the parties suffering losses. We have argued that different anatomies call for different policies, sometimes for significantly different policies. Table 2.1 summarizes the institutional responsibilities we identify as appropriate to each type of catastrophe. Note that in every instance at least one of the institutions has no significant constructive role to play. This categorization highlights the diversity of catastrophic risks and the need to develop and deploy a portfolio of risk policies. Different policy tools are useful with respect to different kinds of risk situations. Generally, it will be fruitful to employ a mix of policy instruments tailored to each particular situation.

Table 2.1. Allocation of Responsibility for Catastrophic Risks

	External risks caused by nature	*External risks caused by humans*	*Internal risks caused by humans*
Markets and Coasean bargains	Yes, but limited for catastrophes due to scale and correlation of risks	Yes, but limited by bargaining impediments	Yes, through information, insurance and personal self-protection
Civil liability	No	Yes, but liability limits for catastrophes. Need first tier of two-tier liability system	Not generally, but sometimes possible for unbalanced internal risks
Regulation, legislation, and taxation	Yes, to provide information, foster self-protection, mandatory or subsidized insurance, and post-disaster relief	Yes, regulate externalities in many ways, but need second tier of two-tier liability for complex risks	Yes, but often there are barriers to policy adoption for unbalanced risks

Civil liability has a critical but restricted area of application, namely, when humans impose risks externally (or internal risk impositions are severely unbalanced). But even in this area, the current liability system falls far short when dealing with catastrophic risks. It cannot cover the largest losses, which—given the fat tails of disaster losses—constitute a significant portion of overall expected losses. We have proposed that, where a responsible party can be identified prior to any accident, liability approaches be augmented with a two-tier liability structure designed to cope with this problem. The tax-tier aspect of the two-tier liability system would be part of the regulatory mechanism. The two-tier liability structure would greatly enhance the current efficacy of government regulation, which is not suited to provide adequate risk incentives for many high-risk activities.

Predominant market approaches play a limited but useful role in dealing with catastrophes. In almost all contexts, there are at least some opportunities for self-protection and for private insurance. Appropriate information can provide the right incentives for controlling self-imposed catastrophes. A variety of approaches, such as agreed-upon self-regulation or taxation of risky activities, can work for balanced commons catastrophes—that is, for situations in which symmetrically situated parties have imposed risks on themselves. Unfortunately, where catastrophes are concerned, a balanced commons is an unlikely situation.

Greater challenges arise with external catastrophes, such as deepwater oil spills, and those arising in an unbalanced commons, such as climate change. As we show in Table 2.1, markets and Coasean bargains are far from adequate for dealing with such problems. Indeed, the general category of externalities serves as a paradigmatic example of market failure in economic textbooks. To achieve the best feasible outcomes in such situations, individual actions must be combined with an array of liability and regulatory interventions.

Catastrophic risks will always be with us. But a judicious choice of policies from the entire portfolio of public and private institutional mechanisms can significantly reduce their frequency, magnitude, and consequences.

Acknowledgment

Cary Coglianese and Howard Kunreuther provided helpful comments.

Notes

1. Studies that address institutional coordination issues generally include, among others, Viscusi (1988, 2002), American Law Institute (1991a, 1991b), Kessler (2011), Posner (2011), and Shleifer (2011).

2. The October 2011 earthquake in Eastern Turkey caused substantial loss of life, in part due to lax building codes (Arsu 2011).

3. Interestingly, equating marginal utilities in this fashion sometimes leads to insuring against bad events, as with life insurance, and sometimes to insuring against good outcomes. For example, annuities and Social Security protect one against living for a long time.

4. It is not evident that such losses even raise the marginal utility of income so that people would not choose to structure insurance policies to provide additional income after such adverse events.

5. For a full list of the most significant wildfires in U.S. history, see the National Interagency Fire Center's website at http://www.nifc.gov/fireInfo/fireInfo_stats _histSigFires.html.

6. In the 1990 Berkshire Hathaway Inc. Shareholder Letter, Warren Buffett explained to shareholders why his firm wrote relatively little insurance in the prior year: "The picture would change quickly if a major physical or financial catastrophe were to occur. Absent such a shock, one to two years will likely pass before underwriting losses become large enough to raise management fear to a level that would spur major price increases. When that moment arrives, Berkshire will be ready—both financially and psychologically—to write huge amounts of business" (Buffett 1990). Subsequently, he observed, "we will [write insurance] only at prices we believe to be commensurate with risk. If competitors become optimistic, our volume will fall. This insurance has, in fact, tended in recent years to be woefully underpriced; most sellers have left the field on stretchers" (Buffett 1990).

7. For a full list of the world's largest earthquakes since 1900, see the U.S. Geological Survey's website at http://earthquake.usgs.gov/earthquakes/world /10_largest_world.php.

8. The second largest spill, at 3.3 million barrels, was Ixtoc I in the Bay of Campeche in the Gulf of Mexico, off the coast of Mexico (Robertson 2010).

9. An overview of the *Exxon Valdez* spill can be found at the federal-state *Exxon Valdez* Oil Spill Trustee Council's website at http://www.evostc.state.ak .us/facts/qanda.cfm.

10. The fires caused by the San Francisco earthquake destroyed 28,000 structures, three-fourths of the developed areas in San Francisco (Canton 2006:S159).

11. The U.S. Geological Survey Earthquake Hazards Program contains historical information about major earthquakes and resulting fatalities and property damage at its website, http://earthquake.usgs.gov/.

12. That is because traditional insurance is provided by insurance companies and reinsurance companies, whose assets may be large but are small relative to the losses from some catastrophic risks. Financial markets have far greater asset levels, and it is possible that catastrophe bonds offer an attractive insurance arrangement. Such bonds pay a premium over regular bonds but do not pay off at all if a specified form of catastrophe occurs.

13. An earlier "doomsday rock," the Chicxulub asteroid, is believed by many scientists to have led to the extinction of the dinosaurs. Future threats of a collision of a large asteroid with the earth also exist. The doomsday rock serves as a principal case study in Posner's (2004) exploration of policies toward catastrophic risks.

14. We leave aside the fact that, although emitters are around today, the majority of sufferers are as yet unborn; we effectively assume that nations represent their citizens, present and future. Were the present–future divide acknowledged, the problem would become one of external impositions.

15. Mahbubani (forthcoming), argues that the vastly increased interdependence of the world calls for greatly enhanced schemes of global governance. He has shared with us the observation that in former times the nations of the world might be thought of as 193 separate boats. However, a metaphor more appropriate for today's world is that they are residents of 193 cabins on a single boat. If so, that would create a balanced commons, and effective global governance might be feasible. Following Mahbubani's boat image, we think of the nations of the world as being on a 10,000-cabin boat, with some nations, such as the United States and China, occupying many hundreds of cabins but other nations having only one or a few. And some nations are giving up cabins and others are taking them over. Moreover, some nations have their cabins on top decks, whereas others are in steerage. Reaching agreement on how the boat should proceed, and who should pay for its operation, would represent an immense challenge.

16. A fuller version of this proposal is presented in Viscusi and Zeckhauser (2011).

17. Thus, unless gross negligence could have been demonstrated, BP's financial responsibility was limited to $75 million. It agreed to establish a compensation fund of $20 billion due to intense political pressures created by President Obama. Such retrospective impositions are hardly the way to run a risk-control regime. Fortunately, BP had the resources to cover the losses it imposed.

18. The Price-Anderson Act also established a separate fund to provide for compensation of up to $12.975 billion. However, such group contributions do not establish private safety incentives.

19. The inadequacies of government regulation in addressing the hazards from deepwater drilling, including a lack of technical expertise and institutional failures, are documented in Oil Spill Commission (2011:250–91).

20. This theme was echoed by the Oil Spill Commission (2011) report as well. Industry experts are paid salaries far above the government pay range.

21. An interesting case involving many forms of government subsidy is that of a development of high-end homes constructed in a known flood plain in South Dakota adjacent to the Missouri River. Some homeowners dropped their insurance, but 172 did not. To fund barriers against current flooding, the community financed much of the cost with a no-interest loan from the state, and they are seeking to obtain reimbursement of 75 percent of the cost from the federal government and 10 percent from the state (Sulzberger 2011).

References

American Law Institute (1991a) *Enterprise Responsibility for Personal Injury: Reporters' Study*, Vol. 1, *The Institutional Framework*. Philadelphia: American Law Institute.

——— (1991b) *Enterprise Responsibility for Personal Injury: Reporters' Study*, Vol. 2, *Approaches to Legal and Institutional Change*. Philadelphia: American Law Institute.

Arsu, Sebnem (2011) "Amid Debris in Turkey, Survivors and Signs of Poor Construction." *New York Times*, October 25, A11.

Berger, Alan et al. (2011) "The Challenge of Degraded Environments: How Common Biases Impair Effective Policy." *Risk Analysis: An International Journal*. http://www.hks.harvard.edu/fs/rzeckhau/Challenge_of_Degraded_Environments.pdf.

Buffett, Warren (1990) "To the Shareholders of Berkshire Hathaway Inc." Chairman's letter, http://www.berkshirehathaway.com/letters/1990.html.

Canton, Lucien G. (2006) "San Francisco 1906 and 2006: An Emergency Management Perspective." *Earthquake Spectra* 22: S159–82.

Coase, Ronald (1960) "The Problem of Social Cost." *Journal of Law and Economics* 3: 1–44.

Donahue, John D. (2008) *The Warping of Government Work*. Cambridge, Mass.: Harvard University Press.

Hardin, Garrett (1968) "The Tragedy of the Commons." *Science* 162: 1243–48.

Harvey, Steve (2010) "California's Legendary Oil Spill." *Los Angeles Times*, June 13.

Kessler, Daniel P. (2011) "Introduction." In D. P. Kessler, ed., *Regulation Versus Litigation: Perspectives from Economics and Law*. Chicago: University of Chicago Press.

King, Rawle O. (2010) "*Deepwater Horizon* Oil Spill Disaster: Risk, Recovery, and Insurance Implications." *Congressional Research Service Report*, July 12, 2010. http://http://www.cnie.org/NLE/CRSreports/10Aug/R41320.pdf.

KPMG Global Energy Institute (2011) *After the Gulf of Mexico Oil Spill: Recent Developments in the Oil and Gas Industry*. http://www.kpmg.com/Global/en/Issues AndInsights/ArticlesPublications/Documents/gulf-of-mexico-oil-spillv2.pdf.

Mahbubani, Kishore (forthcoming) *The Great Convergence: Asia, the West, and the Logic of One World*. New York: PublicAffairs.

National Commission on the BP *Deepwater Horizon* Oil Spill and Offshore Drilling (2011) *Report to the President, Deepwater: The Gulf Oil Disaster and the Future of Offshore Drilling*. http://www.gpo.gov/fdsys/pkg/GPO-OILCOMMISSION /pdf/GPO-OILCOMMISSION.pdf.

Posner, Richard A. (2004) *Catastrophe: Risk and Response*. New York: Oxford University Press.

——— (2011) "Regulation (Agencies) Versus Litigation (Courts): An Analytical Framework." In D. P. Kessler, ed., *Regulation Versus Litigation: Perspectives from Economics and Law*. Chicago: University of Chicago Press.

Revkin, Andrew C. (2010) "Disaster Awaits Cities in Earthquake Zones." *New York Times*, February 24, A1.

Robertson, Campbell (2010) "U.S. Puts Oil Spill Total at Nearly 5 Million Barrels." *New York Times*, August 2.

Shleifer, Andrei (2011) "Efficient Regulation." In D. P. Kessler, ed., *Regulation Versus Litigation: Perspectives from Economics and Law*. Chicago: University of Chicago Press.

Sulzberger, Arthur G. (2011) "In Flood Zone, but Astonished by High Water." *New York Times*. July 31, A1.

Taylor, John (2010) "Origins and Policy Implications of the Crisis." In R. Porter, ed., *New Directions in Financial Services Regulation*. Cambridge, Mass.: MIT Press.

U.S. Department of Homeland Security, Federal Emergency Management Agency (1995) "Oklahoma City Bombing, 1995." http://www.fema.gov/emer gency/usr/usrok95.shtm.

U.S. Geological Survey (2003) *Natural Disasters—Forecasting Economic and Life Losses*. http://pubs.usgs.gov/fs/natural-disasters/index.html.

Viscusi, W. Kip (1988) "Product Liability and Regulation: Establishing the Appropriate Institutional Division of Labor." *American Economic Review* 78: 300–204.

——— (2002) "Overview." In W. K. Viscusi, ed., *Regulation Through Litigation*. Washington, D.C.: AEI-Brookings Joint Center for Regulatory Studies.

————— (2011) "Policy Challenges of the Heterogeneity of the Value of Statistical Life." *Foundations and Trends in Microeconomics* 6: 99–172.

Viscusi, W. Kip, and Richard J. Zeckhauser (2011) "Deterring and Compensating Oil Spill Catastrophes: The Need for Strict and Two-Tier Liability." *Vanderbilt Law Review* 64: 1717–65.

Zeckhauser, Richard (2011) "Causes of the Financial Crisis: Many Responsible Parties." In R. Glauber, T. Healey, and R. Porter, eds., *New Directions in Financial Services Regulation.* Cambridge, Mass.: MIT Press.

Statutes Cited

Oil Pollution Act of 1990, 33 U.S.C. 2701 et seq.
Price-Anderson Act of 1957, 42 U.S.C. 2210.

Chapter 3

Beyond Belts and Suspenders

Promoting Private Risk Management in Offshore Drilling

Lori S. Bennear

On April 20, 2010, eleven workers were killed in an explosion on the *Deepwater Horizon* rig in the process of drilling the Macondo well off the Gulf of Mexico. The blowout resulted in between four and five million barrels of oil leaking into the Gulf of Mexico. Early estimates of the damages from the oil spill are in the range of $20 billion with an additional $17 billion in fines (*Economist* 2010). There are many entities at blame for the significant human and environmental disaster in the Gulf, and regulators have not escaped unscathed. Regulators at the Minerals Management Service (MMS), the federal agency charged with issuing permits and overseeing safety of offshore oil drilling, appeared compromised by conflicts of interest and unqualified to ensure safety in operations (CNN 2010; Leonnig 2010; U.S. Department of the Interior 2010). The magnitude of the damages from the Gulf oil spill, combined with perceptions of regulatory capture at MMS, has brought into question the sufficiency of current regulatory approaches to offshore oil drilling.

Prior to the Gulf oil spill, the primary form of regulation that applied to offshore oil drilling was a set of highly prescriptive command-and-control regulations requiring significant redundancy in safety systems, an approach I call "belts and suspenders." The belts-and-suspenders regulations were coupled with a strict liability regime where the operating company—BP in this case—was strictly liable for damages up to $75 million, with additional damages covered by a government pool of funds generated through taxes on oil (Hargreaves 2010). Arguably, this coupling of regulatory systems should have created the correct incentives for companies to manage risks. The required safety technologies should have been in place and, given the financial liability for damages, BP and its contractors should have had the incentives to ensure that all these systems were working properly. Nonetheless, a disaster occurred.

To advance the search for better ways to prevent such disasters in the future, I analyze in this chapter three ways of regulating offshore drilling in the United States. The first approach is the belts-and-suspenders approach used both prior to and in response to the Gulf oil spill. I argue that the belts-and-suspenders approach is flawed because it fails to account for the inherent risk derived from drilling technologies' dependence on human control. The belts-and-suspenders approach may even encourage greater risk taking by human operators because it creates the impression that multiple safety systems will catch any errors before a significant accident occurs.

The second approach is management-based regulation, which requires drilling operators to develop detailed safety and risk management plans. This approach has been used to regulate offshore drilling in other countries and has been adopted by the United States as a supplemental response to the Gulf oil spill. I consider the suitability and likely effectiveness of management-based regulation for regulating offshore drilling, concluding that such an approach by itself does little to ensure that risk management plans are fully implemented.

The third approach would be to apply a deposit-discount-refund system, which would require an up-front establishment of a project-level "safety deposit." Operators can earn "discounts" on the size of their safety deposit by earning high grades on independent third-party assessments of their safety management plans. And upon successful completion of the project, the safety deposit is refunded to the company. In this way, the deposit-discount-refund system provides an incentive for companies to carry out effective risk management practices.

The Blowout at *Deepwater Horizon*/Macondo

Before turning to the three policy approaches, I offer a brief overview of the *Deepwater Horizon*/Macondo accident, focusing on the multiple failures in redundant safety systems that occurred. Of course, a highly detailed description of all the factors that contributed to the oil spill in the Gulf would be beyond the scope of any book chapter, and in any event, such accounts can already be found in various governmental reports on the disaster (U.S. Chemical Safety and Hazard Investigation Board 2010; U.S. Department of the Interior 2010; Bureau of Ocean Energy Management, Regulation and Enforcement 2011; Oil Spill Commission 2011). However, a brief narrative of some of the key decisions that contributed to the disaster is necessary to understand the potential effectiveness of alternative regulatory responses.

The blowout at the Macondo well occurred while the exploration well was being prepared for temporary abandonment prior to preparing the well for ongoing oil extraction operations. Evidence collected during the exploratory drilling suggested the well had reached a pool of hydrocarbons that warranted preparing the site for future production that would use a different drilling rig than the *Deepwater Horizon*. To switch rigs, the well needed to be sealed off and temporarily abandoned until extraction operations would begin at the site (Oil Spill Commission 2011).

To prepare a well for extraction, a steel casing is lowered from the wellhead on the seafloor down into the hydrocarbon pool. Cement is then pumped down the casing and back up the sides. The cured cement then acts as a plug, isolating the hydrocarbons—that is, the oil—from the opening of the well (Oil Spill Commission 2011).

The Macondo well failed primarily because the cement job failed to properly seal the hydrocarbons from the well. At least three major changes in the engineering design of the well that occurred in the period prior to the disaster may have contributed to this failure:

- Production casing design: Results from different engineering models used by BP and its contractor, Halliburton, argued for different types of casings. BP engineers decided to stick with the original design despite concerns about its suitability (Oil Spill Commission 2011). However, there is not universal agreement that the production casing design was a proximate cause of the blowout (U.S. Department of the Interior 2010).
- Number of centralizers: If the casing is not perfectly centered in the well, the cement will not flow evenly up all sides of the casing, and the risk of hydrocarbon intrusion into the well will increase. BP's original design included sixteen centralizers. At the time the casing was to be lowered into the well, only six centralizers were available. Despite model results suggesting that up to twenty-one centralizers were required, only six centralizers were used (U.S. Department of the Interior 2010; Oil Spill Commission 2011).
- Cement slurry: The exact formulation of the cement slurry depends on the characteristics of the individual well. At the Macondo well there was concern about the fragility of the rock formation, and a decision was made to use cement that had been "levened with tiny bubbles of nitrogen gas" (Oil Spill Commission 2011). In addition, BP and Halliburton made changes to the pressure at which the cement was pumped and the way in which the well was prepared before cementing. All

these changes were designed to reduce the risk of fracturing the rock formation, which could lead to hydrocarbon leakage (U.S. Department of the Interior 2010; Oil Spill Commission 2011).

These three decisions increased the risk of a blowout at the Macondo well. However, there were several systems in place that should have detected hydrocarbon leakage into the well before the situation became dire. These signals included laboratory analysis of the nitrogen foam cement slurry, visual tests of fluid flow, and two negative pressure tests on the well (Oil Spill Commission 2011). These tests were performed and each had abnormal results, yet these abnormalities were dismissed or rationalized (U.S. Department of the Interior 2010; Oil Spill Commission 2011).

In addition, there were multiple safety systems in place to minimize the size of the blowout should one occur—in particular, the blowout preventer (BOP), which contains blind-shear rams that cut through the well and seal it off. The BOP should have been activated manually when staff on the rig triggered the emergency disconnect system. When that failed, it should have activated automatically using the deadman system. Neither system activated the blind shear rams and the well remained opened, resulting in a massive oil spill (Oil Spill Commission 2011).

It is tempting to write off the sequence of failures at Macondo as a rare occurrence—the result of a perfect storm of carelessness and bad luck that is unlikely to occur again. Indeed, before the Macondo blowout, the view was that safety of deepwater drilling had progressed far enough that the risk of a major oil spill was zero. In a speech on the economy in Charlotte, North Carolina, on April 2, 2010 (a mere eighteen days before the catastrophe), President Barack Obama said: "I don't agree with the notion that we shouldn't do anything. It turns out, by the way, that oil rigs today generally don't cause spills. They are technologically very advanced. Even during Katrina, the spills didn't come from the oil rigs, they came from the refineries onshore" (Obama 2010). But this optimistic view is inherently based on a belief in the independence of safety system failure probabilities. Under these conditions, we can observe a situation like Macondo, but only very rarely. However, as the accounts of the events leading up to the Macondo blowout illustrate, the probabilities of multiple failures are not independent, precisely because the same set of people are managing all of these systems.

Belts and Suspenders

Risks of environmental catastrophes, be they from nuclear power, offshore oil drilling, or shale gas drilling, are frequently viewed as technological risks. The primary regulatory approach to preventing systemic technological failures and their resulting catastrophic damages has been to require significant redundancy in safety systems, that is, the "belts-and-suspenders" approach.

Belts-and-suspenders regulations were the primary form of regulating offshore drilling in the United States before the Gulf oil spill. Even after the oil spill, when MMS was reorganized and replaced with the new Bureau of Ocean Energy Management, Regulation and Enforcement (BOEMRE), one of BOEMRE's first actions was to enact the Drilling Safety Rule (DSR), which contains an additional set of belts-and-suspenders regulations designed to reduce the chance of a blowout on a deepwater oil rig (BOEMRE 2010). For example, these regulations include

- requirements to control potential flows during well construction
- certification of casings and cement by a professional engineer
- two independent barriers across the flow path
- measures to ensure proper installation of casings and liners
- third-party verification that the blind-shear rams can cut drill pipe at anticipated pressures
- requirements for a BOP that can be controlled by a remotely operated vehicle (ROV)
- an ROV that is capable of closing the pipe rams and the blind-shear rams and of unlatching the lower marine riser
- requirements for autoshear and deadman systems
- requirements for training and documentation

This extensive set of prescriptive requirements is a classic example of the belt-and-suspenders approach to regulating technological risks. Significant redundancy in safety systems is required, based on the idea that all of the systems are unlikely to fail at the same time. This approach seems further motivated by the idea that with sufficient technological redundancies, the "human" element in catastrophes, which cannot be directly regulated, is minimized. The particular laundry list of regulations in the DSR is also directly responsive to the particular series of technological and human failures at the Macondo well.

There are several problems with the belts-and-suspenders approach. First, as with command-and-control regulation generally, the technological requirements imposed by belts and suspenders are costly. In order to address safety in a manner that will be applicable to all drilling operations, additional redundancies are built into the regulations than may actually be needed in any particular drilling operations. These additional redundancies are costly ways of maintaining safety.

More important, there is concern that prescriptive belts-and-suspenders regulations fail to work as intended. The key assumption underlying the belts-and-suspenders approach is that the probabilities of safety-system failures are independent. That is, the failure of one system does not affect the probability of failures in other systems. From a purely technological standpoint this assumption is often reasonable. What is missing from this technological view is the human dimension of risk. On a given deepwater oil rig, a nuclear power plant, or a shale gas drilling operation, all the technologies and redundant systems are operated and maintained by the same company—the same people. Human errors that interfere with the successful operation of one safety system may well predict similar problems at other safety systems. The human dimension makes the risk of system failures dependent. If the risks are not independent, then the probability of catastrophic failure of all systems does not approach zero rapidly. There remains a nontrivial probability of a large-scale failure—a fat-tail risk.

Still more troubling, the requirements of multiple safety systems may actually encourage risk taking. If we assume that decision makers are profit maximizers, then at each decision point that presents potential safety or environmental consequences, a decision maker must weigh the expected costs of taking a conservative, safety-focused approach with the expected costs of more aggressive decisions. The expected costs of the safety-focused approach may be time spent waiting for a second opinion, further analysis, or additional materials and equipment—costs that may be quite salient. The expected costs of more aggressive decisions are some expectation of the fines from any accident resulting from the decision as well as private costs, including lives lost, property damage, and other liabilities. Calculating these costs requires making an estimation of the likelihood of an accident, the likely magnitude of the accident, and the resulting fines and damages. When the probability of an accident from any one decision is small, especially when the conditional probability of an accident given other safety systems is viewed as close to zero, the expected costs of more aggressive decisions will be extremely low. Accidents, after all, are rare—and large accidents even rarer—so the likelihood that any one shortcut leads to catastrophic costs will also be very low. This is particularly true if you believe that any error from taking a shortcut will be caught by another safety system before a significant accident occurs. Of course, if everyone making decisions uses this calculus, things can go very wrong.

A specific example from the Macondo well was the decision to use only six centralizers on the well despite models indicating that up to twenty-one centralizers were required. The decision to use six centralizers was complex, but it was based in part on the additional time that would have been needed to obtain the additional centralizers (and the additional costs associated with that time). In retrospect, the correct decision would have been to use more centralizers or, at minimum, spend more time determining whether using only six centralizers would be safe. But from the vantage point of the BP decision makers, the risk might well have been viewed as worth taking. If the cementing job was not sufficient with six centralizers, there should have been other signals. In particular, the negative pressure test should have revealed that fluids were leaking back into the well. The negative pressure tests did reveal anomalies, but the anomalies were overlooked or misinterpreted. The presence of multiple belts and suspenders appears to have led to a sense of overconfidence in the safety of the whole system, which encouraged risk taking.

Management-Based Approaches

Given the failure of multiple safety systems at the Macondo well and the lack of qualified government personnel to review permits and inspect wells, the Oil Spill Commission and others have argued, convincingly, that long-term improvements in safety and environmental protection from deepwater drilling must come from within industry. Several policies have been proposed to try to promote a stronger culture of safety within the offshore energy industry. The most widely discussed policy is a form of management-based regulation (MBR).

MBR does not mandate specific means to achieving a regulatory end but instead mandates that firms engage in systematic planning efforts designed to better achieve the regulatory end (Coglianese and Lazer 2003). A stylized model of MBR is provided in Figure 3.1. In this model, the regulatory requirements are on the front end—firms are required to engage in systematic safety or environmental planning before they begin risky operations. These plans are designed to connect to certain actions and activities; however, the actions and activities themselves are unobserved (at least most of the time) and hence remain unregulated. Finally, the actions and activities can lead to outcomes, which if negative are typically associated with fines and penalties.

The umbrella of policies that can be considered "management-based" is quite large. Each of the following could be considered an MBR:

- Regulated firms must consider options to promote the regulatory goal and issue a public statement that outlines their plans.
- In addition to the requirements above, regulated firms must review their production process, identify alternative production techniques or input mixes that would achieve the public goal, evaluate the feasibility of these alternatives, and report on these evaluations (Bennear 2007).

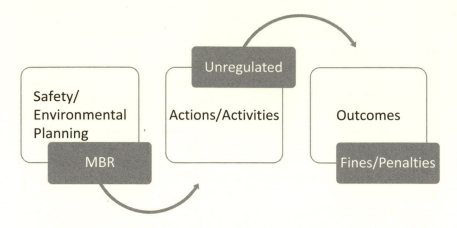

Figure 3.1. A Stylized Model of Management-Based Regulation.

- In addition to the requirements above, regulated firms must review supply chains and distribution chains including all subcontractors, identify changes in all operations that could promote the public goal, evaluate the feasibility of these alternatives, and report on these evaluations.
- In addition to the requirements above, regulated firms must also obtain periodic third-party review and certification of their management plans and evaluations.

Each of these variants has a common emphasis on improving firms' management of their own operations, leaving the ultimate decisions about specific safety practices up to the firms themselves, in accordance with the plans they develop.

Variants of MBRs are already in use to regulate food safety, pollution prevention, and occupational health and safety. In the area of food safety, the Hazard Analysis and Critical Control Point (HACCP) system has been used to control pathogen contamination in the food supply since the 1990s. The HACCP program requires that food processors evaluate their production process and identify potential sources of food contamination, develop systems to eliminate or reduce those risks, and develop detailed records of their safety activities (Bennear 2007). The Occupational Safety and Health Administration adopted a set of regulations that required firms to implement management systems to assess the risk from chemical accidents and to develop rules and procedures to reduce those risks. Fourteen states have also adopted MBR to reduce toxic chemical use and release from manufacturing. For example, the

Massachusetts Toxics Use Reduction Act requires that manufacturing facilities develop detailed pollution prevention plans and examine the use of toxic chemicals throughout the production process, identify alternatives for reducing toxics chemical use, and evaluate those alternatives in terms of economic feasibility (Bennear 2006, 2007).

Indeed, MBR is already in use to regulate offshore drilling in other countries, particularly the United Kingdom, Norway, and Canada. The "safety case" approach in the United Kingdom is an example of MBR for offshore drilling. The exact requirements for each safety case vary slightly by the type of drilling facility; there are separate MBR requirements for fixed, mobile, and combined operations. However, all of the safety case regulations contain the same basic set of requirements. Each drilling installation must provide

- A basic narrative description of the ways in which the installation was designed and will be operated to minimize risk.
- Descriptions and diagrams of the installation and all connections and wells that are planned for the installation.
- Information on the meteorological and oceanographic conditions as well as geologic conditions of the seabed.
- Descriptions of the types of operations and the number of people on board the installation.
- Description of methods to control pressure, prevent leaks and blowouts, and minimize the effects on the sub-seabeds.
- A description of any pipeline capable of causing an accident, with information on the dimensions and layout, the evacuation plan, and the location of temporary refuge for workers.
- A completed risk assessment with respect to all the pipelines capable of causing an accident.
- Plans for detection of toxic and flammable gases and plans to detect, mitigate, and prevent fires.

Similar regulations were proposed by MMS in July 1991 as the Safety and Environmental Management Program (SEMP), but apparently under pressure from industry these regulations were postponed. After the *Deepwater Horizon* spill, these regulations were finally and swiftly promulgated. But how well can offshore drilling risks be managed by this kind of regulation?

Theory of MBR

Theory suggests that MBR is best suited to policy domains with significant heterogeneity in the sources or risk and the methods of mitigating that risk (Coglianese and Lazer 2003). The costs of command-and-control regulations increase with heterogeneity (Newell and Stavins 2003). However, if heterogeneity is the only concern, then MBR is not the only policy choice. Several policy instruments are well suited to handling heterogeneity and achieving cost-effective risk reductions that are site- or entity-specific. These include market-based instruments, such as cap and trade, taxes, or performance standards (Stavins 2003). But all three of these approaches require some measure of policy outcomes—that is, some measure of performance.

MBR, in contrast, can accommodate significant heterogeneity among regulated entities and can also be used when there are no measures (or poor measures) of policy outcomes (Coglianese and Lazer 2003). The regulated entities ultimately must construct some measure of performance, but this can be site-specific or context-specific and does not need to be monitored by regulators. It is largely for this reason that we observe adoption of MBR in cases where outcomes—for example, catastrophic accidents—are difficult to measure because these outcomes happen infrequently. Observing that a plant has no accidents does not necessarily reveal much about the safety of the plant's underlying operations if accidents are infrequent events.

Given that these two conditions, heterogeneity and absence of outcome data, also apply in offshore drilling, MBR does seem well suited to regulating in this context. But this begs the question of whether, in the absence of outcome data and outcome-based mandates, MBR can actually deliver improvements in health and environmental safety. Referring back to Figure 3.1, how does MBR actually motivate better actions/activities to lead to better outcomes?

The first way MBR may improve safety is through changes in internal decision making within regulated entities. In order for MBR to be effective through this channel, it must be the case that the businesses are not already (voluntarily) engaged in the level of environmental management prescribed by the regulation and that there is a strong complementarity between management effort and planning and environmental quality (Bennear 2006). Here I use the economic meaning of the word *complement*, which requires that increased consumption of one good (or service) either increases the marginal benefits or decreases the marginal costs of consuming the complementary good. This means that additional expenditures on safety planning either increase the marginal benefits of expenditures on safety (by better targeting these efforts) or decrease the marginal costs of safety expenditures (by revealing lower cost alternatives), or both. The key is that once the firms engage in the planning, on average they discover opportunities for improvement that are in their own best interest to undertake. Thus, once planning is required, the improvements in actions and outcomes are entirely voluntary and occur only if in the profit-maximizing or cost-minimizing interest of the firm.

The second way MBR may be effective is through information sharing between the regulated entities and the regulator. The information generated through the development of required plans may reveal something important to regulators about the costs and benefits of safety improvements. Information sharing can also allow for comparison across regulated entities, which can, in turn, improve performance through targeted inspections or technical assistance (Karkkainen 2001; Bennear 2006).

How Well Has MBR Worked?

Although theory suggests that MBR may be a good regulatory tool for offshore drilling, the catastrophic consequences of safety failures in offshore drilling operations make it reasonable to ask for more than a theoretical justification and to evaluate how well MBR has actually performed in practice. This raises an interesting analytic dilemma. How does one evaluate the success or failure of a policy designed to regulate risks that are not themselves directly or easily measurable? In typical program evaluations (also called impact evaluations), the outcomes of the "treated" group are compared with the outcomes of a similar "control" group. But all of these methods require detailed and comprehensive data on outcomes.

Following the *Deepwater Horizon* accident, the U.S. Chemical Safety Board, an independent government agency tasked with investigating all chemical accidents in the United States, convened a public hearing that focused on regulatory approaches to offshore oil drilling. At the hearing, representatives from the United Kingdom, Norway, and Australia discussed the use of the safety case approach in those countries. Without exception the representatives believed that the safety case approach had improved safety and reduced the likelihood of a large-scale disaster in their countries. But almost equally without exception, these views were based on anecdotes and some limited (and not fully disclosed) analysis of near-miss data (U.S. Chemical Safety and Hazard Investigation Board 2010). More detailed research, perhaps using international data on near misses, could help illuminate the impact of the safety case on offshore drilling risk.

In the meantime, empirical analysis of MBR has focused primarily on state pollution prevention programs because of the existence of a time series of data on toxic chemical releases from the Toxics Release Inventory (Coglianese and Lazer 2003; Bennear 2006, 2007). The cumulative evidence from these analyses suggests that MBR can lead to significant reductions in toxic chemical releases (Natan et al. 1996; Keenan et al. 1997; Bennear 2006, 2007). Bennear (2007) uses panel data analysis to compare toxic chemical releases, source reduction activities, and numbers of chemicals reported among plants subject to MBR and those not subject to MBR, controlling for a number of other plant and location characteristics. Firms subject to MBR engaged in more source reduction activities and reported statistically significantly larger reductions in total toxic chemical releases but did not report fewer chemicals relative to their non-MBR counterparts. However, the gains from MBR appeared primarily in the earlier years of a program, with no statistically significant differences detected after six years of program implementation (Bennear 2007). Other research has demonstrated that smaller firms are less likely to see environmental benefits from the planning effort (Natan et al. 1996; Keenan et al. 1997).

Because of infrequent outcomes data, there is very limited evidence on the impact of management-based standards on reducing workplace accidents or the incidence of food-borne illness. Data on accidents at chemical facilities showed a "modest decline in reported accident frequency and worker injury rates" but "no change in reported accident severity" following introduction of management-based requirements (Kleindorfer et al. 2007:222); however, the question of whether management-based standards caused any effects remains unanswered. Several studies have investigated the economics of HAACP standards, but these studies tend to focus on costs and simulate estimation on the benefits using assumptions of the decrease in pathogen count between 10 and 100 percent (Crutchfield et al. 1997; Unnevehr and Jensen 1999). When estimating benefits, assuming a 50 percent reduction in pathogen count from the HAACP standards, the benefits of the standards outweigh the costs (Crutchfield et al. 1997). However, concerns have been raised that the large up-front costs of HAACP regulations may result in consolidation in the industry as HAACP standards are too costly for small producers.

The take-home message from the empirical literature is that, in cases that most resemble offshore drilling, anecdotal evidence suggests that MBRs may reduce risk, but no rigorous empirical evidence can confirm the effectiveness of these regulations. In large part, this absence of evidence is due to absence of outcomes data, which means we have no evidence on success or failure of alternative regulatory mechanisms either. In the one case where MBR was used when outcomes were observable (i.e., toxic emissions), there is some evidence of success. However, some reasonable concerns may remain about the ability of MBR to translate regulation of management effort and planning into systematic changes in behaviors that reduce risk of rare but catastrophic events.

The largest concern about the use of MBR under these conditions is that it relies quite heavily on industry safety planning and proper execution of plans—but that the execution of plans is hard to inspect and ensure. MBR also requires sustained attention over time to safety even when costs may be lower by not following the safety plan. In short, there is concern that MBR may not provide adequate incentives for operators to manage risk over the long term.

But MBR is not the only regulatory approach to offshore oil drilling. MBR for oil drilling is currently added onto a broader regulatory regime that includes prescriptive belts-and-suspenders regulations, inspections and fines, and strict liability (up to a cap) on damages. One might argue that firms will have the incentive to execute their plans properly when MBR is one element of this larger regulatory mix, a mix that together will be sufficient to prevent future safety failures of the magnitude of the blowout at the Macondo well.

Certainly inspections and fines could increase compliance not only with belts-and-suspenders regulations but with a firm's own safety plan. But inspections and fines depend on a level of expertise in inspections that was shown lacking at MMS and likely remains in short supply at BOEMRE. That said, perhaps MBR combined with the existing rule of strict liability for damages will adequately increase the expected costs of failure to adhere to safety plans and regulatory guidelines. Of course, that liability—perhaps because it is currently capped—was not sufficient to prevent the blowout of the Macondo well. Perhaps if the cap is raised or eliminated, industry would have the correct incentives to make better choices. Maybe MBR would make those "better choices" easier to make, or harder to avoid following, because it requires that companies document safety steps and plan for multiple contingencies. But the underlying incentives for safe drilling operations would be driven by the change in or elimination of the strict liability cap, not MBR.

In the end, whether MBR, even in combination with other liability or regulations, will induce sufficient safety precautions is an empirical question, and it is an empirical question that will be nearly impossible to answer well. However, given that MBR adds no new incentives for following safety precautions, there is some reason to continue to be concerned about its ability, even when combined with strict liability and belts-and-suspenders regulations, to change the fundamental decision calculus of managers and operators throughout the drilling industry.

Safety Deposits

How can the calculus of these many individual decisions be reframed to provide greater weight to environmental and safety risks? In the high-paced and dynamic environment of the drilling well, how can we better ensure that careful safety and environmental planning is actually executed? I argue that strict liability is insufficient over the long term to properly incentivize these individual choices. In the immediate aftermath of a large-scale accident, we are likely to see more attention paid to safety, but over time, as the memory of those costs fades, the cost savings calculus remains stacked against safety and the environment. If society wants to encourage stronger private risk management—such as the proper execution of a thorough environmental and safety management plan—then the costs of not following the plan need to be more immediate to decision makers in two ways: the costs need to be moved up front, and there need to be consequences for mistakes even if they do not result in accidents.

In thinking of how to design a regulatory system with those incentives, it is helpful to remember another market-based regulatory instrument that is frequently used in circumstances of high costs of mitigating damage after it occurs. That instrument is the deposit-refund system. The idea behind a deposit-refund system is that the regulated entity (consumer, firm, etc.) pays an up-front deposit that is refunded if and only if the entity follows through on required actions. Deposit-refund systems are frequently used in waste disposal to help ensure proper disposal of consumer products that present environmental hazards in landfills.

The theory behind the deposit-refund system is well developed. It is frequently used when there are many regulated entities, so enforcement of standards is expensive, and when costs of mitigating damage are high (e.g., getting lead out of the aquifer after the lead batteries decompose in landfill). For economic efficiency, the deposit is set equal to the marginal social costs of improper disposal (Bohm 1981; Russell 1988; Macauley 1992). In a context that more resembles offshore drilling, safety bonds have been proposed to hold companies accountable for the quality and safety of goods they import (Baker 2009). An example would be requiring a toy manufacturer to provide a safety bond as insurance that imported toys do not contain lead.

In the context of offshore drilling, the deposit-refund system would involve an up-front "safety deposit" for all permitted well operations. The deposit is refunded when the well drilling is complete and a safety inspection has occurred. Assuming the safety deposit is set at a magnitude equal to the expected costs of a significant accident, this system is not terribly different from a strict liability system. In theory, one might even say that the incentives created by it should be the same.

However, there is significant research in behavioral economics that suggests that responses to these two strategies may be quite different. In a series of studies, Dan Ariely (2008) examined cheating behavior as a function of whether participants were asked to think about ethical behavior (either by recalling the Ten Commandments or by signing an honor code) in advance of their testing. The results of these experiments provide strong evidence that making ethics salient at the onset of an activity will significantly reduce cheating. This research suggests that shifting the payment of the safety deposit up front makes safety more salient and may result in increased attention to safety even if the monetary costs are not changed.

As applied to offshore drilling, the classic deposit-refund system could be modified somewhat to make the consequences of everyday decisions seem even more substantial by rewarding consistent execution of a drilling firm's safety plan. This modification would involve granting a "discount" on the safety deposit to operations that are certified by an independent third-party auditor as consistently in compliance with their safety plan. The notion of an independent third-party audit of safety plan execution was also proposed by the Oil Spill Commission as a key aspect of its proposals for increasing safety of offshore drilling (Oil Spill Commission 2011) and has been suggested more generally as an effective risk management approach (Kunreuther et al. 2001). Under the safety deposit system, firms with audits that received high marks could earn a discount on the size of their deposit. In theory, firms with consistently high marks on safety audits could even be required to offer no safety deposit, leaving them no worse off than under the current system. Tying a deposit system to a system of independent audits in this way would provide a direct monetary reward for consistent safe behavior.

An additional advantage of a safety deposit system along the lines suggested here is that it can even empower other market actors to inspect and enforce private risk management standards (Baker 2009; Bamberger and Guzman 2009). One might expect insurance and bonding companies to become sources of capital for safety deposits, but then they will also assume a financial stake in ensuring that operations they have bonded are safe. Under these conditions, the need for specific government-imposed management-based mandates for risk and safety planning could be reduced, if not even perhaps eliminated. Notably, the American Petroleum Institute (API) has for years made recommendations for safety planning similar to what MMS had proposed with SEMP (API 2004). The problem has not been that industry is unaware of how to engage in risk management planning; the problem has been that some parts of the industry have not felt sufficiently motivated to undertake such rigorous analysis voluntarily. By creating a set of market-based incentives for risk management planning through a well-crafted safety deposit system, direct government mandates for risk planning may be unnecessary.

Conclusion

The disaster onboard the *Deepwater Horizon* and the subsequent environmental and economic losses highlight the limitations of the current regulatory approach to offshore drilling. At the same time, the importance of oil for the U.S. economy and the importance of this industry in certain parts of the country, including the Gulf Coast, make permanent banning of offshore drilling unlikely and even undesirable. What is required is sufficient regulation of this industry to balance the benefits it provides with the low-probability but high-consequence risk that it creates. In this chapter, I have presented three alternatives for regulating offshore drilling.

The first regulatory approach is the belts-and-suspenders approach, which requires multiple redundant safety systems. This has been the primary approach in the United States, but it works only if probabilities of failure of any one system are independent. On an offshore oil rig, however, probabilities of failures are linked by the humans who operate them. Furthermore, the presence of multiple redundant systems can encourage risk taking because any one shortcut is perceived as very low risk given the existence of other safety systems and backups.

The second regulatory approach takes the form of management-based regulations that require detailed environmental and safety planning to address the unique risks each drilling operation. MBR has been used in other countries, but evidence of its success is still nascent. This is largely due to the fact that accidents are rare events, so it is difficult to statistically analyze whether any regulatory system results in lower accident frequency. Anecdotal evidence from countries that use MBR, combined with evidence of MBR's success in pollution prevention programs, suggest that this may be a promising alternative. One concern with MBR, however, is that the planning process itself may do little to ensure that day-to-day operational decisions follow those plans and are sufficiently safety focused. In order to change the calculus of individual, day-to-day decisions, MBR will need to be operationalized in a way that provides proper incentives for safety at each decision point.

A third alternative would address the need for better incentives by imposing a safety deposit requirement for all drilling operations. The required up-front safety bond would be refunded upon safe completion of the drilling activity, and firms could earn rebates on the amount of the safety bond by earning high scores on an independent third-party review of their operational practices. Such a safety deposit would likely promote still further improvements in private risk management by providing incentives for risk management in day-to-day operations and by empowering other market actors, including insurance companies and bonding companies, to help inspect and enforce safety activity.

Deciding how to address the regulatory failures that were partially responsible for the disaster at the *Deepwater Horizon* rig is critically important. As we have recently seen, failures in regulatory approaches carry large costs, but these costs may not manifest themselves for many years. It is important therefore to cast a broad net when considering policy changes and to focus particularly on those policies that are likely to provide incentives for better private risk management in day-to-day operations. Further theoretical and empirical research on the alternatives presented in the chapter would be of great value.

References

American Petroleum Institute (2004) "Recommended Practice for Development of a Safety and Environmental Management Program (SEMP) for Offshore Operations and Facilities." http://www.api.org/aboutoilgas/sectors/explore/safetymanage.cfm, accessed November 30, 2011.

Ariely, Dan (2008) *Predictably Irrational: The Hidden Forces That Shape Our Decisions.* New York: HarperCollins.

Baker, Tom (2009) "Bonded Import Safety Warranties." In C. Coglianese, A. M. Finkel, and David Zaring, eds., *Import Safety: Regulatory Governance in the Global Economy.* Philadelphia: University of Pennsylvania Press.

Bamberger, Kenneth A., and Andrew T. Guzman (2009) "Importers as Regulators: Product Safety in a Globalized World." In C. Coglianese, A. M. Finkel, and David Zaring, eds., *Import Safety: Regulatory Governance in the Global Economy.* Philadelphia: University of Pennsylvania Press.

Bennear, Lori S. (2006) "Evaluating Management-Based Regulation: A Valuable Tool in the Regulatory Toolbox." In C. Coglianese and J. Nash, eds., *Leveraging the Private Sector: Management-Based Strategies for Improving Environmental Performance.* Washington, D.C.: Resources for the Future Press.

———— (2007) "Are Management Based Regulations Effective? Evidence from State Pollution Prevention Programs." *Journal of Policy Analysis and Management* 26: 327–48.

Bohm, Peter (1981) *Deposit-Refund Systems: Theory and Applications to Environmental, Conservation, and Consumer Policy.* Washington, D.C.: Resources for the Future Press.

Bureau of Ocean Energy Management, Regulation and Enforcement (2010) *Fact Sheet: The Drilling Safety Rule, an Interim Final Rule to Enhance Safety Measures for Energy Development on the Outer Continental Shelf.* Washington, D.C.: Bureau of Ocean Energy Management, Regulation and Enforcement.

———— (2011) *Report Regarding the Causes of the April 20, 2010 Macondo Well Blowout.* Bureau of Ocean Energy Management, Regulation and Enforcement, http://www.boemre.gov/pdfs/maps/DWHFINAL.pdf, accessed November 30, 2011.

CNN (2010) "MMS Was Troubled Long Before Oil Spill." http://articles.cnn.com/2010-05-27/politics/mms.salazar_1_salazar-oil-spill-rig?_s=PM:POLITICS, accessed November 30, 2011.

Coglianese, Cary, and David Lazer (2003) "Management Based Regulation: Prescribing Private Management to Achieve Public Goals." *Law and Society Review* 37: 691–730.

Crutchfield, Stephen R. et al. (1997) "Economic Assessment of Food Safety Regulations: The New Approach to Meat and Poultry Inspection." *Agricultural Economics Reports*, AER755.

Economist (2010) "The Oil Well and the Damage Done." http://www.economist.com/node/16381032, accessed November 30, 2011.

Hargreaves, Steve (2010) "Cap on Oil Spill Damages Under Fire." CNN, http://money.cnn.com/2010/05/25/news/economy/BP_liability/index.htm, accessed November 30, 2011.

Karkkainen, Bradley C. (2001) "Information as Environmental Regulation: TRI and Performance Benchmarking, Precursor to a New Paradigm." *Georgetown Law Journal* 89: 257–370.

Keenan, Cheryl et al. (1997) "Survey Evaluation of the Massachusetts Toxics Use Reduction Program." Methods and Policy Report #14, Lowell, Mass.

Kleindorfer, Paul R. et al. (2007) "Accident Epidemiology and the RMP Rule: Learning from a Decade of Accident History Data for the U.S. Chemical Industry." Final Report for Cooperative Agreement R-83033301 Between Risk Management and Decision Processes Center, the Wharton School of the University of Pennsylvania and Office of Emergency Management, U.S. Environmental Protection Agency. http://opim.wharton.upenn.edu/risk/library/2007_EPA-Wharton_RMPRule.pdf, accessed November 30, 2011.

Kunreuther, Howard et al. (2002) "Improving Environmental Safety Through Third Party Inspection." *Risk Analysis* 22: 309–18.

Leonnig, Carol D. (2010) "Oil Spill Highlights Conflict Issue." *Washington Post*, July 31, A2.

Macauley, Molly K. et al. (1992) *Using Economic Incentives to Regulate Toxic Substances*. Washington, D.C.: Resources for the Future Press.

Natan, Thomas E., Jr., et al. (1996) *Evaluation of the Effectiveness of Pollution Prevention Planning in New Jersey*. Alexandria, Va.: Hampshire Research Associates.

National Commission on the BP Deepwater Horizon Oil Spill and Offshore Drilling (2011) *Deep Water: The Gulf Oil Disaster and the Future of Offshore Drilling*. National Commission on the BP Deepwater Horizon Oil Spill and Offshore Drilling. http://www.oilspillcommission.gov/, accessed November 30, 2011.

Newell, Richard G., and Robert N. Stavins (2003) "Cost Heterogeneity and the Potential Savings from Market-Based Policies." *Journal of Regulatory Economics* 23: 243–59.

Obama, Barack (2010) *Remarks by the President in a Discussion on Jobs and the Economy in Charlotte, North Carolina*. http://www.whitehouse.gov/the-press-office/remarks-president-a-discussion-jobs-and-economy-charlotte-north-carolina (April 2), accessed November 30, 2011.

Russell, Clifford S. (1988) "Economic Incentives in the Management of Hazardous Wastes." *Columbia Journal of Environmental Law* 13: 257–74.

Stavins, Robert N. (2003) "Experience with Market-Based Environmental Policy Instruments." In K.-G. Maler and J. Vincent, eds., *Handbook of Environmental Economics*, Vol. 1. Amsterdam: Elsevier Science.

Unnevehr, Laurian J., and Helen H. Jensen (1999) "The Economic Implications of Using HACCP as a Food Safety Regulatory Standard." *Food Policy* 24: 625–35.

U.S. Chemical Safety and Hazard Investigation Board (2010) *Public Hearing: Regulatory Approaches to Offshore Oil and Gas Safety.* Washington, D.C.: U.S. Chemical Safety and Hazard Investigation Board. http://www.csb.gov/assets /document/Transcript_of_Public_Meeting_12_15_2010.pdf, accessed November 30, 2011.

U.S. Department of the Interior, Office of the Inspector General (2010) *Investigative Report—Island Operating Company, et al.* Washington, D.C.: U.S. Department of the Interior. http://www.eenews.net/public/25/15844/features /documents/2010/05/25/document_gw_02.pdf, accessed November 30, 2011.

Chapter 4
Regulation or Nationalization?
Lessons Learned from the 2008 Financial Crisis

Adam J. Levitin and Susan M. Wachter

The U.S. housing finance system presents a conundrum for the scholar of regulation, as it simply cannot be described in traditional regulatory vocabulary. Regulatory cosmology has long had but a limited number of elements: direct command-and-control legislation (including substantive term and feature regulation, disclosure, and licensing), Pigouvian taxation and subsidies, tradable Coasean quantity permits, and regulation via litigation.

None of these traditional regulatory approaches, however, are adequate to describe the regulation of housing finance in the United States. Instead, to understand U.S. housing finance regulation, it is necessary to conceive of a distinct regulatory approach—that of the "public option"—whereby the government competes in the market against private enterprises for the provision of goods and services.

Since the New Deal, the fundamental approach of U.S. housing finance regulation has been this public option. The government, as a market participant with substantial market power, has been able to set the terms on which much of the market functions (Levitin 2009:143).

This chapter examines the use of public options in housing finance. It does so by tracing the arc of housing finance regulation from the Depression to the present, showing how public options were adopted during the Depression. Starting in the late 1960s, the public option regulatory approach began to be undermined, first by the privatization of Fannie Mae and the creation of Freddie Mac, then by the relaxation of the remaining command-and-control regulations on mortgage lending, and finally by the emergence of a private securitization market. The result was a wholly private market in housing finance with simply no effective regulatory framework in place to address the risks attendant to that market.

The collapse of the housing finance market in 2008 returned us to a world of inadvertent public options. Going forward, as the United States rebuilds its housing finance market, it is important to consider how the combination of the traditional regulatory tools of command-and-control, Pigouvian taxation and subsidies, quantity limitations, and litigation might be best deployed to ensure a stable, liquid market for housing finance.

This chapter commences with a discussion of the housing finance crisis that was part of the Great Depression. It then considers the Hoover and Roosevelt regulatory response, which was to create government institutions in the market rather than to engage in direct regulation or Pigouvian taxation. The chapter then traces the fate of the public option approach through the privatization of public options and emergence of a new form of private competition. It shows that while the market developed, the regulatory framework did not—instead, housing finance regulation continued to rely on a public option approach even as there was no longer a public option.

The result was a functionally unregulated space in which housing finance's endemic information and agency problems returned in a déjà vu fashion to Depression-era mortgages. At the very time of the private-sector emergence and takeover of what had been a public option for housing finance, the regulatory framework was dismantled. The end result was that no regulator exercised power over the market, and agency and information problems encouraged a rapid and unsustainable race to the bottom in lending standards and financial instability.

Housing Finance Before the Depression

The shape of the U.S. housing market before the Great Depression was substantially different than after it. First and foremost, prior to the Depression, home ownership rates were substantially lower than they are today. From 1900 to 1930, home ownership rates hovered around 46 percent and then declined slightly during the Depression. Renting, rather than owning, was the pre-Depression norm, and those who owned their homes often owned them free and clear of liens. The prevalence of renting, and of free-and-clear ownership, was largely a function of the scarcity of mortgage finance.

The pre-Depression funding of mortgages through depositaries, life insurance companies, and individuals was intensely local, yet the availability of financing was still vulnerable to national waves. Interest rates and the availability of financing varied significantly by locality and region. This was because of the local nature of the lending base, which resulted in highly cyclical and geographically based mortgage financing.

Compounding the local nature of funding for many mortgage lenders was its flighty nature, which exposed them to a liquidity risk if liabilities could not be rolled over.

Before the Depression, there was also no national secondary home mortgage market. Although individual lenders could contract with private investors, the norm was for originators to retain mortgages on their books—hence the liquidity risk.

A series of attempts were made prior to the Depression in the United States—between the 1870s and 1920s—to create secondary mortgage markets based on European models (Brewer 1976:356–57). All were purely private enterprises, virtually unregulated, and unable to maintain underwriting standards. All failed and resulted in ever-larger scandals. This failure to develop a secondary mortgage market prior to the New Deal compounded the U.S. problem of locality in mortgage lending.

The typical pre-Depression mortgage was a short-term, non-amortizing loan (Keehn and Smiley 1977:474, 478–79; Bogue 1963:176). The ratio of the loan amount to the value of the collateral property (the loan-to-value ratio, or LTV) was relatively low, meaning that a high down payment was required for a purchase. Down payments of less than 50 percent were rare, although mortgages from savings and loan (S&L) as-

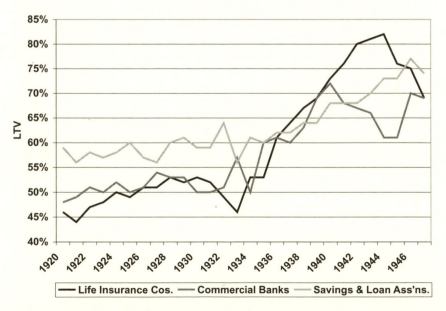

Figure 4.1. Average Mortgage Loan-to-Value Ratio, 1920–47. *Source:* Grebler et al. (1956:503).

sociations had slightly lower down payments (see Figure 4.1). Thus, D. M. Frederiksen (1894:204–5) reported that the average mortgage loan in the late nineteenth century was between 35 and 40 percent of the property's value.

The pre-Depression mortgage was generally a short-term, fixed-rate loan. Although there was some variance across different lending institutions, loans were typically for five years or less (see Figure 4.2). The short term limited lenders' exposure to interest rate risk, but the fixed rate increased this exposure.

The pre-Depression mortgage was also typically not fully amortizing—the borrower would make only periodic interest payments during the term of the mortgage, with most or all of the principal due in a lump sum at the end (a "balloon" or a "bullet"). Not surprisingly, foreclosure rates were substantially higher on non-amortized or partially amortized loans (Saulnier 1950:83, 85) (see Figure 4.3).

Pre-Depression foreclosure rates were quite low: around 0.3 percent in 1929 (Saulnier 1950:80) compared with an average of around 1 percent since 1978. For 1920–46, however, cumulative foreclosure rates were nearly double, and for loans with an LTV of 40 percent or more they

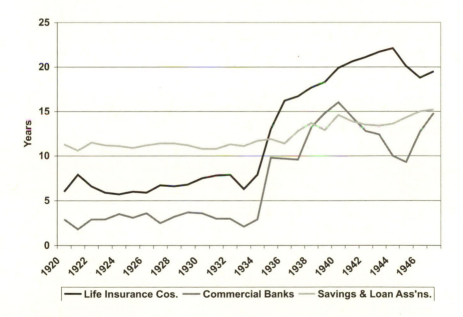

Figure 4.2. Average Contract Length of Mortgages on 1–4 Family Residences, 1920–47. *Source:* Grebler et al. (1956:23).

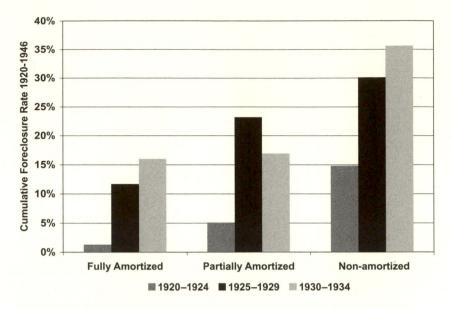

Figure 4.3. Cumulative Foreclosure Rates, 1920–46, by Amortization and Loan Origination Year. *Source:* Saulnier (1950:140).

were almost 20 percent. The default risk engendered by adjustable rates, particularly in a volatile monetary environment, offset the protection of high LTV ratios.

The New Deal and the Inadvertent Rise of the Public Option

The New Deal response to the market failures in the housing finance market was for the federal government to create new institutions that were active as market participants, offering liquidity and insurance to financial institutions.

The New Deal regulatory response to the market failures in the housing market is notable for what it did not do. It did not proceed through command-and-control regulation. For example, it did not prohibit non-amortizing mortgages. Nor did it contain individual mandates for the purchase of private mortgage insurance. Instead, the Hoover–Roosevelt response was to use government to fill the gap in the market: where the market did not produce services and products, the government would.

The Hoover–Roosevelt response involved the creation of four distinct public options. These disparate elements were not part of a master plan devised beforehand. The initial two components were responses to different exigencies and interest groups, while the later two were responses to the problems created by the first two components.

Liquidity and Diversification: The Federal Home Loan Bank

In 1932, Congress created the Federal Home Loan Bank (FHLB) system. This was a credit reserve system modeled after the Federal Reserve, with twelve regional FHLBs mutually owned by their member institutions and a central FHLB Board to regulate the system (Federal Home Loan Bank Act 1932).

The FHLBs provided liquidity to mortgage lenders by rediscounting mortgages—in other words, lending against mortgage collateral. FHLB rediscounting was initially restricted to lending against long-term mortgages. The FHLB system created a secondary market for mortgages in the United States, solving the problems of locality in mortgage lending. Starting in 1933, the FHLB system also assumed regulatory oversight of the new federal S&L associations authorized by the Home Owners' Loan Act (1933). Federal thrifts were restricted to making only fixed-rate loans.

Deposit Insurance: Federal Deposit Insurance Corporation and Federal Savings and Loan Insurance Corporation

Oversight authority over the federal S&L institutions included resolution authority for failed institutions (Home Owners' Loan Act 1933). Resolution authority was bolstered in 1934 with the creation of the Federal Savings and Loan Insurance Corporation (FSLIC; National Housing Act 1934:Title IV). FSLIC provided deposit insurance for S&Ls, just as the Federal Deposit Insurance Corporation (FDIC), created in 1932, provided for commercial banks. Deposit insurance was critical because it helped depositary institutions address the duration mismatch between their assets (often long-term) and liabilities (short-term deposits). Deposit insurance helped make deposits less flighty and thereby enabled depositaries to better manage maturities without keeping significant liquid assets on hand.

Market Clearing: Home Owners' Loan Corporation

Faced with a growing mortgage default problem, Congress responded in 1933 by authorizing the FHLB Board to create the Home Owners' Loan Corporation (HOLC), a U.S. government corporation, authorized to refinance troubled mortgages. HOLC purchased defaulted mortgages from financial institutions in exchange for tax-exempt 4 percent eighteen-year bonds (Home Owners' Loan Act 1933). HOLC received applications from 40 percent of all residential mortgagors in its first year of operation and refinanced half of them (Snowden 1988:292; Harriss 1951:11). HOLC resulted in a sudden and massive government entrance into the mortgage market, resulting in the government directly holding one in ten mortgages. Nonetheless, "it was well understood that in the H.O.L.C. no permanent socialization of mortgage lending was intended and no attempt to preserve home ownership irrespective of public cost" (French 1941:54). It represented a deliberately temporary public option to help mortgage finance markets clear other than through foreclosure, but the standards it set—long-term, fixed-rate, fully amortized mortgages— became ingrained in U.S. housing finance.

Because HOLC would not refinance at a 100 percent LTV ratio, HOLC refinancings required the consent of the existing mortgagee. At first, the federal government guaranteed only the timely payment of interest on HOLC securities but not repayment of principal—hence lenders were reluctant to accept HOLC refinancing. Therefore, in order to facilitate HOLC refinancings, the federal government began to guarantee the principal on HOLC securities, too, and HOLC securities eventually traded at par (Home Owners' Loan Act 1933; Home Owners' Loan Act Amendments 1934).

HOLC wound down by 1951, but by then it had changed the U.S. housing market in four major ways. First, it had forced a market clearing. Second, it had turned a large pool of mortgages into marketable securities. Third, it had set the long-term, fully amortized, fixed-rate mortgage as the federal government standard and demonstrated its feasibility (Jackson 1985:196). And fourth, HOLC standardized many mortgage lending procedures, including national appraisal methods, mortgage forms, and origination, foreclosure, and real estate owned (REO) management processes (Carrozzo 2008:1, 23).

HOLC created the template for a national mortgage market out of necessity, not forethought. It also rapidly made the federal government into the largest single mortgagee in the United States. The federal government did not want to hold the HOLC-modified mortgages for the long term.

There was little market appetite for the risk on these new long-term, fixed-rate, fully amortized products featuring borrowers with recent defaults, especially in the Depression economy. Therefore, to make the mortgages marketable, the federal government had to provide credit enhancement. The government was thus willing to assume the credit risk on these mortgages if private investors would assume the interest-rate risk.

Mortgage Insurance: Federal Housing Authority

The vehicle through which the government assumed mortgage credit risk while leaving borrowers with interest-rate risk was federal mortgage insurance from the Federal Housing Authority (FHA). The FHA, a government agency created in 1934, was mandated to insure payment of principal and interest on mortgages in exchange for a small insurance premium charged to the originator and passed on to the borrower.

Because of the credit risk assumed by the FHA, FHA insurance was available only for loans that met certain characteristics, modeled on the terms of HOLC mortgages. FHA insurance then reallocated the bundle of risks attendant to a mortgage loan. The government and the borrower split the credit risk, while the lender took the interest-rate risk. Of course, the taxpayer stood behind the government risk retention.

The FHA insurance system was a response to several problems. First, it was a reaction to the government finding itself a major mortgagee as the result of the HOLC refinancings. The government hoped to be able to sell the HOLC-refinanced mortgages to private investors, but no investors would take the credit risk on these mortgages. Offering a credit guarantee of the mortgages served to move them off the government's books. Second, the government was hoping to attract more capital into the battered mortgage sector. The FHLB system and FSLIC insurance encouraged S&L mortgage lending, but further action was needed to encourage commercial bank capital deployment in the mortgage sector. Commercial banks were reluctant to become deeply committed to mortgages, not least because of the illiquidity of mortgage assets.

Standardization via FHA insurance was intended to transform mortgages into assets that were more liquid. Notably, FHA insurance was not originally intended as a long-term intervention in the housing market—hence the original temporary duration of the Treasury guarantee of FHA debentures. Instead, the FHA was intended to deal with the problem of unloading the pool of HOLC mortgages and jumpstarting the housing sector. Only when it became apparent that the sector needed longer-term care did the FHA evolve into an ongoing guarantee program aimed at ensuring greater housing affordability going forward.

FHA insurance requirements, along with HOLC refinancing, played a major role in standardizing mortgage terms. The importance of standardization cannot be overstated because it was the precondition for the development of a secondary mortgage market. Secondary markets are built around liquidity, and nonstandard instruments are not liquid because each individual instrument must be examined, a requirement that adds transaction costs.

FHA insurance also eliminated credit risk for investors. FHA insurance alone, however, was not sufficient for a secondary mortgage market to develop. For that, the final New Deal innovation, Fannie Mae, was required.

Liquidity Again: The Federal National Mortgage Association (Fannie Mae)

Investors had little appetite for buying individual mortgages in the secondary market, even if they were insured, because of the liquidity and interest-rate risk involved as well as the transaction costs of diligence on individual mortgages. Therefore, the National Housing Act (1934) provided for a federal charter for national mortgage associations to purchase these insured mortgages at par. The goal was to create a secondary market that would encourage mortgage originators to make new loans by allowing them to capitalize on future cash flows through a sale of the mortgages to the mortgage associations, which would fund themselves by issuing long-term fixed-rate debt with maturities similar to those of the mortgages.

The federal national mortgage association charter was made available to all comers. When no applications for a federal national mortgage association charter were forthcoming by 1938, the Reconstruction Finance Corporation created under federal charter provisions a subsidiary called the Federal National Mortgage Association of Washington—later simply the Federal National Mortgage Association, which has since been shortened still further to "Fannie Mae."

Fannie Mae purchased mortgages from financial institutions in exchange for its debt securities, which were backed in this period by the full faith and credit of the U.S. government. Fannie Mae would either keep the mortgage loans in its own portfolio—against which it issued bonds that it used to fund its operations—or resell the loans whole to private investors. This meant that Fannie Mae was able to pass on some of the interest-rate risk on the mortgages to its bondholders, because their bonds had fixed-rate coupons. Neither the Fannie Mae bondholders nor the lenders that sold mortgages to Fannie Mae in exchange for its debt securities assumed any credit risk, however, because Fannie Mae was a government corporation.

Fannie Mae's activities before World War II were fairly limited. During World War II, it largely ceased purchase operations. Its prewar accumulation of mortgages (as well as those of the Reconstruction Finance Corporation Mortgage Company) "were expected to decrease as soon as the FHA type mortgage had proved itself" (Lindholm 1951:5–57). Fannie Mae was virtually reborn in 1948, when Congress amended its charter to authorize the purchase of mortgages guaranteed by the Veterans Administration (VA; Lindholm 1951:58). Fannie Mae entered the VA-guaranteed market in force. From June 30, 1948, to June 30, 1949, its holdings increased 809 percent because it extended purchase commitments in order to stimulate the construction market (Lindholm 1951:56–57).

Fannie Mae thus set the stage for three longer-term structural features of the mortgage market. First, it provided liquidity for mortgage originators by creating a secondary market that linked capital market investors to mortgage lenders to mortgage borrowers. Second, the Fannie Mae secondary market reduced regional discrepancies in interest rates and financing availability (Lindholm 1951:260). It harnessed capital of investors from capital-rich regions to purchase or invest in mortgages from capital-poor regions. And third, Fannie continued the work of HOLC in establishing the 20 percent down, self-amortizing, thirty-year fixed-rate mortgage as the national standard. Thanks to Fannie's government backing, the subsidized cost of funds for the thirty-year fixed mortgage helped lead to the crowding out of other mortgage products.

When the thirty-year fixed-rate invention was first introduced during the Depression, the long-term, fixed-rate, self-amortizing mortgage was an exotic product. The product was introduced at a time of tremendous market uncertainty about future incomes and the economy. Even with FHA insurance, many lenders were reluctant to make long-term, fixed-rate loans because of the interest-rate and liquidity risk. Fannie Mae relieved the liquidity problem by offering to buy any and all FHA mortgages at par. By buying long-term, fixed-rate, self-amortizing mortgages and issuing bonds, Fannie Mae transformed what were then exotic mortgage products into plain vanilla, government-backed corporate bonds, something for which the market had a strong appetite.

The thirty-year fixed-rate mortgage was the product of a moment when the entire financial system was at risk, but it had advantages that helped give it staying power. The long term of the mortgage made it possible for individuals to borrow against their long-term earnings. Indeed, the advent of the thirty-year fixed-rate mortgage arguably established the middle class as a class of property owners—and as a class of debtors. Although individuals are not able to secure credit by indenturing themselves, the long-term mortgage serves as a proxy for long-term payment commitment. The fixed rate allows families to avoid interest-rate shocks against which they have little ability to hedge. Self-amortization protects against overleverage by constantly reducing the LTV ratio. Self-amortization also serves as the perfect hedge for families who do not want to be exposed to payment shocks, the way they would be as renters.

By stabilizing consumer finances, the thirty-year fixed-rate mortgage also helped guard against the systemic risk that can result from mass defaults stemming from payment reset shock on variable-rate mortgages. Thus, the thirty-year fixed-rate mortgage stabilized not only individual consumers' finances but also those of communities and the entire economy.

Taking stock of this history, we see a largely unprecedented regulatory response to the failure of the housing market during the Great Depression. Although the creation of the Federal Reserve System, the farm mortgage system, and the U.S. Housing Corporation during World War I had pioneered the federal public option model in financial services, the scope of federal intervention in housing finance markets during the New Deal was unparalleled. The federal intervention was somewhat haphazard and uneven, responding to particular problems and building on the splintered nature of U.S. financial regulation, with its multiple-chartering options and regulators, rather than effectuating a comprehensive overhaul of housing finance. The federal intervention was also largely intended to be temporary. Nonetheless, by the late 1940s, the U.S. housing finance system was run through and by public options. Some command-and-control regulations remained, on both the state and federal levels, but there was no command-and-control regime that covered the entire market. Instead, public options substituted as a type of market-wide regulatory regime.

The Decline of the Public Option

Coming out of the New Deal, the primary mode of regulation of the U.S. housing finance system was through the public option in the secondary market. There was still a variety of regulatory cobwebs on the state and federal regulations for particular types of lenders. Federal thrifts, for example, were prohibited from making adjustable-rate loans, and some states prohibited all lenders from making adjustable-rate loans, but by and large, mortgage regulation was a matter of what the government-sponsored enterprises (GSEs) would buy and what the FHA would insure. Even if other loan products could formally be made, there was no secondary market for them, and lenders were generally unwilling to assume the risk themselves. Thus, through the domination of the secondary market by public options, the federal government was able to effectively regulate the mortgage market.

Between the late 1960s and the 2000s, however, U.S. housing finance underwent a series of further changes that undermined the effectiveness of the public option approach. Nonetheless, regulation via public options remained virtually the exclusive mode of regulation.

Privatization of Public Options

First, in 1968, the Johnson administration, eager to clear room in the federal budget for Great Society spending and the Vietnam War, split Fannie Mae up into two entities. One entity was privatized as Fannie Mae. The other remained government owned and was christened "Ginnie Mae." Ginnie Mae's mission was restricted to the securitization of FHA-insured and VA-guaranteed mortgages. Fannie Mae, under a revised charter, became privately capitalized but operated under government regulation.

The privatization of Fannie Mae meant that its management would be subject to pressure from shareholders, and it was also subject to some command-and-control regulation. It was required to maintain minimum capital levels of 2.5 percent for on-balance sheet obligations and 0.45 percent for off-balance sheet obligations. Fannie Mae's loan purchases were also subject to single-exposure limitations (conforming loan limits) and LTV limitations absent mortgage insurance. Otherwise, however, underwriting was left up to Fannie Mae. The potential menu of loans that Fannie Mae could purchase was determined by what was possible in the loan origination market, so it was in effect constrained by state and federal regulation of the primary market. The privatization of Fannie Mae had the effect of creating a secondary market for non-FHA/VA mortgages, thereby significantly loosening regulatory control over housing finance.

Creation of a Private Public Option: The Federal Home Loan Mortgage Corporation (Freddie Mac)

In 1971, the federal government chartered another GSE, the Federal Home Loan Mortgage Corporation, more commonly known as "Freddie Mac." Freddie Mac was originally a subsidiary of the FHLB system, designed to enable the securitization of mortgages originated by the S&Ls that belonged to the FHLBs. But Freddie Mac was soon privatized.

Initially Freddie Mac operated differently from Fannie Mae. Freddie Mac engaged in securitization via pass-through certificates issued against dedicated pools of mortgages, whereas Fannie Mae funded the mortgages it purchased by issuing corporate debt. By the 1980s, however, Fannie Mae had begun to engage in securitization and Freddie Mac was issuing corporate debt, so the two models converged.

The critical move presented by both Fannie and Freddie was the division of credit risk from interest-rate risk. Investors in these two GSEs' mortgage-backed securities assumed interest-rate risk on the securitized mortgages but not credit risk on them. Instead, they assumed the GSEs' credit risk, which was implicitly backed by the federal government. Similarly investors in GSE debt were really investing in interest-rate risk plus an implied government security.

The emergence of Freddie Mac exacerbated the problems caused by privatizing the public option of Fannie Mae without ensuring the existence of another market-wide regulatory system. Freddie Mac competed against Fannie Mae, which put pressure on the GSEs to loosen their underwriting standards to gain market share. Into the late 1980s, however, the GSEs still had a fairly small market share; most mortgages were still held in portfolio, particularly by S&Ls. It was only with the collapse of the S&L industry in the 1980s that the GSEs truly emerged as market giants.

The Savings and Loan

From the 1950s to the 1970s, the S&L institution dominated U.S. housing finance. The S&Ls were unequipped to handle rising interest rates in the 1970s. As rates rose, depositors sought rates of return that kept pace with inflation. The advent of money market funds resulted in a tremendous disintermediation from the depository system into the securities system. In order to retain their deposit base in the face of disintermediation, the S&Ls were forced to offer ever higher interest rates. The S&Ls' assets, however, were long-term, fixed-rate mortgage loans. The result of paying higher interest rates on liabilities than those received on assets was the decapitalization of the S&Ls.

Congress and federal regulators responded to this problem through S&L deregulation, including the undoing of usury laws. In 1982, Congress passed legislation that enabled the underwriting of second mortgages and preempted state laws that prohibited adjustable-rate mortgages, balloon payments, and negative amortization (Alternative Mortgage Parity Transactions Act 1982; Renuart and Keest 2005:679). The FHLBB also rewrote its regulations for federal thrifts, allowing them to underwrite adjustable-rate mortgages and to invest in assets with potentially higher yields than home mortgages. The result was that the decapitalized S&Ls doubled down on their bets and expanded into markets in which they lacked experience—commercial real estate, junk bonds, race horses, and so on. This, plus a regulatory environment in which both Congress and the FHLBB engaged in playing ostrich, significantly increased the damage done to the S&Ls.

The lesson from the S&L crisis was that depositories were poorly suited for making long-term, fixed-rate loans. Instead, they could make adjustable-rate loans or sell their loans in the secondary market. At the same time that adjustable-rate lending increased, consumers evinced a strong taste for fixed-rate loans, around which they can budget. The result, then, was the rapid growth of the secondary market, which, in the 1980s consisted primarily of GSEs.

Emergence of Private Secondary Market: Private-Label Securitization

While the GSEs dominated the secondary market until 2003–6, a completely private, unregulated secondary mortgage market started to emerge in 1977. This was the private-label securitization (PLS) market. The PLS market began with the securitization of ultra-high-quality mortgages that were too large to meet the GSEs' conforming loan limits. Although this market remained quite small for many years, PLS began to take off in the mid-1990s as a result of the S&L crisis, and it began to experiment in the securitization of loans to ever-riskier borrowers. Rapid growth started in the early 2000s, so that by 2006, almost one-half of all mortgage originations were nontraditional products and PLS had grown to 56 percent of the securitization market.

Reregulation and Deregulation via Preemption

Though limited, the early growth in subprime lending led to a national legislative response—the Home Ownership and Equity Protection Act of 1994, or HOEPA—which prohibited certain predatory lending practices for "high-cost" refinancing loans.

HOEPA's narrow scope limited its effectiveness because lenders easily avoided its application by pricing loans just under the HOEPA cost thresholds. Many states, however, passed their own "mini-HOEPA" statutes (McCoy and Renuart 2008). Yet between 1996 and 2007, federal banking regulators pursued a single-minded campaign of deregulation via preemption, unraveling both state consumer protection laws and state attempts to enforce federal laws.

Unlike the case with preemption by the Home Owners' Loan Act (1933) that enabled FHA-insured lending with national standards, federal preemption was not coupled with substitute federal regulation. Instead, a regulatory vacuum was substituted for disparate state regulations. The result, by 2000, was a multitrillion-dollar national mortgage market with little remaining regulation.

Return of the Bullet Loans and the Debacle

Freed of its post-Depression regulations, the U.S. mortgage market quickly reverted to Depression-era bullet loans, shifting interest rate

and refinancing risk back to borrowers: non-amortizing and even negatively amortizing loans proliferated in the private-label market, as did
loans like 2/28s and 3/27s, which had short-term, fixed-rate teaser periods before resetting to a much higher adjustable rate. These mortgages
were designed to be refinanced upon the expiration of the teaser period, just like bullet loans, and they carried the risk that the borrower
would not be able to refinance either because of a change in the borrower's finances, a decline in the value of the property, or a market freeze.
As these new bullet loans were at high LTVs, only a small decline in
property values was necessary to inhibit refinancing.

The new bullet loans were also tied into a global financing system that
amplified their performance but lessened market discipline on underwriting, as securitization separated economic ownership from underwriting, which created agency and information problems that encouraged
riskier underwriting and underpricing for risk (Levitin and Wachter
2012). The result was disaster.

There is a tradeoff between (1) the benefits of expanded national
and international markets in housing finance and (2) the impacts from
a failure in either the public management or regulation of those markets. The expanding markets in housing finance over the history of the
United States contributed to the impact suffered in 2008.

The post–New Deal U.S. mortgage market was built around regulation by public option, not command-and-control regulation. The public
option was eroded through privatization and market developments,
while the existing elements of command-and-control regulation were
removed first by Congress and then by federal regulators. The end result
was that no regulator exercised complete power over the market, and
agency and information problems encouraged a rapid and unsustainable race to the bottom in lending standards.

Looking Forward

In the wake of the financial disaster, the U.S. housing finance system
had by 2008 returned to a public option model. The PLS market was
dead. Fannie Mae and Freddie Mac were in federal conservatorship. The
remaining public entities—the FHA/VA, Ginnie Mae, and the FHLBs—
continued to function, but the mortgage market had become almost an
entirely government-supported market. Public option regulation once
again corresponds to what has become a public option market. And once
again, the public option is an inadvertent, reactionary approach adopted
in response to a crisis, rather than a deliberate, methodical approach.

Going forward, however, it is not clear that public option regulation
will continue to be the order of the day. The Dodd-Frank Wall Street

Reform and Consumer Protection Act (2010), which is the major legislative response to the financial crisis, signaled a different regulatory approach: command-and-control regulation. The Dodd-Frank Act creates a new set of command-and-control rules for both mortgage origination and mortgage securitization. For mortgage origination, the Dodd-Frank Act (2010:§ 1693c(a)) prohibits residential mortgage loans unless the lender has verified the borrower's ability to repay. Failure to do so is a defense against foreclosure (Dodd-Frank Act 2010:§ 1640). The Dodd-Frank Act provides a safe harbor for lenders to the ability-to-repay requirement, which does not apply to "qualified mortgages" as defined by Federal Reserve Board regulations (Dodd-Frank Act 2010:§ 1693c(b)). Nonqualified mortgages do not benefit from a presumption that the borrower was able to repay and are also prohibited from bearing prepayment penalties (Dodd-Frank Act 2010:§ 1693c(b)&(c)).

Dodd-Frank also undertakes a reform of the securitization market by requiring that securitizers have "skin-in-the-game," meaning that they must retain some risk exposure to their securitized assets (Dodd-Frank Act 2010:§ 70–11). Under regulations promulgated by a consortium of federal financial regulators, securitizers must retain a certain portion of credit risk on assets securitizations (or retain near identical deals) unless the securitized assets fall into certain exempt categories. The most important of those exemptions is for "qualified residential mortgages," another term to be defined by the federal financial regulatory consortium.

The Dodd-Frank Act also created a new Consumer Financial Protection Bureau (CFPB), which has broad powers to regulate all mortgage origination and insurance markets (Dodd-Frank Act 2010:§ 5491). If and when the CFPB does regulate, it will be either regulation through command and control or regulation via litigation.

The Dodd-Frank Act's reforms aside, it remains to be seen what will happen to the public options that today are the mortgage market. Will Fannie Mae and Freddie Mac be nationalized, privatized, or recapitalized as hybrid entities? What role, if any, will government guarantees have? Will the market divide into a public option (such as FHA/VA) for the poor and private options for others? Or will the temporary measures taken in 2008–10 end up lasting for decades, just like those of the New Deal?

A consideration of the options for housing finance reform is far beyond the scope of this chapter, but it seems patent that the regulatory paradigm should track the market. If the market is to be privatized, command-and-control and Pigouvian taxation makes sense as the regulatory approach. If the market is to be nationalized, then the public option model makes sense. And if we end up with a combination, where public options coexist and compete with private actors, then the lesson to be learned from the collapse of 2008 is that command-and-control and Pigouvian taxation need to be combined with public option regulation. A public option is effective at shaping competition in the market only if all parties in the market have to compete according to the same rules and standards—otherwise the result is merely market segmentation. Moreover, without basic standards that apply to all parties, the result can quickly become a race to the bottom that can damage not only private parties but also governmental entities and the overall economy.

The public option has been associated with long-standing structural changes that transformed the shape of American home ownership and mortgages. It created the long-term, fixed-rate, fully amortized mortgage as the standard American housing finance product. In so doing, it made possible sustainable home ownership for American households and the economy (Jackson 1985). But for public options to succeed as policy tools and not turn into liabilities, they need to function in a market that has standards for all.

References

Bogue, Allan G. (1963) *From Prairie to Corn Belt.* Chicago: University of Chicago Press.

Brewer, H. Peers (1976) "Eastern Money and Western Mortgages in the 1870's." *Business History Review* 50: 274–79.

Carrozzo, Peter M. (2008) "A New Deal for the American Mortgage: The Home Owners' Loan Corporation, the National Housing Act, and the Birth of the National Mortgage Market." *University of Miami Business Law Review* 17: 1–46.

Frederiksen, Ditley M. (1894) "Mortgage Banking in America." *Journal of Political Economy* 2: 203.

French, David M. (1941) "The Contest for a National System of Home-Mortgage Finance." *American Political Science Review* 35: 53.

Grebler, Leo et al. (1956) *Capital Formation in Residential Real Estate.* Cambridge, Mass.: National Bureau of Economic Research.

Harriss, C. Lowell (1951) *History and Policies of the Home Owners' Loan Corporation.* Cambridge, Mass.: National Bureau of Economic Research.

Jackson, Kenneth T. (1985) *Crabgrass Frontier: The Suburbanization of the United States.* New York: University of Oxford Press.

Keehn, Richard H., and Gene Smiley (1977) "Mortgage Lending by National Banks" *Business History Review* 51: 474–91.

Levitin, Adam J. (2009) "Hydraulic Regulation: Regulating Credit Markets Upstream." *Yale Journal of Regulation* 26: 143–228.

Levitin, Adam J., and Susan M. Wachter (2012) "Explaining the Housing Bubble." *Georgetown Law Journal* 100: 1177–258.

Lindholm, R. W. (1951) "The Federal National Mortgage Association." *Journal of Finance* 6: 54–61.

McCoy, Patricia A., and Elizabeth Renuart (2008) "The Legal Infrastructure of Subprime and Nontraditional Home Mortgages." Harvard University Joint Center for Housing Studies, Working Paper Series Paper #UCC08-5, Boston.

Renuart, Elizabeth, and Kathleen E. Keest (2005) *The Cost of Credit: Regulation, Preemption, and Industry Abuses.* Boston: National Consumer Law Center.

Saulnier, Raymond J. (1950) *Urban Mortgage Lending by Life Insurance Companies.* Cambridge, Mass.: National Bureau of Economic Research.

Snowden, Kenneth A. (1988) "Mortgage Lending and American Urbanization, 1880–1890." *Journal of Economic History* 48: 292.

Statutes Cited

Alternative Mortgage Parity Transactions Act of 1982, 12 U.S.C. § 3801 et seq.

Dodd-Frank Wall Street Reform and Consumer Protection Act of 2010, 12 U.S.C. §§5491 et seq., 15 U.S.C. §§ 780-11, 1640, 1693.

Emergency Relief and Construction Act of 1932, Ch. 520, § 201(a)(2), 47 Stat. 709, 711.

Federal Home Loan Bank Act of 1932, Ch. 522, 47 Stat. 725.

Home Owners' Loan Act Amendments of 1934, Ch. 168; 48 Stat. 128, 129, 643.

Home Owners' Loan Act of 1933, Ch. 64, 48 Stat. 128, 132.

Home Ownership and Equity Protection Act of 1994, 15 U.S.C. § 1639.

National Housing Act of 1934, Ch. 847, 48 Stat. 1246, 1256.

Chapter 5
Regulating in the Dark

Roberta Romano

How should one regulate in the midst of a financial crisis? This is a fundamental question for financial regulation, but it is not readily answerable as the issues implicated are truly complex, if not intractable. Yet foundational financial legislation tends to be enacted in a crisis setting (Romano 2005:1591–94), and over the past decade, when confronted with this question, the U.S. Congress has answered it reflexively by enacting legislation that massively increases the scope and scale of the regulation of business firms, especially financial institutions and instruments, in a manner seemingly oblivious to the cost and consequences of its actions. A simple but telling comparison of a commonly used measure of legislative complexity, a statute's published length, conveys what Congress has wrought. The Sarbanes-Oxley Act of 2002 is sixty-six pages long and the Dodd-Frank Wall Street Reform and Consumer Protection Act of 2010 is an astounding 848 pages, whereas the twentieth-century foundational federal banking legislation—the Federal Reserve Act and the Glass-Steagall Act—are twenty-four and thirty-seven pages, respectively (Perry 2010).[1]

In addressing how to regulate in a financial crisis, there is a related question: whether there is something about financial institutions and markets that is different from other regulatory domains, which makes regulation more challenging and crisis responses more prone to legislative failure. This chapter addresses both questions by contrasting three recent examples of financial regulation that, I contend, are, in the main, misguided: Sarbanes-Oxley, the response to the accounting scandals and bankruptcies of several large public corporations accompanied by a sharp stock market decline in the early 2000s; Dodd-Frank, the response to the global financial crisis originating in the subprime mortgage crisis of the late 2000s; and the Basel capital accords, through which central banks and banking regulators of the leading industrial nations have sought to harmonize international financial regulation since the late 1980s.

The answer to the two questions regarding crisis-generated financial regulation is, I believe, not really an issue of institutional competence— that is, of Congress's lack of the requisite expertise to understand technically complicated financial products and markets. After all, financial regulators, in promulgating permutations of internationally harmonized capital requirements, have not fared much better in protecting the global financial system from catastrophic systemic risk and, I would contend, have contributed to it, albeit unintentionally—though one would have a hard time figuring that out from media accounts (Romano 2012).

Rather, the nub of the regulatory problem derives from the fact that financial firms operate in a dynamic environment in which there are many unknowns and unknowables and state-of-the-art knowledge quickly obsolesces. In such a context, even the most informed regulatory response—which Congress's reaction in the recent crises was not—will be prone to error and is likely to produce backward-looking regulation that takes aim at yesterday's perceived problem, rather than tomorrow's, for regulators necessarily operate under considerable uncertainty and at a lag behind private actors. But using market actors' superior knowledge to inform regulation is not necessarily an effective solution either, as indicated by the utter failure in the recent crisis of Basel II, which relied on banks' internal risk ratings to measure capital requirements. This only further highlights the fluid, fast-moving, and uncertain environment in which financial institutions operate—even firms' state-of-the-art risk management techniques proved inadequate in the confluence of events that produced the global financial crisis.

In order to understand financial regulation undertaken in a crisis, we need to take account, as Frank Knight (1965:270) put it, of "human nature as we know it." Human nature in this context is that legislators will find it impossible to not respond to a financial crisis by "doing something," that is, by ratcheting up regulation, instead of waiting until a consensus understanding of what has occurred can be secured and a targeted solution then crafted, despite the considerable informational advantage from the latter approach, which would, no doubt, improve the quality of decision making (see Carrigan and Coglianese this volume). Compounding the problem, Congress tends not to move nimbly to rework financial legislation when it becomes widely acknowledged as flawed or seriously deficient. For instance, it took decades to repeal the Glass-Steagall Act's separation of commercial and investment banking; eleven years to make relatively small revisions to accounting and bribery provisions of the Foreign Corrupt Practices Act; and eight years to amend the Sarbanes-Oxley Act to exempt only the smallest firms from the auditor attestation of internal controls' effectiveness requirement, despite substantial consensus regarding the statutes' problems.

In this chapter, I contend that the best means of responding to the typical pattern of financial regulation—legislating in a crisis atmosphere under conditions of substantial uncertainty followed by status quo stickiness—is for Congress and regulators to include as a matter of course in financial legislation and regulation enacted in the midst or aftermath of a financial crisis procedural mechanisms that require automatic subsequent review and reconsideration of those decisions, along with regulatory exemption or waiver powers that create flexibility in implementation and encourage, where possible, small-scale, discrete experimentation to better inform and calibrate the regulatory apparatus. Such an approach, in my judgment, could mitigate, at least at the margin, errors that invariably accompany financial legislation and rulemaking originating in a crisis atmosphere. Given the fragility of financial institutions and markets and their centrality to economic growth and societal well-being, this is an area in which it is exceedingly important for legislators acting in a crisis with the best of intentions to keep from making matters worse.

Legislating Financial Regulation in Times of Crisis

Most significant financial regulation is adopted in response to financial crises (Banner 1998:257; Romano 2005:1591–94). This pattern is consistent with the political science literature on policy agendas. According to that literature, issues move to the top of the legislative policy agenda in conjunction with "focusing events" and shifts in national mood, which render the public receptive to government action to redress a specific problem (Kingdon 2011:19–20). This constellation of events opens a "window" through which individuals (referred to as "policy entrepreneurs") present their preexisting preferred policies as "solutions" to the problem at hand (Kingdon 2011: 20). A typical pattern in a financial crisis is a media clamor for action, reflecting, if not spurring, a similar popular demand and, as a crisis intensifies, an accompanying suggestion that government inaction is prolonging the pain and suffering.[2] A risk-averse legislator whose objective is reelection will, no doubt, conclude that there is a need to respond without seeking to ascertain, if it were even possible, whether such demands are media-driven, or popularly shared, or, in fact, necessary to resolve the problem.

There is a theoretical and empirical political science literature, based on agency models of political representation, supporting that hypothesized course of legislators' action: it indicates a close connection between an issue's salience in the media, election outcomes, and implementation of policy.[3] For a legislator, "doing something" in response to a crisis is both easier to explain to anxious constituents, and more likely to be positively reported in the media, than inaction, and therefore it would appear to be a clear-cut superior route to reelection, which is the posited focus of legislators.

The heightened issue saliency, or in the vernacular "media frenzy," that accompanies the exigency of a financial crisis compels legislators not only to respond but to respond quickly, even though they will be aware that they cannot possibly determine what would be the best policy to adopt in the circumstances as there will be considerable uncertainty in the first place about what has just occurred and why. Yet without an understanding of the causes of a crisis, regulatory fixes, except by fortuity, are bound to be off the mark. Indeed, paralleling the political science literature's explanation of how policy proposals reach the congressional decision-making agenda, legislation adopted in financial crises typically contains recycled proposals fashioned to resolve quite unrelated problems, imagined or real, which policy entrepreneurs advance as ready-made solutions to immediate concerns, to a Congress in need of off-the-shelf proposals that can be enacted quickly (Kingdon 2011:139–43, 181–82; Bainbridge 2011:1796–819,1821; Romano 2005:1568–85). Given this reality, the repeated legislative failures that we have witnessed with regard to financial regulation should not be a surprising outcome.

Sarbanes-Oxley, for instance, is a case study of legislative failure. The statute's highly touted governance mandates of independent audit committees, restrictions on auditor services, and certifications of internal controls—essentially "off-the-rack" initiatives that had been advocated by policy entrepreneurs for some time—had minimal support in the academic literature publicly available both before and even more so after the legislation's enactment, regarding their efficacy at improving performance or reducing audit failures (Romano 2005). Not surprisingly, those ostensible reforms apparently had no bearing on financial institutions' ability to withstand the 2007–9 financial crisis (Beltratti and Stulz 2009; Cheffins 2009). Yet Sarbanes-Oxley's governance mandates are still law, imposing considerable costs on firms (Ahmed et al. 2010; Bargeron et al. 2009; Linck et al. 2009; Romano 2009), and it will take a Herculean effort to repeal them given the organization of government.

In addition, a considerable portion of Dodd-Frank and, to a far lesser extent, Sarbanes-Oxley consist of substantive rulemaking instructions to federal regulators. Dodd-Frank requires four hundred final rulemakings and sixty-seven studies, the vast majority of whose legislative deadlines will, no doubt, be missed (Davis Polk 2011:10–11; Davis Polk 2010:ii).[4]

Indeed, at the statute's one-year anniversary, 104 rulemaking deadlines had already been missed (Davis Polk 2011:2). This legislative strategy of delegation would appear, at first glance, to be attentive to the informational concern regarding decision making in a crisis that I have mentioned, as the contemplated rulemaking process could generate, in theory, needed information to improve the quality of policymaking. Such an explanation works hand in glove with the conventional rationale for delegation and deference, that among government institutions, "agencies are the repositories of expert knowledge and experience" (Eskridge and Ferejohn 2010:276).

However, it is difficult to posit seriously that in delegating so extensively Congress was concerned with improving the information available for decision making, given the statute's absurd demands on agencies, in both the plenitude of rulemakings and implementation timetable.[5] An illustration, underscoring the fact that agencies cannot be expected to accumulate, let alone assimilate, relevant, available information in the rulemaking process contemplated by the statute, involves the Securities and Exchange Commission (SEC) proxy access rule, which Dodd-Frank expressly authorized. The rule was struck down by the U.S. Court of Appeals for the D.C. Circuit in *Business Roundtable v. SEC* (2011), as "arbitrary and capricious" for having been adopted with an inadequate cost-benefit analysis of its effect. Yet the proxy access rule had been in the making by the SEC for well over a decade, in contrast to the vast majority of the statute's required rulemakings.

A strand of the political science literature provides an alternative rationale for regulatory delegation, that it is a means by which legislators can avoid responsibility for adverse policy consequences (Fiorina 1982:46–52). That explanation offers a more compelling account of Dodd-Frank's large-scale delegation strategy than the interpretation of a Congress earnestly seeking to cope with having to legislate under uncertainty by creating a window for additional information gathering and regulatory fine-tuning. Rather, in this scenario, delegation enables legislators to "do something" in a crisis, by passing "something" and thereby mollifying media and popular concerns, while at the same time shifting responsibility to an agency for potential policy failures—outcomes that legislators may well suspect to be possible, given the paucity or poor quality of information available concerning the causes of a crisis when the legislation is being crafted. If that possibility were to be realized, legislators, without missing a beat, would be positioned to criticize the agency, with the policy failure attributable to faulty implementation rather than an ill-conceived congressional mandate, and would have the further possibility of providing valuable constituent services, assisting firms and individuals to navigate difficulties created by administrative action (e.g., Fiorina 1982:47, 53). But if policy implementation were to be successful, legislators could, of course, still take credit (Nichols 1982:68). In short, by means of delegation, legislators can have their cake and eat it too, so to speak.

From a legislator's perspective, the delegation strategy would appear to have minimal cost, under both the benign and more manipulative explanations. But many members of the business and academic communities view Dodd-Frank as having exacerbated the severe economic downturn that has followed the global financial crisis. As banks are spending in the billions of dollars on Dodd-Frank compliance (Protess 2011), the statute quite plausibly adversely affects the price or availability of credit. But more important is the increase in business uncertainty generated by the immense number of required rulemakings. Until proposed, let alone promulgated, regulatory compliance costs cannot be estimated with any confidence, which deters investment. Moreover, because Dodd-Frank was enacted on a party-line vote, in contrast to the bipartisan, unanimous, or near unanimous, support crisis-driven financial legislation has typically received, an additional source of uncertainty affecting business investment is the possibility that, in the near future, control of Congress and the presidency could shift before all of the required rulemakings are completed and dramatically alter the implementation of the law.

The full cost of Dodd-Frank is rendered more opaque by regulators finding, as they attempt to implement the statute, that Dodd-Frank's mandates pose unanticipated operational issues that create new risks, complicating implementation. For example, in order to decrease the risk of trading customized off-exchange derivative securities, Congress required derivative trades, wherever possible, to be cleared on exchanges (Dodd-Frank Act: Title VII). Yet, this requirement, it turns out, increases risk for pension funds and asset managers due to the way exchanges handle margin collateral, and changing exchange brokerage arrangements to reduce the risk significantly increases costs (Grant 2011).

In short, by requiring agencies to enact a multitude of rules often devoid of guidance and consideration of how the rules would interact with institutional practice, Dodd-Frank's delegation strategy has created a minefield for business planning. Moreover, adding insult to injury, Dodd-Frank does not even attempt to address the financial crisis's ground zero, Fannie Mae and Freddie Mac, the government-sponsored enterprises (GSEs) that back mortgages, which are estimated to require hundreds of billions of dollars in taxpayer support by the end of the decade (Acharya et al. 2011; Congressional Budget Office 2011; Wallison

2011a, 2011b). Perhaps that omission should not be surprising: throughout their pre-bailout existence, the GSEs have been considered "too influential and too politically connected to be regulated," with "each successive presidential administration turn[ing] a blind eye" to their unconstrained, highly leveraged, and increasingly risky lending activities (Acharya et al. 2011:22, 28).

But there are also in the Dodd-Frank Act delegations to agencies (along with statutory provisions that require agency action without discretion in implementation) that have at least some connection to the financial crisis, those explicitly directed at reducing systemic risk, such as the creation of a Financial Stability Oversight Council (Dodd-Frank Act: Title I), and regulatory directives on minimum leverage and risk-based capital requirements (Dodd-Frank Act:§ 171). This suggests that a helpful comparative benchmark would be the efforts of the international financial regulatory community to reduce systemic risk by harmonizing capital requirements in the Basel accords. Given the greater technical expertise of regulatory agencies compared with Congress, if institutional competence were to explain flaws in legislated financial regulation, then financial regulators would be expected to do a better job than Congress.

Moreover, the negotiations of financial regulators over the Basel accords do not receive as intensive media coverage and accompanying popular attention, pressing for immediate action, as does congressional deliberation in times of financial crisis. Basel II, for example, the 1998 initiation of which Daniel Tarullo (2009:90–9) contends "was not impelled by a crisis specific to banks in member countries," was not ultimately approved until 2004.[6] However, even Basel initiatives motivated by crises took years to bring negotiations to conclusion, in contrast to Congress's relatively quick crisis-response legislative output.[7] The notable exception—the rapid approval of Basel III in 2010, within two years of the onset of the global financial crisis—contains an extended timetable for implementation and observational reassessment, which, for some key provisions, ranges from five to ten years (Basel Committee on Banking Supervision 2010:77). Therefore, in further contrast with Congress, international regulators have more time to obtain additional information concerning a crisis's causes and consequences, to refine their regulatory responses.

Despite the seemingly decisive differences between financial regulation initiated by Congress and central bankers, which would suggest that the latter might be better positioned to get things right, the ongoing financial crisis suggests, to the contrary, that such an expectation would be misplaced. In fact, the harmonized international financial regulation produced by the Basel accords contributed to the ongoing global financial crisis, perversely increasing systemic risk, by encouraging banks to hold, in levered concentrations, the assets at the epicenter of the ongoing crisis: residential mortgages and residential mortgage-backed securities and sovereign debt (Friedman and Kraus 2011; Romano 2012). Because the accords were global, banks worldwide were incentivized to follow broadly similar business strategies, so when the value of the mortgage-related assets preferred by Basel collapsed, it led to a global financial crisis, rather than one more localized, where the subprime mortgage crisis originated. Basel's flawed regulatory architecture has also been implicated in the eurozone sovereign debt crisis, as sovereign bonds have an even greater preference in the Basel risk-weighted capital schema than residential mortgages and mortgage-backed securities.

Why would financial regulation produced by central bankers and banking regulators of the most developed economies, with sophisticated technical knowledge and resources at their disposal and without media demands for quick action, end up so profoundly mistaken? One possible answer is bad luck. Although there may well have been some bad luck, the answer seems to me to be more a function of dynamic uncertainty in financial markets and explicit political considerations affecting the Basel agreements. "Dynamic uncertainty," a term used in the literature on terrorism,[8] refers to the fact that the action of the regulated in response to regulation alters risk in unanticipated ways that evolve nonlinearly, rendering it extremely difficult to predict the impact of regulation over time.

The truth is that the current state of knowledge does not permit us to predict, with any satisfactory degree of confidence, what the optimal capital requirements or other regulatory policies are to reduce systemic risk or, indeed, what future categories of activities or institutions might generate systemic risk. Regulations that are appropriate when initiated can rapidly become inappropriate as a financial system's business, legal, and technological conditions change. Moreover, institutions and individuals adapt their behavior in response to regulation, and their reactions change over time, interacting with the regulatory environment, in nonlinear ways, greatly complicating analysis.

Notwithstanding considerable advances in knowledge, the fast-moving and constantly changing dynamic of financial markets also renders it improbable that any future state of knowledge would enable us to make predictions with confidence. Risk management in today's context of large and interconnected financial institutions and complex financial instruments must grapple with unknown and unknowable, and not simply known, risks (Diebold et al. 2010:3). Yet the Basel approach has focused the attention of the private sector, regulators, and academic researchers on knowns—that is, on measuring capital adequacy through statistical probabilities of risks, disregarding the equal, if not more important, need to create internal control and regulatory systems that emphasize adaptability to the challenge of unknown, and unknowable, risks (Diebold et al. 2010:5). Moreover, knowledge of past relations across asset returns, used in risk management, can be misleading, for in times of financial stress, asset correlations not only change (Diebold et al. 2010:25) but also increase significantly (Erdorf and Heinrichs 2010). In such an environment, regulators are bound to make mistakes, and Basel's global harmonization template is poorly suited to catch them, as it neither adapts readily to change nor fosters diversity, strategies that increase system survivability (Haldane 2009:4); rather, it may well increase the likelihood of systemic failure (Romano 2012; Herring and Litan 1995:134–35).

But the failure of the Basel accords is not solely the result of the inappropriateness of a top-down harmonized regulatory approach for the dynamic uncertainty of financial markets; the accords are also informed by political judgments (Romano 2012:39, 43–44; Tarullo 2008:87), which have had adverse consequences for financial system stability. The most critical terms in the accord, the definition of core (tier one) capital and the choice of risk weights, have been a subject of repeated political logrolling. A case in point is the tripartite agreement devised under Basel I in which Japanese negotiators obtained their desired core capital treatment for deferred tax assets, the U.S. negotiators their desired treatment for mortgage servicing rights, and European (French and German) negotiators their preferred treatment for minority interests in other financial institutions, a logroll carried forward in Basel III, with all three assets continuing to qualify as tier one capital, albeit limited to the precise same 10 percent (Basel Committee on Banking Supervision 2010:26). There is no economic or prudential justification for the three asset categories to be treated equivalently, let alone characterized as equity capital. And, as earlier mentioned, favorable Basel risk weights for residential mortgages are illustrations of political considerations influencing risk weight assignments so as to be in conformance with, and furtherance of, national policies (Dewatripont et al. 2010:30).

By tending to enact comprehensive financial legislation only in reaction to an immediate financial crisis, Congress acts most swiftly precisely when greater deliberateness is called for, given the paucity of information available to produce a high-quality decision. The Basel regulatory architecture premised on global harmonization is equally poorly suited for the need, as it is not designed for generating information concerning what new risks might require regulation, let alone what regulation would be best suited for specific risks. Nor is it nimble enough to adapt and change course rapidly to scotch looming problems, when information becomes available that a regulatory approach is likely to be mistaken or no longer appropriate. Although Congress is not about to restrain itself from acting in a crisis, and Basel committee members are not about to abandon their commitment to harmonization any time soon, the unintended consequences likely to accompany their decisions can, in my judgment, be mitigated by deploying systematically procedural mechanisms that require the revisiting of enactments and by fostering experimentation in regulatory approach.

Improving the Quality of Crisis-Based Financial Regulation

There are two key components that should be included in financial regulation to mitigate the effect of legislative and regulatory failure: (1) a sunset requirement that regulation be reviewed and reconsidered within a fixed period after enactment (e.g., five to six years) in order to stay on the books; and (2) a structure that is hospitable to regulatory experimentation wherever possible. By permitting legislators and regulators to incorporate new information into the decision-making process, and simultaneously increasing the likelihood that new information will be generated from the regulatory variety generated by experimentation, the quality of future decision making has a better chance of being improved.

Sunsetting Financial Regulation

Sunsetting—providing that a statute expires on a specified date unless reenacted—is a time-honored legislative tool.[9] It has been used by Congress and state legislatures since the nation's founding, although its use as a lawmaking strategy has ebbed and flowed over time. For instance, in the late 1970s, sunset legislation rapidly coursed through the states, with thirty-five legislatures enacting sunset laws to review administrative agencies, widely perceived to be ineffective and wasteful (Davis 1981; Price 1978). At the same time, Congress considered, but did not enact, a broad sunset statute, yet it still followed the trend in sunsetting the newly created Commodity Futures Trading Commission (CFTC) in the Commodity Futures Trading Commission Act of 1974.

By 1990, enthusiasm for administrative agency sunsetting waned, given the time and cost of reviews, but over twenty states still have some form of active sunset review, and in recent years, as states' fiscal situations have deteriorated, they have once again adopted or reinvigorated the process (Kearney 1990; Weaver 2011). Articles discussing the effectiveness of state sunset reviews in their heyday in the 1970s indicate that they were on balance successful, resulting in the termination of agencies (although no major entities were terminated) and improvements in agency operations, even in states that discontinued sunset reviews (Kearney 1990:52–55; Price 1978:440).[10]

Sunsetting is particularly well suited for crisis-driven financial legislation. Of the rationales for adopting a sunsetting strategy, the key justification in the financial regulatory domain is that sunsetting mitigates the predicament of legislating with minimal information and therefore running the risk of getting things seriously and, for all practical purposes permanently wrong. Congress can, of course, in principle modify crisis legislation that turns out to be misplaced. But the U.S. political system's organizing principles of separation of powers and checks and balances create numerous veto points throughout the legislative process (e.g., approval of both chambers, then presidential approval or approval by a supermajority of both chambers) that make repealing a statute extremely arduous. Sunsetting loosens the institutional stickiness of the status quo by putting a statute in play, with a need for affirmative legislative action at a specific date to remain in effect.

But more important, in the financial regulation context, sunsetting sets in motion a process by which post-enactment information can be incorporated into the regulatory regime. For instance, by the time of a statute's sunset review, several years after enactment, there should be a better understanding of the causes of the crisis that the legislation sought to address, along with knowledge of the enacted legislation's consequences, information indispensable for getting regulation right but unavailable when a crisis necessitates a response. In addition to permitting a more clear-eyed assessment, with the benefit of hindsight, of the crisis-enacted regulation, economic and technological conditions may have dramatically changed in the interim, with financial innovation occurring apace. That information can also be taken advantage of in the legislative "second look," for the most appropriate regulatory responses will undoubtedly have shifted as well.

John Coffee (2012) critiques sunsetting crisis-driven financial regulation on two grounds.[11] First, he maintains that the review process will be captured by financial institutions and produce outcomes at odds with the public interest that he contends characterizes emergency legislation.[12] Second, he asserts that flaws in crisis legislation go away over time because the administrative process through which the legislation is implemented will eventually revise the more problematic parts. Although the significance Coffee draws from this second claim with regard to sunset review is not made explicit, he would appear to be arguing that over time bad laws can be undone by administrative agency action. Whatever the intended interpretation, his bottom line is that the "greater danger" is that too little or no regulatory "reform" will be enacted in a crisis, because "overbroad" regulation "is usually repealed or curtailed relatively quickly (and without the need for mandatory sunsets)" and the "forces of inertia will veto or block all change" (2012:79–80).

Coffee's first claim regarding the legislative process is, however, mistaken, in depicting crisis-driven financial legislation as a triumph of a dispersed public interest, unrepresented in times of normal politics, against the concentrated interest of business.[13] There are, in fact, highly organized and powerful interest groups on both sides of financial regulation issues, and solutions appearing in crisis-driven legislation are often policies that a range of those groups have advocated, sometimes for an extended period of time (Bainbridge 2011), and not simply the work of "champions" of investors whose voice would never be heard by Congress or regulators in the absence of a crisis, as Coffee (2012:13) contends.

In particular, the counterpart in the political arena of Coffee's "concentrated" business interest is certainly not a dispersed investor public in need of a crisis-induced "political entrepreneur" to be represented against business but, rather, well-funded and politically influential labor unions, public pension funds,[14] and the plaintiff's bar, along with the corporate governance cottage industry and a variety of trade groups, whose leadership regularly is called to testify in congressional hearings (Romano 2005). Moreover, these groups are full-time political players and do not just spontaneously emerge as a counterweight to business interests solely in a crisis, as Coffee would have it. Such groups are equally active in the normal politics of the administrative process that Coffee contrarily characterizes as the domain of one concentrated interest— "business." Although the objectives of those groups in relation to the public good or the interests of individual investors can be deeply problematic (Agrawal forthcoming; Anabtawi and Stout 2008; Coffee 1985, 2006; Romano 1993b; Rose 2007), their prominent presence in the policy process, in crisis and noncrisis times, is an incontrovertible fact, and it tends to counterbalance business influence.

In addition, business is not a monolithic interest group (Hart 2004), as Coffee's invocation of Mancur Olson suggests. Rather, business firms are quite often divided on legislative issues, including those related to financial regulation. For example, large and small companies split over supporting Sarbanes-Oxley (Romano 2005), and the securities, futures, and banking sectors of the financial industry were in continual conflict over the regulation of derivatives in the 1990s (Romano 1997). Of course, even if business was united on a specific proposal, it would be incorrect to assume, as does Coffee, that simply because business supports a particular policy, it cannot be good public policy. To the contrary, a comprehensive study of business lobbying found that when a united business front "wins" in a deliberative process over controversial regulation, it is because the public supports business's policy position, rather than business's having "captured" legislators (Smith 2000).[15]

Coffee's second contention, that problematic components of crisis-driven financial legislation are revised over time through the administrative process, is inconsistent with his first claim, that the administrative process is captured by business: an administrative process that is properly revising problematic legislation would not simultaneously be eviscerating legislation in the "public" interest. Coffee cannot have it both ways. Moreover, the example Coffee provides of "quick" regulatory adjustment to the problematic internal controls provision of Sarbanes-Oxley proves the precise opposite of what he claims. It took eight years and an act of Congress to undo costly regulation by a bit, and much of the agency action that was directed at the problem in the intervening years was not self-correcting administrative action, as Coffee contends, but rather undertaken in response to action, or the threat of action, by Congress (see Romano 2009).[16]

Finally, and most important, both of Coffee's concerns that motivate his objection to sunsetting, contrary to his contention, would, in fact, be addressed, not exacerbated, by a sunset requirement. If his first objection to sunsetting were correct and the post-crisis administrative implementation process is captured by business interests that undo publicly regarding legislation, then sunsetting should, all the more, be endorsed. Sunset review entails a far more transparent public process than administrative action, with congressional hearings that would attract media attention, rendering it more difficult for any single organized interest group or groups to control the process. And if Coffee's second objection were accurate and the post-crisis administrative process is one in which all or nearly all statutory flaws are eventually ironed out, as he claims, then sunset review would reduce the cost of such errors by further facilitating and accelerating the revision process.

But to be effective, it is important that the sunsetting process be crafted in light of the states' experiences with what works. To guide the collection and analysis of information in a sunset review, and hence the reassessment of whether legislation should be retained or revised, evaluative criteria for the sunset review, and not simply an expiration date, need to be specified in the statute responding to the crisis. Otherwise, a review will lack focus and may become a pro forma process, as legislators will often have more immediate concerns that they wish to pursue rather than undertaking a serious reassessment, especially if, as is probable, constituent concerns in a crisis that motivated the statute in the first place have drifted to new matters (Davis 1981:394, 396–401). The evaluative criteria will, of course, vary depending on the specific legislation.

Taking Dodd-Frank as an illustration, a crisis-specific evaluative criterion could be whether implemented regulations have had a positive (or at least nonnegative) effect on financial system stability (banks' safety and soundness), along with a more general criterion of whether the benefits (e.g., the increase in bank soundness) outweigh the costs. An example of the latter might be whether there has been an increase in the cost of credit to small businesses, which, because they are more reliant on bank financing than large corporations that can access public capital markets, are considered the parties most at risk from a reduction in bank lending that the statute may cause. Estimation of the economic effect of financial regulation is a quite feasible, albeit most certainly imperfect, endeavor, as academics and bank regulators' technical staff routinely analyze the impact of regulatory changes on individual banks and the economy. In any event, such a calculation is not only simply better than operating in total darkness but essential for attempting to evaluate what crisis-driven regulation has wrought.

The availability of new information at the time a second vote on a statute is required for it to remain in force does not guarantee that legislators will engage in a serious reassessment, rather than a pro forma review, of course (Breyer 1982:365). To increase the likelihood that new information will be conscientiously acted upon, there is another component that should be included in a sunset provision, in addition to an expiration date and evaluative criteria: the establishment of a sunset review panel to perform the review along with a timetable for action (Breyer 1982:366). A sunset review panel should be tasked to recommend what action—repeal, reenactment, revision—Congress should take, and a timetable should set out the interval in which a panel recommendation would be considered by the House and Senate committees with jurisdiction over the legislation, after which the panel's recommendation would be automatically discharged as a bill for a floor vote if the committees do not themselves bring it, or an amended version, to the floor.[17]

The sunset review panel should consist of independent experts, who are neither government employees nor officials, and be empowered to obtain information from relevant regulatory agencies and firms to undertake its review. The advantage of independent experts is that they tend to self-identify more strongly with professional norms, and are more concerned about reputational damage if peers perceive them to be doing the bidding of interest groups or party politics, than government employees who are in a hierarchical chain of command. For the review panel to be both politically accountable and independent, it should be appointed by Congress and the president, paralleling the practice used for creating blue ribbon government panels. Although Congress could establish a standing blue ribbon review panel, which would reduce the cost to future Congresses of forming a panel, reviews would be more effective if undertaken by panels created specifically for the legislation to be evaluated, as the relevant expertise is likely to vary with a statute's focus. For example, expertise in macroeconomics would be pertinent for reviewing much of Dodd-Frank but not Sarbanes-Oxley.

To ensure that the sunset process is meaningful, the authorizing legislation would need to include adequate funding for a review. Budgets of prior congressionally appointed blue ribbon investigatory panels could be used to provide guidance. Given budgetary concerns, Congress could impose a fee on the relevant sector affected by the legislation to cover a review panel's operating cost. It could also mandate that governmental research organizations, such as the Congressional Research Service or General Accounting Office, and the relevant regulatory agencies provide evaluations of the sunsetting regulations to the panel, for use in its review. But that would probably not substantially reduce the expense of a sunset review, as the panel would likely want to seek to conduct its own evaluation de novo.

The rationale for this review mechanism, an expert panel and a timetable, is that the threat of a required floor vote on a recommendation made by outside experts would compel a higher-quality reassessment of a statute by all concerned, and in particular by congressional committee members who know they cannot prevent a vote on a recommendation they might otherwise be able to oppose merely by inaction. It should also better incentivize review panel members, as they would know that a floor vote on their work product is assured. The use of a review panel has a further benefit, of reducing the time required by legislators and their staff to engage in a sunset review, for the panel would collect data and perform the analyses necessary for the legislature's reassessment. It would thereby mitigate a key operational problem experienced by states in their 1970s sunset reviews, which led several states to abandon the procedure: legislators, particularly in states where they were part-time, did not have the time or resources to engage in the demanding process of reviewing numerous state agencies (Kearney 1990:55).

A variant of legislative sunset, which would reduce even further demands placed on Congress of a required review, would be to impose the sunset review on agencies implementing the regulation. In this alternative, crisis-driven financial legislation would mandate agency reassessment of regulations implemented under the statute, with an automatic expiration in five years unless they are found to be cost-effective, and with the technical analysis undertaken by independent experts, rather than agency staff, to minimize potential bias from an agency's being too closely involved in the rules it administers to evaluate them objectively (Coglianese 2011; Romano 2005:1601). Further, to guard against an agency's inherent bias in interpreting the independent experts' analysis in support of the regulatory status quo or its agenda, a congressional vote on the agency's determination should be required in an administrative sunset review regime.

The availability of sunsetting as a well-known technique in the congressional playbook suggests a puzzle: why, given the compelling informational benefit from sunsetting crisis-driven financial regulation, has Congress chosen not to do so? I offer three possible explanations: one prudential, one political, and one pragmatic. First, there may be a prudential concern that a sunset law would impose costs on firms and individuals by decreasing regulatory certainty, given an expiration date. I do not find this to be a plausible explanation. In the financial regulation context, the multiyear interval before a sunset is often long enough for the completion of business planning surrounding the regulated financial investments and instruments, especially given how rapidly the financial environment changes. The business planning affected by financial regulation, in short, does not typically consist of projects with a long development lead, such as the research and development of a pharmaceutical drug. Furthermore, experience teaches otherwise. The CFTC's being a sunset agency, with the possibility that it would cease to exist, along with its regulatory framework, did not hinder a remarkable degree of innovation in financial derivatives that were under the agency's jurisdiction.

Second, and in my judgment a more compelling explanation, sunsetting imposes political costs on legislators because it shifts decisional control over the content of a statute from current legislators to a future Congress.[18] That creates a strong disincentive to permit a second look. This might have been especially so in the case of Dodd-Frank, enacted by a Congress with very large Democratic majorities not likely to be of the same margin in the future, because it contains provisions of great interest to Democrats' core political supporters but with minimal support in the broader electorate, and that, more likely than not, would not have survived separate up-or-down votes. Instances of this type of provision are the requirement that public companies hold shareholder votes on executive compensation (Dodd-Frank Act:§ 951; a labor union issue, which had been introduced as a bill in prior sessions but had languished in the Senate) and the requirement of affirmative action in hiring by federal financial agencies and any business (e.g., banks and law firms) regulated by, or participating in programs or contracts of, the financial regulatory agencies (Dodd-Frank Act:§ 342; a black caucus issue, advocated by Representative Maxine Waters [2011], a member of the House committee responsible for drafting the bill). Legislators, recognizing that the crisis environment guaranteed passage of a bill, opportunistically worked to include those provisions and would not have wanted to tempt fate with a subsequent reconsideration that might cull their legislative contributions.

Finally, human nature and practical concerns of party leadership would seem to have a role in explaining the puzzle. Lawmakers drafting emergency financial statutes may think, out of hubris, that they have indeed crafted landmark legislation that is the best of all possible regulatory solutions. As a consequence, the idea of including a sunset provision would not cross their minds and, if suggested, would most likely be perceived as a rebuke of their work product, rather than a needed mechanism for improving rules that are bound to be imperfect. In addition, drafters typically personally identify with legislation, which sometimes bears their names. In such a setting, legislators would perceive sunsetting as potentially diminishing or threatening what they consider to be their "legacy." Reinforcing such foibles of human nature, party leadership rarely has a strategic interest in entertaining a need to employ sunsetting in financial legislation enacted in a crisis, for it is typically supported by large majorities, with the backing of the media and a panicked public. Such pragmatic considerations would seem to explain why the USA PATRIOT Act had a sunset provision but Sarbanes-Oxley, enacted less than a year later, did not. Not only was the USA PATRIOT Act an administration bill with no legislator's name attached, but also party discipline alone could not lock up passage because a sufficient number of members in both parties felt uneasy about its considerable expansion of law enforcement powers, provisions also considered problematic by the media.

Given that lawmakers' incentives often work at odds with sunsetting, a key item on an agenda for improving the quality of financial regulation decision making, then, is the development of public awareness and suasion to overcome those hurdles. A starting point would be to educate the media, political elites, and public concerning what is needed for value-enhancing financial regulation: that sunsetting, at least in this context, is good governance. The view that sunsetting and good government go hand in hand was, for a brief time, widely shared by political elites, when then President Jimmy Carter espoused the approach and Common Cause assisted the Colorado state legislature in drafting a sunset statute (Kysar 2005:353).

Because there is a literature indicating that the media can and does influence policy outcomes by affecting an issue's salience (see Baum this volume; Romano 2009:255–57), pursuing a media educational campaign to foster an ethos of sunsetting would seem to be an excellent initial strategy for advancing sunsetting on the legislative agenda. However, this task will not be easily accomplished. To affect public opinion, the benefits of sunsetting would need to be concretized in a vivid example or event, for the literature further suggests that public attention is more likely to be engaged, and thereby influenced, by concrete issues, such as the drama of human interest stories, rather than abstractions (Severin and Tankard 2001:228–29). In keeping with this observation, the media tends to cover items of interest to, and information in the form preferred by, its audience (Hamilton 2004).

Opening Financial Regulation up to Experimentation

The harmonization premise of contemporary international financial regulation is inhospitable to regulatory innovation: notwithstanding an absence of an enforcement mechanism, nations agreeing to comply with the Basel accords implement the standards through domestic legal processes (in the United States, for instance, through administrative rulemaking), incorporating them into domestically enforceable obligations (Barr and Miller 2006). As a consequence, negotiations over changes to the accord tend to be intense and extended, as nations vie for provisions that will advantage, or at least not disadvantage, domestic financial institutions and that are consistent with national policies. Such an understandably politically infused process makes the outcome less than ideal and revision cumbersome, and at the same time it blocks experimentation or encourages violations of the accords.

Yet the dynamic environment in which financial institutions operate calls for a nimble regulatory apparatus that can both adapt to new products and accompanying risks and safeguard the international financial system from systemic regulatory error. Regulatory experimentation and diversity are safety valves that address both concerns. But to introduce the capacity for regulatory diversity into international financial regulation, the Basel architecture needs to be altered: experimentation deviating from the accord's strictures should be permitted and encouraged, albeit in a structured fashion, to mitigate the possibility that a nation's experiment could adversely impact system-wide stability.

A mechanism for introducing diversity and experimentation into the international financial regulatory architecture, while safeguarding against an increase in systemic risk, is a peer review process with three components.[19] First, a nation wishing to adopt a rule or regulatory approach different from that taken by Basel would submit to a Basel Committee–designated committee of peer regulators a proposal that would include a description of the proposed departure accompanied by an econometric forecast (or formal modeling, where the requisite data for forecasting are unavailable) of its effect on financial system stability. Second, the review process in which a committee would evaluate a proposal, seeking further information or undertaking its own economic analysis, would operate with a presumption of approval: unless it found concrete evidence that the proposed departure would increase systemic risk and thereby adversely affect financial system stability, a departure would be approved. Third, approved departures would be subject to ongoing monitoring and periodic reassessment, so that approvals could be withdrawn, for instance, when an approved regulatory departure is seen to have a negative systemic impact, which could not have been ascertained in an initial review, or when the regulatory impact has changed with new economic and technological conditions.

All the documentation in the three stages of the review process should be made publicly available. A transparent decision process should improve the quality of regulatory decision making, as participants will have a stronger incentive to provide well-reasoned justifications, with analytical support, for their positions on deviations from Basel requirements, and other nations will be able to learn from that experience and thereby be better able to make informed regulatory choices. The transparency of the ongoing review process offers a critical additional benefit to that of the initial review procedure: it provides a mechanism for comparing the efficacy of the Basel regime to departures from it. Because the reassessment should provide data on the effectiveness of alternative regulation, it will also encourage a reevaluation of the Basel requirements by other nations and emendations to Basel itself.

I have provided a thumbnail sketch of how regulatory experimentation could be introduced into international financial regulation, but experimentation could also be incorporated into domestic financial legislation. It is the genius of the federal organization of the U.S. government that makes it quite amenable to such an approach (Romano 1993a). Moreover, structuring financial regulation to be more hospitable to experimentation is consistent with a contemporary trend in economics to introduce experimentation into policymaking as the gold standard for policy evaluation (Greenstone 2009). Greenstone (118) advocates implementing regulatory initiatives through a process that either starts with small-scale randomized experiments or permits states to implement different regulatory approaches. The expectation is that coverage would be expanded nationwide were these initial experiments successful, essentially on a cost-benefit metric. Although this approach, he notes, is most feasible for environmental, health, labor market, and safety regulations, where discrete programs can be implemented using randomized trial experiments or "quasi" experiments, on the model of Food and Drug Administration testing requirements for new drugs, there is, I think, an analogue in the financial setting. That could be done by providing agencies with expanded exemptive and waiver power and an accompanying directive to use the authority to permit individual or classes of institutions to operate under different regulatory arrangements.[20]

Congress has, in fact, used such an approach in crisis-driven financial legislation, but it has been limited in scope. For example, Sarbanes-Oxley's mandate of independent audit committees (by requiring the SEC to direct stock exchanges to prohibit the listing of any firm without an independent committee) states that the SEC can establish exemptions to the statutory criteria of director independence (Sarbanes-Oxley Act:§ 301). Such an approach could be more broadly applied and agencies instructed to implement rules along the lines of a small-scale experiment, with incremental expansion only after a cost-benefit analysis undertaken by independent experts.

One means by which experimentation could be implemented within a waiver setting is by permitting a firm or class of firms to request a regulatory waiver and by not leaving the matter solely to an agency's initiative. The standard for approval of an exemption could be an assessment of minimal adverse impact on the statutory objective (e.g., on systemic risk or financial statement fraud—objectives, respectively, of Dodd-Frank and Sarbanes-Oxley). Because an agency could be expected to be predisposed to believe that whatever regulation exists is good and hence to oppose exemptions, it could be required to accept, or at least to have to rebut in a meaningful way, an analysis of the proposed waiver provided by independent experts. Maintenance of the statutory purpose would be safeguarded by having the agency engage in ongoing monitoring and review of approved waivers, to make sure no adverse impact developed. And paralleling Greenstone's (2009) contemplated regulatory reform process, were the waivers deemed successful, the agency would be expected to extend them to more, or all, firms or sectors. Where the proposed waiver is a private-sector initiative, the firms could be required to cover the agency's cost of evaluating and administering the experiment.

The interaction between statutory experimentation through waivers and required sunset reviews can, however, be complicated. When exempted firms are nonrandom, one cannot evaluate properly either the impact of the waiver with an eye to generalization or the efficacy of the regulation under sunset review, for the analysis would be subject to selection bias, as covered and excluded firms would not be comparable. For instance, firms that request a waiver would most likely be those that would be most adversely affected by a rule. This difficulty could be addressed if regulatory waivers were constructed as natural experiments, in which firms receiving a waiver were selected by lot.[21] But such an approach would, in my judgment, in many instances be politically infeasible and inappropriate, as it could seriously interfere with market competition, where the exempted firms' operating cost would be less than that of the regulated firms. In addition, if the exemption was for a limited time frame—for instance, until the "experiment" could be evaluated by the agency for its effectiveness—then firms' behavior might not represent how they would respond to a permanent rule, as they strategize to affect the outcome. In short, there is an inherent tension between sunset reviews and experimentation. But I do not believe the potential conflict is sufficient to reject the proposed dual-pronged regulatory approach.[22] Given the sunset review panel's expertise, it should be well attuned to the selection issue and able to recalibrate the analysis when undertaking its regulatory evaluation in the context of experimental data.

Although I believe that a review mechanism permitting departures from, and thereby introducing experimentation and diversity into, financial regulation requirements, and especially into the Basel international financial regulatory regime, is quite feasible, as with sunsetting there are powerful incentives working against its adoption. Financial regulators, in particular, confront determined lobbying by banks and legislators to harmonize rules in order to not impact negatively large, internationally focused domestic banks. This is, in essence, an attempt to legislate modern-day mercantilism and ought to be resisted. In addition, regulators may be subject to a status quo bias (Samuelson and Zeckhauser 1988), leading them to evaluate adversely waiver requests, particularly those that are most innovative, and legislators, out of hubris, may resist permitting deviation from mandates. This is, then, another area in which a media and public educational campaign, on the value added by financial regulation experimentation and diversity, will be critical.

Conclusion

Determining how to regulate financial institutions effectively is challenging under the best of circumstances, given the uncertain and dynamic environment in which they operate. What would appear to be an optimal regulatory policy can become a serious mistake as new risks materialize as financial institutions and products interact with regulation in unanticipated ways. Yet Congress typically legislates on financial matters in a crisis environment, which is not conducive to high-quality decision making. International financial regulators have not fared better, as their focus on harmonizing global financial regulation has limited the generation of information on regulatory alternatives and hindered the making of a nimble and adaptable rulemaking process better suited to the environment.

There is a useful legislative tool that could mitigate legislative failure in the field of financial regulation: a sunsetting statute. One could also make headway in improving the quality of decision making in international financial regulation through the adoption of a structured peer review process that permits regulatory experimentation and diversity, subject to procedural safeguards. Experimentation and diversity could be incorporated into the legislative process as well, by Congress directing agencies to use regulatory exemptive and waiver powers to foster such objectives. In tandem with sunsetting, the greater flexibility arising from use of such tools would facilitate timely updating of the legislative and regulatory architecture, which is a matter particularly appropriate to financial regulation.

Acknowledgments

I would like to thank Alain Pietrancosta for suggesting what became the title of this chapter and Cary Coglianese, Jill Fisch, Jonathan Macey, Andrew Verstein, and participants at the Penn Program on Regulation conference, the Quinnipiac University School of Law Federalist Society Student Chapter Lunch Lecture, and the Yale Law School Graduate Student Seminar for helpful comments.

Notes

1. The Dodd-Frank figure is a single-spaced page count; a longer count of 2,319 pages, often publicized in the media and provided by Perry (2010), references an official bill format that is double-spaced. Perry's page counts for the two earlier statutes are undercounts in relation to the two newer statutes, because the page margins are narrower; but even if we were to adjust for a formatting difference, the point is still broadly accurate: Dodd-Frank dwarfs those pieces of legislation.

2. For example, a media frenzy over corporate accounting scandals, calling for a government response, was a key factor in the enactment of the Sarbanes-Oxley Act (see Romano 2005:1559, 1567). In the ongoing global financial crisis, media coverage on a daily basis includes repeated calls for a wide variety of government actions to resolve the crisis.

3. The models suggest that by raising the salience of an issue, the media facilitates citizens' ability to monitor their elected representatives and thereby bring about government adoption of policies the citizenry prefers. There are numerous empirical studies that support the theory, finding a link between policy, election outcomes, and media coverage. For a summary of the literature, see Romano (2009:255–57). Kingdon (2011:58–61) contends that rather than affecting a policy issue's movement onto a legislative agenda directly, the media exerts an indirect

effect on policy either by affecting public opinion on an issue and thereby influencing legislators, who pay attention to public opinion, or by magnifying "movements that had already started elsewhere" in the policy process.

4. The mind-boggling number of regulatory actions mandated by Dodd-Frank is so daunting for a business to follow that law firms have introduced paying client services that track agencies' progress on the statute's required rulemakings and reports.

5. Congress frequently imposes unrealistic deadlines. There is no compelling explanation for the widespread use of this practice. One theory is that Congress, fully aware that its deadlines will not be met or will produce "incomplete or flawed" rules, uses deadlines as a mechanism of accountability, by providing a tactical advantage for constituents to challenge rulemaking in court, and to exert influence over the content of the rule (Kerwin and Furlong 2011:226). The one Dodd-Frank-related rulemaking litigated so far, the SEC's proxy access rule, did not have a deadline, and although the *Business Roundtable* litigation technically comports with the explanation, it is the opposite of what its legislative proponents intended, as their political supporters—labor unions— were vigorous advocates of the SEC's adoption of the rule.

6. Although some might contend that Basel II was initiated in response to the Asian financial crisis of 1997, Tarullo (2008) maintains that the crisis was not the causal initiating factor because Basel members' banks were not seriously impacted by that crisis.

7. For example, Tarullo (2008:91 n. 9) notes that Basel I, adopted in 1988, was set in motion as a response to the Latin American debt crisis of the early 1980s.

8. In the literature on terrorism, "dynamic uncertainty" has been commonly used to differentiate terrorist risk from natural disasters: the materialization of risk in both instances is highly uncertain but terrorists adapt their behavior in response to targets' protective actions and thus affect risk over time (Michel-Kerjan 2005).

9. For an overview of the use of temporary legislation, of which sunset statutes are one variety, see Gerson (2007). The U.S. income tax code is, in fact, rife with time-delimited provisions, often referred to as "extenders" (because they typically are automatically rolled over), rather than "sunsets." For a critical appraisal of the political dynamics of tax sunsets, which, being related to evasion of restrictive budgetary rules, is orthogonal to the issues concerning the use of sunsets in this chapter's context of crisis-driven legislation, see Kysar (2005).

10. John Coffee (2012:19 n. 39) questions the intellectual consistency of my critique of Sarbanes-Oxley and my advocacy of sunsetting as a means of mitigating the adverse consequences of emergency legislation, quoting another article criticizing my advocacy of sunsetting for offering "no empirical evidence that sunshine laws provide any benefits on balance," and commenting that "[i]t seems ironically inconsistent for Professor Romano to criticize Congress for enacting many of SOX's provisions without (in her view) adequate empirical support and then for her to propose a legislative remedy (a mandatory sunset rule) that has no empirical support." Coffee and the authors to whom he refers (Prentice and Spence 2007) ignore the long and well-established U.S. experience with sunset legislation as an instrument in legislators' conventional toolkit, as well as the literature, such as it is, evaluating the results. Although empirical research on sunset reviews is limited, those studies that do exist, noted in the text, provide positive, albeit mostly qualitative, assessments. My response to the

Prentice and Spence (2007) article that Coffee cites can be found in Romano (2009:260–61).

11. Coffee also sweepingly seeks to dismiss the scholarship with which he disagrees by engaging in name calling, referring to Steve Bainbridge, Larry Ribstein, and me as "the 'Tea Party Caucus' of corporate and securities law professors" (a claim that would have been humorous had it not been said earnestly) (e.g., Coffee 2012:7) and "conservative critics of securities regulation" (a claim, at least in my case, that would be accurate if he had dropped the adjective) (Coffee 2012:5), and by further referring to Bainbridge and Ribstein, as "[my] loyal allies" (Coffee 2012:7).

One should at least get labels right when attempting to disparage intellectual foes. In point of fact, in the American political tradition and academic literature, advocacy of sunsetting in general, as well as in particular as a means to implement cost-effective regulation, has historically cut across political party lines. It has had a distinguished liberal pedigree, having been advocated by, among others, President Jimmy Carter, Senator Edward Kennedy, political scientist Theodore Lowi, and the "good government" advocacy organization Common Cause (Breyer 1982; Kysar 2005). A more recent instance is the bipartisan support of sunset provisions in the USA PATRIOT Act (O'Harrow 2002). Moreover, the aim of sunsetting is to eliminate regulations that are either ineffective, lack intelligence, or have had perverse consequences—not all regulation, as Coffee (2012:7) suggests with his comment: "Such an outcome [a sunset review of the federal securities laws undertaken in the 1930s that would result in their elimination in entirety] seem[s] sensible only if one believes (as she [Romano] may) that markets need little regulation (and thus that regulatory interventions should be short-lived, disappearing like snowflakes in the sun)." The historical experience with sunsetting demonstrates that Coffee misunderstands the legislative technique: states did not terminate all or even most administrative agencies subject to their sunset reviews in the 1970s, as opposed to specific programs, practices, and entities thought to not be cost-effective (see, e.g., Kearney 1990), nor has Congress eliminated the Commodity Futures Trading Commission, which, created as a sunset agency, comes up for periodic reconsideration and renewal.

Coffee (2012:5) further claims that I (and others who have similarly critiqued Sarbanes-Oxley) see democratic politics as "dismaying, dangerous, and need[ing] to be discouraged." He has it precisely backward. Advocacy of sunset review in this context—emergency financial legislation—perfects democratic politics by seeking to have elected representatives—legislators—make decisions. It is Coffee who would leave the revision of flawed crisis-driven legislation or its inept implementation to unelected functionaries, with their own private and institutional agendas, whose decisions are often beyond public scrutiny or when visible so technical as to be beyond public comprehension. Coffee's critique, in the very same paper, of regulators' implementation of Dodd-Frank's executive compensation rules, among others, for eviscerating Congress's objectives makes my point.

12. Coffee asserts that his argument about the administrative process's undoing or "watering down" of crisis-driven financial legislation does not assume that regulators are captured (e.g., Coffee 2012:13, 82). But rather, much like Hamlet's mother and the player queen, despite his protestations, Coffee's analysis bespeaks otherwise. For example, he states that "financial regulators are often so closely intertwined with those they regulate that they respond

in an equivocal and even timid fashion" (Coffee 2012:81); by most lights, that description aptly conveys what is conventionally understood to be a "captured" agency.

13. Coffee (2012:5–6 n. 11) cites Mancur Olson's (1965) celebrated work on the collective action problem in support of his claim that emergency financial legislation is in the public interest whereas interest groups will dictate the output of sunset review, asserting that my analysis of the emergency legislative process and the role of policy entrepreneurs is not used in "any theoretical sense" and "seems unaware of the political science literature and focuses exclusively on empirical economics." This is a strange assertion. The work that he is criticizing (Romano 2005) refers extensively to both the economics and political science literature. It just does not cite or discuss Olson's work on collective action because, in this context, it would be a mistake to do so, as elaborated in the text.

14. Coffee (2012:17) dismisses the political significance of public pension funds because they do not make campaign contributions. But that misses the point: public pension funds are often led by prominent state political figures (Romano 1993b), whose positions and contacts provide considerable clout and a bully pulpit that can further political ambitions.

15. Coffee (2012:16–17 n. 35) cites a law review article (Apollonio et al., 2008) in support of his view that business dominates politics, for the proposition that business outspends unions on lobbying. Apparently he is unaware of the comprehensive research on lobbying by Baumgartner et al. (2009) that details the offsetting lobbying resources that coalesce against large organized lobbying expenditures by business, and the data indicating that resources spent do not explain lobbying success. The error in relying on the article Coffee cites is that Apollonio et al. (2008) use aggregate lobbying expenditures, without examining how the funds were allocated across issues, to ascertain how they line up: not only are businesses affected by many more issues than unions because there are many different business sectors affected by different laws, but also on many issues business and unions are not at odds. More important, contrary to that article's correlative claim that business outspends unions in campaign contributions, and Coffee's contention that unions are outspent by banks, the Center for Responsive Politics (2012), which tabulates campaign contributions, has constructed a list of the "all-time" top campaign contributors over 1989–2012. Of the top fifteen donors, nine are unions, one is the trial bar, one is the national realtors' trade association, and the number one contributor is Act-Blue, a collector of funds for Democratic party candidates. Only three are corporations (AT&T, Goldman Sachs, and Citigroup). Another three unions, but no corporations or corporate trade groups, are in the top twenty on the list. And of course, these contributions do not include the in-kind campaign contributions that unions, not businesses, make in the form of "get out the vote" and other candidate support efforts.

Coffee further cites as a "smoking gun" for his thesis that emergency legislation is the ideal working of democracy while post-crisis government action is dictated by business interests, the fact that financial firms are spending large sums lobbying on Dodd-Frank's required rulemaking, in contrast to members of the general public or unions. Although it is a self-evident proposition that financial firms will expend more resources due to their keener interest than any other entities in the Dodd-Frank rulemaking process, as their economic viability is at issue, Coffee misses the correlative irony embedded in his assessment of these expenditures. Much of the expenditure has been called for by the agencies themselves, as their multitude of regulatory proposals contain hundreds of questions directed to the private sector to assist in their proposed rulemaking. Most important, Coffee's position regarding the import of business lobbying is incoherent. He is contending—in favor of the "democratic" nature of emergency legislation over a more deliberative legislative process as would be occasioned by sunset review—that business lobbying of agencies post-crisis enables industry to dominate the rulemaking process, but a few pages later, in arguing against sunsetting and advocating that any reconsideration of crisis-driven legislation should be left to agencies, he buttresses his position against sunsetting by asserting that the only reason to support sunsetting would be a belief that an agency is "captured" (Coffee 2012:22).

16. Coffee (2012:26–29) contends that the problem with the internal controls provision was not the fault of Congress and the crisis-based haste in which the statute was crafted, but rather due to the Public Company Accounting Oversight Board's (PCAOB) implementation. As I discussed earlier in the text, emergency legislation often adopts a delegation strategy in order to deflect blame for the consequences of a poorly thought out legislative strategy by placing it on the implementing agency, as Coffee has done. In making such a distinction, Coffee misunderstands the scope and intention of sunset review of crisis-driven legislation: it encompasses problems in regulatory implementation as well as in statutory drafting. Moreover, what Coffee regards as a problem of implementation cannot be readily separated from the legislative process as he attempts to do, for the difficulties in implementation are, in fact, a product of hastily drafted crisis-driven legislation that encourages the use of readily available solutions, which, upon more sober reflection, would be recognized as inapt. The internal controls provision is an illustration of this phenomenon. It was simply lifted from a provision in the Federal Deposit Insurance Corporation Improvement Act of 1991 requiring banks to submit reports on their internal controls, with auditor attestation, to banking regulators as part of the bank examination process (Senate 2002: 31); unfortunately, no one attempted to consider, let alone analyze, whether such a template could costlessly be imposed on all sizes and types of public companies as part of the public audit process.

17. I am advocating a modified version of a proposal of Justice (then professor) Breyer (1982:366–67), for review of federal regulatory programs for waste and inefficiency. Breyer rejected a sunset approach because he was concerned that a congressional minority could "destroy" an existing program by preventing a bill from coming out of a committee or by filibustering or otherwise blocking a floor vote to reapprove a majority-supported program (Breyer 1982:367). His proposal therefore would continue a program were Congress not to adopt a recommendation. Breyer's proposed automatic discharge eliminates the issue of committee blocking but not, of course, minority blocking on the floor. But sunset could be retained and the latter issue eliminated with a rule for sunset review analogous to the reconciliation process applicable to budget legislation, which limits debate and bypasses filibusters.

18. Although sunset laws can also be seen as a mechanism by which current Congresses control future Congresses—by forcing legislation to be considered (Gerson 2007)—it seems to me that an enacting majority, particularly if it is risk-averse, would be far more concerned about preserving the legislation it has enacted than influencing the agenda of a future Congress, especially given uncertainty over what a future Congress might do to its "landmark" law. To the extent that sunsetting decreases the present value of a statute to constituents,

it could impose a further political cost by lowering "rents" (such as campaign contributions) legislators can obtain from interest groups seeking a provision's enactment. I do not emphasize this cost as there is dispute in the literature over whether sunsetting decreases or increases such rents. Kysar (2005), for example, contends that sunsetting increases rents because interest groups must lobby for legislation's renewal.

19. For elaboration of the proposed procedural mechanism, including cost implications for international financial institutions, see Romano (2012).

20. In critiquing my advocacy of sunsetting crisis-driven financial regulation, Coffee (2012:21) contends that I "never discuss" what he considers the "most feasible remedy," namely agency exemptive authority. This is an astonishing assertion. Both of my papers that Coffee critiques for this ostensible omission explicitly discuss agency exemptive authority. In my 2005 article, I suggested that the easiest way to revamp misconceived provisions in Sarbanes-Oxley was for the SEC to use its exemptive authority, but noted that it was not likely to do so (Romano 2005:1595). This present chapter advocates congressional directives to agencies to use such authority in implementing emergency regulation. I consider explicit instruction necessary because history teaches that the SEC will not voluntarily use its exemptive powers to remedy flawed rules that it has adopted in implementing emergency legislation. The well-known human cognitive bias to favor the status quo (Samuelson and Zeckhauser 1988) aids in explaining why agency exemptive power alone is not, as Coffee contends, an effective means of revising flawed legislation. Indeed, Coffee's principal example of the administrative process's remedying flawed legislation refutes his contention: Congress mandated the exemption of non-accelerated filers from Sarbanes-Oxley's internal controls auditor attestation requirement because the SEC failed to do so.

Coffee's odd assertion regarding my supposed ignorance of the SEC's exemptive authority is part of a piece: his paper contains numerous misstatements of my position regarding emergency-based legislation. To take an example, Coffee depicts my critique of crisis-driven financial legislation as directed at Sarbanes-Oxley's creation of the PCAOB (Coffee 2012:24) and Dodd-Frank's resolution authority-related provisions (Coffee 2012:58). But my 2005 article critiquing Sarbanes-Oxley was directed solely at corporate governance mandates, for which the best available empirical evidence indicates they would not have remediated the accounting frauds that motivated the legislation. The PCAOB's creation is never mentioned in my article because, of course, as the regulator of auditors, it has no relation to corporate governance mandates. I have never written on Dodd-Frank's resolution authority-related provisions, nor has Stephen Bainbridge, whose critique of Dodd-Frank, like mine of Sarbanes-Oxley, was directed solely at its corporate governance mandates; yet Coffee links Bainbridge's critique of the statute along with mine of crisis-driven legislation, as directed at the resolution authority-related provisions. Coffee's strategy would seem to be to minimize the meliorating properties of sunset review by implying that the position entails treating every provision in crisis-driven legislation as equally wrongheaded. But blanket repeal is not the gist of sunset proposals. The point of sunsetting is to produce a more deliberative drafting process that weeds out the ill-founded from the wise, a reflection impossible to undertake in the heat of a crisis, and not likely thereafter to be willingly undertaken by an agency, given limited time and resources that work hand in glove with the aforementioned status quo bias to blunt reconsideration.

21. The SEC undertook a random experiment to investigate the effect of relaxing restrictions on short selling in 2004 (SEC Office of Economic Analysis 2007). The experimental results led the agency to repeal the uptick rule restricting short sales (SEC 2007). Despite the change in policy's grounding in a "gold standard" natural experiment, in the wake of the financial crisis, pressed by opponents of the rule change, the SEC reinstated a limited version of the rule (SEC 2010).

22. Greenstone (2009), it should be noted, recommends automatic sunsets along with experimentation in his regulatory reform agenda and does not view them to be in tension. This is most likely because he envisions experiments undertaken on a randomized, small-scale basis, which would not be likely to interfere, but rather would assist, in the cost-benefit evaluation of the sunset review he contemplates. In addition, he advocates automatic sunset for all regulations, many of which would not have been subjected to experimentation.

References

Acharya, Viral V. et al. (2011) *Guaranteed to Fail: Fannie Mae, Freddie Mac, and the Debacle of Mortgage Finance.* Princeton, N.J.: Princeton University Press.

Agrawal, Ashwini (forthcoming) "Corporate Governance Objectives of Labor Union Shareholders." *Review of Financial Studies.*

Ahmed, Anwer S. et al. (2010) "How Costly Is the Sarbanes-Oxley Act? Evidence on the Effects of the Act on Corporate Profitability." *Journal of Corporate Finance* 16: 352–69.

Anabtawi, Iman, and Lynn A. Stout (2008) "Fiduciary Duties for Activist Shareholders." *Stanford Law Review* 60: 1255–308.

Apollonio, Dorie et al. (2008) "Access and Lobbying: Looking Beyond the Corruption Paradigm." *Hastings Constitutional Law Quarterly* 36: 13–50.

Bainbridge, Stephen (2011) "Quack Federal Corporate Governance Round II." *Minnesota Law Review* 95: 1779–821.

Banner, Stuart A. (1998) *Anglo-American Securities Regulation: Cultural and Political Roots, 1690–1860.* New York: Cambridge University Press.

Bargeron, Leonce et al. (2009) "Sarbanes-Oxley and Corporate Risk-Taking." *Journal of Accounting and Economics* 49: 34–52.

Barr, Michael S., and Geoffrey P. Miller (2006) "Global Administrative Law: The View from Basel." *European Journal of International Law* 17: 15–46.

Basel Committee on Banking Supervision (2010) *Basel III: A Global Regulatory Framework for More Resilient Banks and Banking Systems.* http://www.bis.org /publ/bcbs189.pdf, accessed August 21, 2011.

Baumgartner, Frank R. et al. (2008). *Lobbying and Policy Change: Who Wins, Who Loses, and Why.* Chicago: University of Chicago Press.

Beltratti, Andrea, and René M. Stulz (2009) "Why Did Some Banks Perform Better During the Credit Crisis? A Cross Country Study of the Impact of Governance and Regulation." European Corporate Governance Institute Finance Working Paper # 254/2009, July. http://ssrn.com/abstract_id=1433502, accessed August 20, 2011.

Breyer, Stephen (1982) *Regulation and Its Reform.* Cambridge, Mass.: Harvard University Press.

Center for Responsive Politics (2012) "Top All-Time Donors 1989–2012," http:// www.opensecrets.org/orgs/list.php, accessed March 14, 2012.

Cheffins, Brian (2009) "Did Governance 'Fail' During the 2008 Stock Market Meltdown? The Case of the S&P 500." *Business Lawyer* 65: 1–65.

Coffee, John C., Jr. (1985) "The Unfaithful Champion: The Plaintiff as Monitor in Shareholder Litigation." *Law and Contemporary Problems* 48 (Summer): 5–81.

——— (2006) "Reforming the Securities Class Action: An Essay on Deterrence and Its Implementation." *Columbia Law Review* 106: 1534–86.

——— (2012) "The Political Economy of Dodd-Frank: Why Financial Reform Tends to Be Frustrated and Systemic Risk Perpetuated," Columbia Law and Economics Working Paper No. 414, http://ssrn.com/abstract=1982128, accessed March 12, 2012.

Coglianese, Cary (2011) "Let's Review the Rules." *Los Angeles Times*, April 29, A23.

Congressional Budget Office (2011) "The Budgetary Cost of Fannie Mae and Freddie Mac and Options for the Future Federal Role in the Secondary Mortgage Market." Testimony Before the House Committee on the Budget (June 2). http://www.cbo.gov/doc.cfm?index=12213andzzz=41781, accessed August 28, 2011.

Davis, Lewis A. (1981) "Review Procedures and Public Accountability in Sunset Legislation: An Analysis and Proposal for Reform." *Administrative Law Review* 33: 393–413.

Davis, Polk (2010) "Summary of the Dodd-Frank Wall Street Reform and Consumer Protection Act, Enacted into Law on July 21, 2010." July 21, https://regulatorytracker.com/regtracker/viewWikiPage.action?metaData.channelId=9andmetaData.siteID=2andmetaData.wikiID=20, accessed August 17, 2011.

——— (2011) "Dodd-Frank Progress Report." July 22, https://regulatorytracker.com/regtracker/viewWikiPage.action?metaData.channelId=9andmetaData.siteID=2andmetaData.wikiID=56, accessed August 17, 2011.

Dewatripont, Mathias et al. (2010) *Balancing the Banks: Global Lessons from the Financial Crisis*. Princeton, N.J.: Princeton University Press.

Diebold, Francis X. et al. (2010) "Introduction." In F. Diebold et al., eds., *The Known, the Unknown, and the Unknowable in Financial Risk Management*. Princeton, N.J.: Princeton University Press.

Erdorf, Stefan, and Nicolas Heinrichs (2010) "Co-Movement of Fundamentals: Structural Changes in the Business Cycle." University of Cologne Graduate School in Management, Economics and Social Sciences Working Paper # 01-01, Köln, Germany, December. http://ssrn.com/abstract=1609570, accessed August 21, 2011.

Eskridge, William N., Jr., and John Ferejohn (2010) *A Republic of Statutes*. New Haven, Conn.: Yale University Press.

Fiorina, Morris P. (1982) "Legislative Choice of Regulatory Forms: Legal Process or Administrative Process?" *Public Choice* 39: 33–66.

Friedman, Jeffrey, and Wladimir Kraus (2011) *Engineering the Financial Crisis: Systemic Risk and the Failure of Regulation*. Philadelphia: University of Pennsylvania Press.

Gersen, Jacob (2007) "Temporary Legislation." *University of Chicago Law Review* 74: 247–98.

Grant, Jeremy (2011) "Buyside Seeks Clearer View of OTC Trading Reconstruction." *Financial Times*, January 10, 15.

Greenstone, Michael (2009) "Toward a Culture of Persistent Regulatory Experimentation and Evaluation." In D. Moss and J. Cisternino, eds., *New Perspectives on Regulation*. Cambridge, Mass.: The Tobin Project.

Haldane, Andrew G. (2009) "Rethinking the Financial Network." *BIS Review* 53: 1–26.

Hamilton, James T. (2004) *All the News That's Fit to Sell: How the Market Transforms Information into News*. Princeton, N.J.: Princeton University Press.

Hart, David M. (2004) "Business Is Not an Interest Group: On Companies in American National Politics." *Annual Review of Political Science* 7: 47–67.

Herring, Richard J., and Robert E. Litan (1995) *Financial Regulation in the Global Economy*. Washington, D.C.: Brookings Institution.

Kearney, Richard C. (1990) "Sunset: A Survey and Analysis of the State Experience." *Public Administration Review* 50: 49–57.

Kerwin, Cornelius M., and Scott R. Furlong (2011) *Rulemaking: How Government Agencies Write Law and Make Policy*, 4th ed. Washington, D.C.: CQ Press.

Kingdon, John W. (2011) *Agenda, Alternatives and Public Policies*, updated 2nd ed. Boston: Longman.

Knight, Frank (1965) *Risk, Uncertainty and Profit*. New York: Harper and Row.

Kysar, Rebecca M. (2005) "The Sun Also Rises: The Political Economy of Sunset Provisions in the Tax Code." *Georgia Law Review* 40: 335–406.

Linck, James S. et al. (2009) "The Effects and Unintended Consequences of the Sarbanes-Oxley Act on the Supply and Demand for Directors." *Review of Financial Studies* 22: 3287–328.

Michel-Kerjan, Erwann (2005) *Report No. 3: Financial Protection of Critical Infrastructure*. Institut Veolia Environnement, http://www.institut.veolia.org/en /cahiers/protection-insurability-terrorism/terrorism-insurability/terrorism -uncertainty.aspx, accessed August 27, 2011.

Nichols, Albert (1982) "Legislative Choice of Regulatory Forms: A Comment on Fiorina." *Public Choice* 39: 67–71.

O'Harrow, Robert Jr. (2002) "Six Weeks in Autumn." *Washington Post*, October 27, W06.

Olson, Mancur (1965) *The Logic of Collective Action: Public Goods and the Theory of Groups*. Cambridge, Mass.: Harvard University Press.

Perry, Mark J. (2010) "Major Financial Legislation: Number of Pages." *Carpe Diem*, July 16. http://mjperry.blogspot.com/2010/07/dodd-frank-aka-lawyers -and-consultants.html, accessed August 17, 2011.

Prentice, Robert A., and David B. Spence (2007) "Sarbanes-Oxley as Quack Corporate Governance: How Wise Is the Received Wisdom?" *Georgetown Law Journal* 95: 1843–909.

Price, Dan R. (1978) "Sunset Legislation in the United States." *Baylor Law Review* 30: 401–62.

Protess, Ben (2011) "Banks Preparing for (and Fearing) Derivatives Rules." *DealB%k*, New York Times Blogs, July 11. http://dealbook.nytimes.com /2011/07/11/banks-preparing-for-and-fearing-derivatives-rules/, accessed August 27, 2011.

Romano, Roberta (1993a) *The Genius of American Corporate Law*. Washington, D.C.: American Enterprise Institute Press.

——— (1993b) "Public Pension Fund Activism in Corporate Governance Reconsidered." *Columbia Law Review* 93: 795–853.

——— (1997) "The Political Dynamics of Derivative Securities Regulation." *Yale Journal on Regulation* 14: 279–406.

——— (2005) "The Sarbanes-Oxley Act and the Making of Quack Corporate Governance." *Yale Law Journal* 114: 1521–611.

――――― (2009) "Does the Sarbanes-Oxley Act Have a Future?" *Yale Journal on Regulation* 26: 229–341.

――――― (2012) "For Diversity in the International Regulation of Financial Institutions: Rethinking the Basel Architecture." Unpublished manuscript, Yale Law School, New Haven, Conn., January.

Rose, Paul (2007) "The Corporate Governance Industry." *Journal of Corporation Law* 32: 887–926.

Samuelson, William, and Richard Zeckhauser (1988) "Status Quo Bias in Decision Making." *Journal of Risk and Uncertainty* 1: 7–59.

Severin, Werner J., and James W. Tankard, Jr. (2001) *Communication Theories: Origins, Methods, and Uses in the Mass Media*, 5th ed. New York: Addison Wesley.

Smith, Mark A. (2000) *American Business and Political Power: Public Opinion, Elections, and Democracy.* Chicago: University of Chicago Press.

Tarullo, Daniel K. (2008) *Banking on Basel: The Future of International Financial Regulation.* Washington, D.C.: Peterson Institute for International Economics.

U.S. Securities and Exchange Commission (2007) "SEC Votes on Regulation SHO Amendments and Proposals: Also Votes to Eliminate 'Tick' Test." Press release 2007-114, http://www.sec.gov/news/press/2007/2007-114.htm, accessed November 12, 2011.

――――― (2010) "Final Rule. Amendments to Regulation SHO," Rel. No. 34-61595. *Federal Register* 75: 11232–325.

U.S. Securities and Exchange Commission, Office of Economic Analysis (2007) "Economic Analysis of the Short Sale Price Restrictions Under the Regulation SHO Pilot." http://www.sec.gov/news/studies/2007/regshopilot020607 .pdf, accessed November 12, 2011.

U.S. Senate (2002) Public Company Accounting Reform and Investor Protection Act of 2002, Report of the Committee on Banking, Housing, and Urban Affairs to Accompany S. 2673 together with Additional Views, 107th Cong., 2d Sess.. Rep. No. 107-205. Washington D.C.: U.S. Government Printing Office.

Wallison, Peter (2011a) "Dissenting Statement." In *The Financial Crisis Inquiry Report: Final Report of the National Commission on the Causes of the Financial and Economic Crisis in the United States.* Washington, D.C.: GPO.

――――― (2011b) "Dodd-Frank and Housing Finance Reform." http://www.aei .org/outlook/101049, accessed August 21, 2011.

Waters, Maxine (2011) "News Release: Congresswoman Waters, FS 10 Bestowed with Political Leadership Award by Black Press," March 26, in Lexis congressional documents and publications library, U.S. House of Representatives Documents, accessed September 4, 2011.

Weaver, Sarah (2011) "Sunset Review in the States." Report for the California Legislature Joint Sunset Review Committee, June 8. http://www.assembly.ca .gov/acs/Committee/C501/Hearings/060811/Sunset%20Review%20in %20the%20States.pdf, accessed August 29, 2011.

Case Cited

Business Roundtable v. SEC, U.S.C.A. Case No. 10-1305 (July 22, 2011).

Statutes Cited

Banking Act of 1933 (Glass-Steagall Act), Pub. L. 73-66, 48 Stat. 162.

Commodity Futures Trading Commission Act of 1974, Pub. L. 93-463, codified as amended at 7 U.S.C. § 4(a) et seq.

Dodd-Frank Wall Street Reform and Consumer Protection Act of 2010, Pub. L. No. 111-203, 124 Stat. 1376.

Federal Deposit Insurance Corporation Improvement Act of 1991, Pub. L. 102-242,105 Stat.2236, codified in scattered sections of 12 U.S.C.

Federal Reserve Act of 1913, 38 Stat. 251 (1913), 12 U.S.C. ch. 3.

Foreign Corrupt Practices Act of 1977, Pub. L. No 95-213, codified as amended at 15 U.S.C. §§ 78dd to dd-3.

Sarbanes-Oxley Act of 2002, Pub. L. No. 107-204, 2002 U.S.C.C.A.N. (116 Stat.) 745, codified in scattered sections of 15 and 18 U.S.C.

Uniting and Strengthening America by Providing Appropriate Tools Required to Intercept and Obstruct Terrorism (USA PATRIOT) Act of 2001, Pub. L. No. 107-56, 115 Stat. 272, codified as amended in scattered sections of 8, 15, 18, 22, 31, 42, 49 and 50 U.S.C.

Chapter 6
Partisan Media and Attitude Polarization
The Case of Healthcare Reform

Matthew A. Baum

By many accounts, partisan polarization in America has rarely been more acute than during President Barack Obama's first term in office. Nowhere have such divisions been starker than with respect to the proper role of the government in regulating the nation's economy and society. The debate over the proper scope and power of the federal government stretches back to the founding of the republic itself. During the Great Depression, Franklin Roosevelt's New Deal—an unprecedented expansion of the federal government's role in regulating the U.S. economy—was as intensely unpopular among Republicans, and popular among Democrats, as President Obama's healthcare reform proposal of 2009 (Baum and Kernell 2001; Cantril 1940).

Recent surveys indicate that the partisan divide on regulatory policy extends across numerous policy areas, ranging from finance to energy to healthcare. For instance, in surveys by the Pew Research Center for the People and the Press conducted in 2010, Democrats were substantially more supportive than Republicans of stricter government regulations on financial institutions (65 vs. 40 percent); oil drilling (82 vs. 56 percent); CO_2 and other greenhouse gas emissions (76 vs. 57 percent); and fuel standards for cars, trucks, and SUVs (89 vs. 73 percent) (Pew Research Center 2010b, 2010d, 2010e).

The partisan gap over reforming the government's role in regulating the healthcare industry—which accounts for over one-sixth of the U.S. gross domestic product—is even larger. In December 2009, Democrats were 56 percentage points more likely than Republicans to support President Obama's proposed reform of the nation's healthcare system (67 vs. 11 percent), with Republicans 66 percentage points more likely than Democrats to indicate that they opposed healthcare reform because it represented "too much government involvement in health care" (86 vs. 22 percent) (Pew Research Center 2009a). Indeed, the overall partisan gap in the percentage of respondents agreeing that "Government has gone too far in regulating business" increased from 22 to 40 percentage points between October 1997 and March 2010 (from 45 vs. 67 percent in 1997, to 39 vs. 79 percent in 2010, among Democrats and Republicans, respectively) (Pew Research Center 2010a).

What accounts for these persistent, and apparently rising, partisan divides in general, and the vast chasm between the parties over health-care reform in particular? In the latter case, a series of Pew Center surveys between July 2009 and March 2010 (when President Obama signed healthcare reform into law) found support for the reform effort fluctuating hardly at all, with 61 percent of Democrats, 34 percent of independents, and 12 percent of Republicans supporting the reform effort in July 2009, compared with 62, 32, and 13 percent, respectively, the following March (Pew Research Center 2009b, 2010a). This raises the additional question of why neither supporters nor opponents of the reform effort appear to have succeeded in moving public opinion, despite intensive public communications efforts.

A possible answer to both questions, which I explore in detail in the present study, concerns the increasing difficulty for both the White House and members of Congress to reach out beyond their own partisan bases. Increasingly, Republicans and Democrats expose themselves to distinct information streams, especially, but not exclusively, in the new media. The streams favored by Republicans, such as the Fox News Channel on cable, as well as conservative talk radio and Internet sites, were more critical of the push toward universal healthcare (as well as other areas of regulatory policy, such as financial and energy regulations) than their more liberal analogues preferred by Democrats (Baum 2011). Such a pattern could enhance attitude polarization in ways that hold important implications for public policy. In the case of healthcare reform, with large majorities of Democrats inclined to support the effort and large majorities of Republicans inclined to oppose it, there were relatively few partisans available to be persuaded by their fellow partisan leaders (that is, Republican leaders in opposition and Democratic leaders in support). And those Republicans who could have reassessed in favor of the reform effort may simply have avoided the president's pitch.

In this chapter, I assess the relationship between political partisanship and attitudes toward President Obama's push for an overhaul of the nation's healthcare system, arguably the most polarized area of federal regulatory policy in recent memory. I argue that increasing partisan polarization characterizes nearly all public policy debates, and especially those, such as regulatory policy, where ideological battle lines are clearly demarked. I further argue that such polarization is in part attributable to the breakdown of the information commons that characterized the U.S. mass media from roughly the 1950s until the early 1990s. In its place has arisen an increasingly fragmented and niche-oriented media marketplace in which individuals are better able to limit their information exposure to attitudes and opinions that reinforce, rather than challenge, their preexisting beliefs.

The Changing Media Landscape

The decline of the traditional news media since the early 1990s is well documented (Baum and Kernell 1999, 2007; Hamilton 2003; Baum 2003). The combined ratings for the evening newscasts of the "big three" broadcast networks (ABC, CBS, and NBC) have fallen from about 52 million viewers in 1980 to 22.3 million in 2009 (Pew Research Center 2010c). Indeed, according to a 2010 Pew Center survey, the percentage of Americans indicating that they regularly watch cable news now exceeds the percentage regularly watching network news by 42 to 31 percent (2010c).

Not only has the overall audience for network news declined dramatically, but the demographics of network news viewers have also shifted starkly. Where the typical network news viewer was once comparable to the median television viewer (after all, the networks enjoyed an oligopoly from the 1950s to the 1980s), by 2008 the network audience was notably older, with a median age of 61.3 (Pew Research Center 2009a), and according to the Pew Research Center (2008), it was composed of more than twice as many Democrats as Republicans (45 vs. 22 percent "regular" viewers).

The so-called new media—by which I refer primarily to cable news channels and the Internet but also to political talk radio—differ in important ways from their traditional media cousins. Most notably, rather than seeking to be all things to all people—as the major networks did during their heyday—new media outlets try to provide a product that more closely fits the preferences of a narrower subset of the public.

In news and politics, the primary dimension upon which new media outlets have sought to differentiate themselves is ideology. Most notably, today there are prominent cable news channels aimed primarily at liberals (MSNBC), conservatives (Fox), and moderates (CNN). Similarly, on the Internet, the political blogosphere is dominated by ideologically narrow websites such as HuffingtonPost.com on the left and Michelle Malkin.com on the right. Political talk radio, in turn, is dominated by conservative voices such as Glenn Beck, Sean Hannity, and Rush Limbaugh, though there are some liberal niches, such as a program hosted by MSNBC analyst Ed Schultz. As the range of options available to consumers seeking political information has expanded, making available media environments that closely match their personal political preferences, audiences—especially those who tend to follow national political debates—increasingly avail themselves of the opportunity to self-select into ideologically friendly political news environments.

Cable News

According to data from Scarborough research, in 2000 the audiences for CNN, Fox News, and MSNBC consisted of fairly similar proportions of Democrats and Republicans. The partisan gaps for viewers of CNN, Fox, and MSNBC were 4, 8, and 2 percentage points, respectively. By 2008–9, these gaps had expanded dramatically, to 30, 20, and 27 points for CNN, Fox, and MSNBC, respectively, with Democrats all but abandoning Fox in favor of CNN and MSNBC and Republicans moving in the opposite direction.[1]

Data from the Pew Center, summarized in Figure 6.1, paint a similar picture. These data indicate that in 2000 there were essentially no partisan gaps in viewership of the three major cable news networks, with differentials between self-reported "regular" Republican and Democratic viewers of CNN, Fox, and MSNBC of 2, 1, and 0 percentage points,

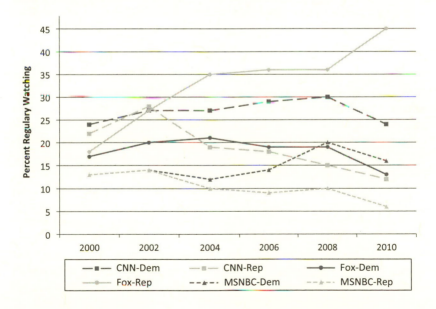

Figure 6.1. "Regular" Cable News Audiences, by Party (2000–10). *Source:* Pew Research Center for the People and the Press.

respectively. By 2010, these gaps had expanded to 12, 32, and 10 points, respectively.

Internet

If niche programming is an important competitive strategy for television news, it is arguably the most consequential such strategy on the Internet. A stunningly small number of political news-oriented outlets dominate news and public affairs traffic on the web (Hindman 2007). Although some of the most heavily trafficked sites—such as CNN.com, MSNBC .com, and Yahoo! News—remain predominantly audience aggregators rather than disaggregators, and collectively make up 27 percent of the top news sites (Pew Research Center 2009a), the political blogosphere functions primarily as an arena for partisan and ideological self-selection.

Baum and Groeling (2008, 2010) report that left-leaning political blogs, such as DailyKos.com, are disproportionately likely to cover news that favors Democrats over Republicans, while right-leaning blogs, such as FreeRepublic.com, are disproportionately likely to feature news favorable to Republicans over Democrats. Perhaps not surprisingly, given the ideological and partisan slant on political blogs, users of these sites are, on average, more likely than typical Americans to prefer news that reinforces their preexisting preferences, more likely to discuss political news with family and friends (Baum and Groeling 2008), and more ideologically extreme (Baum and Groeling 2010).

Also unsurprisingly, the audiences for such outlets are highly skewed based on party affiliation. For instance, according to an April 2007 Nielsen report (All 2007), 77 percent of HuffingtonPost.com readers were registered Democrats; only 3.8 percent were registered Republicans. Although, as with cable news, some Internet consumers seek out news from across the ideological spectrum—and some evidence (Gentzkow and Shapiro 2010) suggests they do so to a greater extent on the Internet than on cable—the Internet is nonetheless a particularly amenable environment for ideological self-selection, and the aforementioned evidence from political blogs suggests that many politically oriented news consumers engage in such self-imposed ideological segregation.

Although the audience for political news on the Internet does not yet match that for television news (Baum and Groeling 2008), it is growing rapidly and is by no means trivial. For instance, according to an October 2010 comScore.com press release, in September 2008 the total number of unique visitors to the top fifteen political blog sites was approximately 206 million. This represents about a 10 percent increase over the prior year (comScore.com 2010). According to data from a Pew Center survey, 41 percent of respondents in 2010 identified the Internet as their primary source of news, compared with 66 percent who identified television (Pew Research Center 2010c). This represents the smallest television advantage ever recorded in Pew Center surveys. According to the same data, the Internet is now the predominant source of news for Americans under age thirty, beating out television by 13 percentage points (65 to 52 percent) (Pew Research Center 2010c).

Political Talk Radio

In one sense, political talk radio is anything but new. It predates other forms of media in targeting niche audiences in general and political niche audiences in particular. The tradition of populist radio dates back to Father Charles Caughlin who, during the Great Depression, railed against everything from Franklin Roosevelt and the New Deal to racial and ethnic minorities and the influence of Jews. Hence, it is something of an awkward fit in the category of "new media," but still it warrants at least a brief mention.

According to Pew's stateofthemedia.org website, twelve of the fifteen most popular talk radio hosts in Fall 2009 were conservative, and none were liberal (Pew Research Center's Project for Excellence in Journalism 2010). The most popular liberal talk show host, Ed Schultz, attracted roughly 2.5 million listeners per day in 2009, down from 3 million in 2008 (Pew Research Center's Project for Excellence in Journalism 2010). This represents roughly a sixth of the audience magnitude of conservative talkers Rush Limbaugh or Sean Hannity. This suggests that despite prominent liberal attempts to crack into the medium—most notably by the Air America Radio Network, which declared bankruptcy and ceased broadcasting in 2010—political talk radio remains largely a medium for conservative populism in the tradition of Father Caughlin.

Partisan Media and Ideological Self-Selection

Although it is certainly the case that there is some partisan overlap in news consumption (Feltus 2009; Prior 2007; Kernell and Rice 2011; Gentzkow and Shapiro 2010), the aforementioned data clearly suggest a fairly strong tendency toward partisan filtering on cable news.[2] Indeed, at least according to a 2010 Pew Center survey, crossing perceived partisan boundaries in news consumption is the exception rather than the rule among cable news audiences. Only a little over 3 percent of respondents indicated that they "regularly" watch Fox News and also regularly watch either CNN or MSNBC, while only about 12 percent indicated that they "regularly" or "sometimes" watch Fox News plus either CNN or MSNBC (Pew Research Center 2010c). These percentages were similar for Democrats, Republicans, and independents.

Yet even these modest figures may somewhat overstate the political consequence of such cross-partisan news consumption. The same Pew Center survey reports that Republicans who regularly watch MSNBC are 10 percentage points more likely than Democrats to report doing so primarily for entertainment and 10 percentage points less likely to report doing so for purposes of hearing the latest news and headlines or in-depth news reporting. Similarly, regular Democratic viewers of Fox News are 11 points less likely than their Republican counterparts to report primarily watching Fox for purposes of hearing "interesting views and opinions."

Although, as with cable news, some Internet consumers seek out news from across the ideological spectrum, the Internet is nonetheless a particularly amenable environment for ideological self-selection. For instance, as noted earlier, most readers of the Huffington Post are Democrats. Moreover, Baum and Groeling (2008) report evidence that some ideological news blogs cover the "other side" primarily to set the stage for making their own political argument, in effect using "opposition" political blogs as straw men. It seems likely that at least some politically sophisticated Internet news consumers are similarly motivated when "crossing over" to ideologically hostile news sources.

In the contemporary media environment, Americans can consume nearly limitless political news from virtually any ideological perspective or alternatively equally limitless entertainment media while rarely if ever encountering politics (Prior 2007). This raises the opportunity costs for typical consumers of seeking out alternative political perspectives. Survey evidence, such as that shown in Figure 6.2, suggests that substantial portions of the public also appear to lack the motive to do so. In these data, nearly one-third of the regular audiences across the twenty-six media outlets included in the figure indicate that they prefer news that reinforces their preexisting beliefs to news with no political point of view. The percentage rises to nearly half among regular viewers of shows hosted by cable news personalities such as Glenn Beck, Sean Hannity, and Rachel Maddow. These results are consistent with the relatively limited ideological crossover viewing described above.

Not surprisingly, as shown in Figure 6.3, these same data indicate that as the strength of an individual's political ideology increases, so too does that individual's preference for news that reinforces her preexisting beliefs (Baum and Groeling 2010).

If, as Figures 6.2 and 6.3 suggest, the current era is significantly characterized by reinforcement seeking among consumers, forging and sustaining bipartisan consensus will likely prove daunting for future leaders, particularly—albeit by no means exclusively—in issue areas such as regulatory policy that have provoked long-standing ideological dissensus.

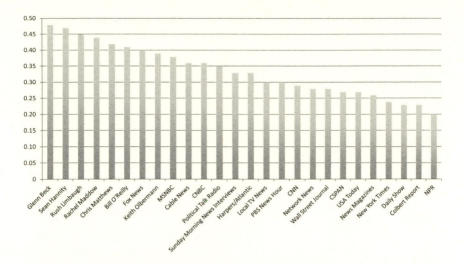

Figure 6.2. Percent of "Regular" Users who Prefer News that Reinforces Their Beliefs. *Source:* Pew Center (2010c).

Evidence of this dilemma emerges even in the traditionally bipartisan area of national security policy. For instance, the 2003 U.S. invasion and subsequent occupation of Iraq produced the greatest partisan divide ever recorded in scientific polling, both in terms of support for a U.S. military conflict and in terms of overall presidential approval (Jacobson 2006). Scholars continue to debate the media's role in sharpening, if not altogether producing, the partisan gulf in evaluations of the president and the Iraq War (Kull et al. 2003–4; Della Vigna and Kaplan 2007; Jacobson 2007). Jacobson (2007), for instance, speculates that a combination of differences in content and partisan self-selection into friendly news environments may have contributed to partisan differences in perceptions of the war and the president leading it.

As the prior discussion attests, self-selection—a concept dating back to Campbell et al.'s (1960) theory of minimalism—may well be sharpening partisan polarization, and this phenomenon seems likely to expand in the future. However, there exists a second, perhaps complementary, culprit: ideologically driven credibility assessments. In other words, contemporary citizens possess, arguably to a greater extent than their predecessors, the means to engage in a multipronged strategy for avoiding information inconsistent with their preexisting beliefs. Selective exposure, or avoiding dissonant information altogether, presumably represents the first such prong. However, even when this first defense mechanism fails and individuals are exposed to ideologically hostile

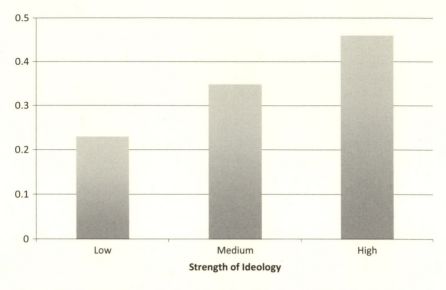

Figure 6.3. Percentage Preferring News that Reinforces their Prior Beliefs over News without an Ideological Slant, by Strength of Ideology (2010). *Source:* Baum and Groeling (2010).

news, they increasingly possess the means—by assigning ideological reputations to individual sources and media outlets—to systematically discount it. In other words, consumers appear also to selectively accept or reject information to which they are exposed based on its perceived credibility (Baum and Groeling 2010). Credibility assessments in turn depend on the perceived ideological leaning of the outlet presenting the information, as well as on the content of the information itself (e.g., its perceived costliness for the outlet and the speaker). The combined influence of selective exposure and acceptance appears, at least in the cases of Iraq and overall assessments of President George W. Bush's job performance, to have contributed substantially to the historically unprecedented levels of partisan polarization in the United States during President Bush's second term and the second half of President Obama's first term.

The combination of means, motive, and opportunity leads consumers toward what I have termed *self-segregated information streams* (SSIS; Baum 2011). In doing so, it contributes to the progressive erosion of the informational commons, that is, the common civic (virtual) space, occupied for roughly four decades by network television nightly newscasts, where a broad cross-section of Americans gathered to learn about the events of the day. This, in turn, seems likely to enhance partisan polarization on an array of public policy issues, including the appropriate role of government in regulating the economy and society.

Healthcare or Obamacare

I now turn to an assessment of the implications of the aforementioned trends for public attitudes about the appropriate role of government in healthcare. To the extent that significant portions of the public are self-segregating into ideologically friendly news environments, I anticipate polarization on these questions to be positively related to consumption of partisan media, even after accounting for respondents' ex ante partisan and ideological attitudes and intensities.

Of course, this implication of SSIS rests on the key assumption that partisan media differed in their coverage of the national debate over healthcare reform. At first glance this seems a reasonable assumption. After all, as noted previously, the appropriate extent of government regulation of individuals and businesses has long been subject to heated debate across partisan and ideological lines. Over three decades ago, conservative Republican president Ronald Reagan came to power with the assertion that government was not the solution to the nation's ills but rather the problem. Nonetheless, it is important to empirically establish at least some baseline plausibility of this assumption with respect to healthcare reform.

One basic means of doing so is to content-analyze healthcare-related coverage from the major television news outlets. In this case, an oft-employed pejorative term for the Obama proposal is "Obamacare." Opponents of the proposal routinely use this term to link it to the president, who is extremely unpopular among Republicans. (His approval rating among Republicans was only 17 percent in a 2009[a] Pew Center survey.) Opponents have also frequently decried the president's proposal as constituting socialism. I thus investigate the frequency of use of the terms "Obamacare" and "socialism" across different outlets.

To do so, I searched the UCLA Television News Archive, which captures the full text (via closed captioning) of all programming airing on a variety of TV networks, including CNN, MSNBC, and Fox News. I searched for the presence of the term "Obamacare" in a story segment on each of these outlets, for the period January 2009 to the most recent date included in the archive at the time of the search (July 18, 2011). I then replicated that search focusing on mentions of the word "socialism" in story segments that also mentioned healthcare reform. Finally, I again replicated the search focusing on mentions of the phrase "government takeover" in story segments that also mentioned healthcare reform. (I required the presence of the phrase "healthcare reform" to eliminate

Table 6.1. Frequency of Use of Terms "Obamacare," "Socialism," and "Government Takeover" in Healthcare Reform Stories, by Network (January 2009–July 18, 2011)

Media outlet	"Obamacare" mentions	Mentions of "socialism" in story segments mentioning healthcare reform	Mentions of "government takeover" in story segments mentioning healthcare reform	Total number of story segments	"Obamacare" mentions as proportion of total story segments	"Socialism" + healthcare reform mentions as proportion of total story segments	"Government takeover" + healthcare reform mentions as proportion of total story segments
Fox News	833	696	802	7,531	.111	.092	.106
CNN	100	87	263	11,850	.008	.007	.022
MSNBC	167	112	157	4,855	.034	.023	.032

Source: UCLA Television News Archive.

stories mentioning socialism or "government takeover" that focused on other topics.) Table 6.1 presents the results.

These results, though far from definitive, nonetheless appear consistent with my assumption, at least if one accepts the added assumption that Fox is more conservative leaning than CNN or MSNBC and hence likely to feature stories that are less supportive of President Obama's healthcare reform initiative than the other networks. In fact, Fox used the terms "Obamacare" and "socialism" (the latter in stories also mentioning healthcare reform) nearly four times more frequently, as a percentage of all story segments, than liberal-leaning MSNBC. MSNBC, in turn, used the term more frequently than CNN. The pattern is similar for the phrase "government takeover," which Fox used within story segments also containing "healthcare reform" more than three times as frequently, as a percentage of all story segments, as MSNBC and nearly five times as frequently as CNN. In each case, MSNBC appears to have used these terms primarily in stories aimed at criticizing opponents of the president's reform effort, thereby using these terms more as straw men than as criticisms of healthcare reform. This suggests that the gaps I identify are likely conservative estimates.

Given the apparent support of the core assumption underlying my SSIS prediction, I turn to testing its aforementioned polarization implication. I investigate two surveys, one by the Pew Center, conducted in December 2009, and a second by the *Washington Post*, conducted in November 2009. Both surveys include questions on respondents' attitudes toward healthcare reform and on their news consumption habits.

Pew Center December 2009 Poll

The Pew Center (2009a) survey asked respondents whether they favored or opposed the "healthcare proposals being discussed in Congress" and included follow-up questions asking why they did so. For my dependent variable, I created a dummy coded 1 for respondents who opposed the reform effort and cited "too much government involvement in healthcare" as a "major" reason for their opposition.

My key causal variables were a series of media consumption questions asking respondents, "on television, do you get most of your news about national and international issues from, local news programming, ABC Network news, CBS Network news, CNN Cable news, MSNBC Cable news, or The Fox News Cable Channel?" Respondents offered as many as five responses. I created a weighted scale, giving respondents five points for mentioning an outlet first, four points for mentioning it second, three for third, and so on.[3] In order to separately assess the effects of media consumption on different partisan subgroups, I interacted the resulting score for a given outlet with party ID dummies. I also included controls for the extent to which respondents had heard about President Obama's healthcare proposal, their political ideology, education, race, religiosity, and consumption of liberal and conservative websites.

Before turning to the results, it is first important to note that, as one might expect, Republicans are far more likely than Democrats or independents to oppose healthcare reform and cite excessive government involvement as a major reason for doing so. Overall, 77 percent of Republicans did so, compared with 45 percent of independents and only 11 percent of Democrats. This creates potential ceiling and floor effects for Republicans and Democrats, respectively. To the extent that nearly all Republicans are inclined to oppose healthcare reform, while nearly all Democrats are inclined to support it, there is relatively little room for Republicans to increase their opposition or for Democrats to increase their support. Hence, we might anticipate that the largest effects of media exposure would be among independents, who are very nearly split down the middle and hence lack either constraint.

With this in mind, I turn to the results of a logit analysis, shown in Table 6.2. The results indicate that all of the controls, except education and frequency of attending religious services, are statistically significant. Not surprisingly, conservatives were more and liberals less likely, relative to moderates, to oppose healthcare reform because of their belief that it entails an excessive government role in healthcare. White respondents were also more likely to oppose healthcare reform and cite excessive government involvement as a major reason. Consuming conservative websites was also positively related to taking this position, while consuming liberal websites was inversely related to opposing the reform effort due to excessive government involvement. These last two results are consistent with the core argument presented in this study. However, due to space limitations, I limit my subsequent analysis to the major cable TV news networks.

Turning to the key relationships, in Table 6.3 I employ Clarify—statistical simulation software operationalized for Stata (King et al. 2000)—to transform the log likelihoods from the logit model into expected probabilities of opposing healthcare reform, with excessive government involvement in healthcare as a major reason for doing so. It is important to keep in mind that for Democrats, MSNBC and CNN are likely to be more credible than Fox, due to the latter's perceived pro-Republican slant, whereas for Republicans, Fox is likely to be more credible than CNN or MSNBC, for the same reason. Perceptions of partisan slant are less likely to influence the persuasiveness of news to independents, who are thus most likely to be influenced by news across the ideological spectrum (Baum and Groeling 2010).

Table 6.2. Logit Analysis of Effects of Cable News Consumption on Likelihood of Opposing Healthcare Reform due to Belief That It Entails Excessive Government Involvement in Healthcare

Causal variables	Coefficient (SE)
Democrat	−1.639***
	(0.288)
Republican	0.856***
	(0.236)
Fox News × Democrat	0.222
	(0.154)
MSNBC × Democrat	−0.104
	(0.234)
CNN × Democrat	−0.194
	(0.144)
Fox News × Republican	0.218^
	(0.130)
MSNBC × Republican	−0.0355
	(0.175)
CNN × Republican	−0.0388
	(0.135)
Fox News × Independent	0.331*
	(0.130)
MSNBC × Independent	−0.137
	(0.152)
CNN × Independent	−0.122
	(0.129)
Heard About Healthcare Proposals Scale	0.929***
	(0.180)
Conservative	0.591**
	(0.187)
Liberal	−0.599*
	(0.284)
White	0.751**
	(0.266)
Education	−0.0374
	(0.0606)
Liberal Website Consumption Scale	−2.132***
	(0.522)
Conservative Website Consumption Scale	1.416**
	(0.486)
Frequency of attending religious services	−0.0542
	(0.0395)
Regularly watch multiple cable news networks	−0.189
	(0.552)
Constant	−2.756***
	(0.523)
Observations	1,485

Note: Robust standard errors are in parentheses.
^p < .10; *p < .05; **p < .01; ***p < .001.

Table 6.3. Probability of Opposing Healthcare Reform due to Belief It Entails Excessive Government Involvement in Healthcare, as Cable News Outlet Consumption Varies

Political affiliation	Minimum	Maximum	Difference
Republicans			
Fox	0.654	0.821	0.167*
CNN	0.654	0.576	−0.078
MSNBC	0.654	0.580	−0.074
Democrats			
Fox	0.141	0.301	0.160
CNN	0.141	0.053	−0.088*
MSNBC	0.141	0.112	−0.029
Independents			
Fox	0.447	0.775	0.328**
CNN	0.447	0.279	−0.168*
MSNBC	0.447	0.279	−0.168^^

$^{\wedge\wedge}p < .15$; $*p < .05$; $**p < .01$.

The results appear to largely support the polarization implication. With all controls held constant at their mean values, and other television network consumption set to zero, Republicans who mentioned Fox News first were 17 percentage points more likely than their counterparts who did not mention Fox News to oppose healthcare reform due in significant measure to a perception of excessive government involvement in healthcare (0.82 vs. 0.65, $p < .05$). The corresponding increase among independents was nearly twice as large (+33 percentage points, 0.45 vs. 0.78), presumably because there were more independents available to negatively reassess healthcare reform based on information consumption.

As one might expect, Fox News consumption had no statistically significant effect on Democrats, for whom the network is least credible and hence the information it presents least likely to be persuasive. Conversely, among Republicans Fox News is highly credible and hence especially likely to be persuasive. However, since most Republicans are strongly inclined to oppose Democratic-sponsored healthcare reform initiatives and tend to oppose increasing the government's role in the economy, including healthcare, there were a limited number of Republicans available to negatively reassess healthcare. In contrast, independents, who lack a partisan incentive to distrust Fox, yet were less inclined, all else being equal, to oppose healthcare reform, the effects of consuming Fox News were larger, presumably, as previously noted, because there were more independents located near the threshold of changing their opinions and hence available to reassess (Baum 2002).

Turning to CNN, once again the results appear consistent with my prior assumptions about partisan credibility. Democrats who mentioned CNN first were 9 percentage points less likely to oppose healthcare reform due in large measure to a perception that it entails an excessive role for government (0.24 vs. 0.05, $p < .05$). Once again, the corresponding effect among independents is larger, a 17-point decline (from 0.45 vs. 0.28, $p < .05$). The reason for the larger effect among independents is similar to that noted above with respect to Fox News: since, as noted earlier, nearly all Democrats are inclined to support healthcare reform, there are simply few available to favorably reassess it in response to new information encountered on CNN. There were more independents available to favorably reassess. As we might expect, given CNN's relatively lower partisan credibility among Republicans, citing CNN first as the most important source of news on television had no statistically significant effect on Republicans' likelihoods of opposing healthcare reform because of a perceived excessive government role.

Citing MSNBC first as the most important source of news on TV had no statistically significant effects on respondents' attitudes toward healthcare reform, though among independents who cited MSNBC first there is a nearly significant ($p < .15$) 18 percentage point decline in opposition, relative to their counterparts who did not mention the network. This makes sense given MSNBC's liberal slant and the absence of a partisan credibility filter that would induce independents to discount information gleaned from that network, all else being equal.

The insignificant effect for MSNBC among partisans may be attributable to the substantially lower likelihood of citing the network as an important source of news in the first instance. Overall, 18 and 20 percent of respondents mentioned CNN and Fox News, respectively, as an outlet where they get most of their news. The corresponding figure for MSNBC is only 4 percent. Among Democrats, the percentages mentioning Fox, CNN, and MSNBC are 8, 29, and 6 percent, respectively, whereas for Republicans the percentages are 39, 10, and 3 percent, respectively. In short, while Republicans are far likelier than Democrats to cite Fox, and Democrats far likelier to cite CNN, neither group is especially likely to cite MSNBC. Among independents, the corresponding percentages show a similar pattern: 15, 15, and 3.5 percent, respectively. The fact that independents are equally likely to watch Fox or CNN makes sense, as this group lacks a partisan motive for eschewing one or the other network. Note also that independents fall in between Republicans and Democrats in their (relatively low) likelihood of citing MSNBC. This makes it far more difficult to find statistically significant effects associated with consuming MSNBC's programming. Notwithstanding the difficulty in estimating viewing patterns for MSNBC, on balance these results clearly indicate that SSIS, combined with individual credibility assessments based on the perceived partisan orientations of news outlets, enhanced polarization with respect to attitudes toward the government's effort to overhaul the nation's healthcare system.

One factor that could potentially mitigate the polarization effects of partisan media is cross-pollination or consuming media across partisan lines. However, at least in these data and with respect to cable news, this pattern appears to be the exception rather than the rule. Overall, only six-tenths of 1 percent of respondents cited both Fox and MSNBC as important sources of news, while only 2.4 percent cited Fox plus either MSNBC or CNN as important sources of news. This figure rises only to 3.6 percent if broadcast network news is added to the mix. The percentages, in turn, vary only modestly for Democrats and Republicans. Although there are, of course, many other potential sources of cross-pollination, it appears that this behavior is not prevalent with respect to television news.

November 2009 *Washington Post* Poll

The *Washington Post* Survey (2009) focuses only on Republicans' attitudes toward a variety of policy issues. Hence, I cannot offer evidence from this survey of cross-party polarization. However, it does include questions that make it possible to investigate the effects of consuming conservative and liberal news on attitudes toward healthcare reform. For my dependent variable, I focus on the following question: "Thinking specifically about the changes to the country's healthcare system proposed by Obama and the Democrats, would you prefer that the Republicans in Congress work with the Democrats on these changes or try to stop these changes from happening? Do you feel that way strongly or somewhat?" In order to maximize my statistical leverage while focusing on the correlates of opposition to healthcare reform, I collapsed the responses into a dichotomous variable, coded 0 for "work with Democrats, strongly," "work with Democrats, somewhat," or "don't know/no opinion" and 1 for "try to stop changes, strongly" or "try to stop changes, somewhat."

My first pair of key causal variables code how frequently the respondent claims to watch the Fox News Channel or MSNBC: regularly, sometimes, hardly ever, or never. (The several responses of "don't know/no opinion" are set to the median value in the scale.) The second key causal variable is based on the following question:

> Thinking about the Republican Party in general and not just the people in Congress, for each issue area I name, please tell me if you think the party in general puts (too much) emphasis on the issue, (too little) emphasis on the issue, or about the right amount? The first issue is [federal spending]: Does the Republican Party put (too much) emphasis on [federal

spending], (too little) emphasis, or about the right amount? (Responses are coded 1 = too little emphasis, 2 = about the right amount, or don't know/no opinion, and 3 = too much emphasis.)

I interacted the "emphasis on federal spending" variable—which serves as my best-available proxy for attitudes toward the government's role in regulating society and the economy—with Fox and MSNBC consumption. My goal in doing so was to determine whether the influence of consuming Fox or MSNBC on attitudes toward healthcare reform is larger among individuals who are concerned that the government is too large or intrusive than among their counterparts who are less concerned with the size and scope of government. My expectation was that exposure to conservative news ought to have a larger (anti–healthcare reform) effect on those who are not ex ante prone to worry about the size and scope of government, while exposure to liberal news ought to have a larger (pro–healthcare reform) effect on those who *are* concerned ex ante about the size and scope of government. The reason is simply that in the former case there are likely to be more marginal reform supporters available to turn against the policy in response to anti-reform news, while in the latter there are likely to be more marginal reform opponents available to turn in favor of the policy in response to pro-reform news. Control variables for this analysis include income, education, attitudes toward President Obama's policies, political conservatism, and social conservatism.

Table 6.4 presents two logit analyses. The first (Model 1) excludes the interactions between news consumption and attitudes toward federal spending, and the second (Model 2) adds the interaction terms. The results strongly suggest that news consumption does indeed influence attitudes toward healthcare reform among Republicans in the anticipated directions, and that the extent of this influence is itself mediated by attitudes toward federal spending, also in the anticipated directions.

Beginning with Model 1, again employing Clarify to transform the results into probabilities, the results indicate that as Fox News consumption increases from "never" to "regularly," with MSNBC consumption held constant at "never," the probability of preferring that Republicans work with Democrats to pass healthcare reform declines by 16 percentage points (from 23 to 7, $p < .01$). Conversely, as MSNBC consumption increases from "never" to "regularly," with Fox News consumption held constant at "never," the probability of preferring that Republicans work with Democrats to pass healthcare reform increases by 32 percentage points (from 23 to 55, $p < .01$).

Of course, these results could be endogenous, in that Republicans more prone to support healthcare reform may be more likely to watch MSNBC, while their counterparts who are prone to oppose it are more

Table 6.4. Logit Analysis of Effects of Cable News Consumption on Likelihood of Favoring Republican Cooperation with Democrats to Pass Health Care Reform

Variable	Model 1 Coef. (SE)	Model 2 Coef. (SE)
Watch Fox	−0.471***	0.142
	(0.114)	(0.293)
Watch MSNBC	0.471***	0.519^
	(0.117)	(0.290)
Social ideology	−0.235	−0.252
	(0.175)	(0.172)
Political ideology	−0.265	−0.242
	(0.202)	(0.198)
Education	−0.0306	−0.0383
	(0.118)	(0.117)
Income	−0.192*	−0.196*
	(0.0761)	(0.0773)
Too much Republican	0.480**	1.703**
emphasis on gov't spending	(0.176)	(0.639)
Enthused–Angry About	−1.456***	−1.432***
Obama Policies Scale	(0.207)	(0.204)
Watch Fox × Too much		−0.391*
Republican emphasis on		(0.177)
gov't spending		
Watch MSNBC × Too much		−0.0535
Republican emphasis on		(0.172)
gov't spending		
Constant	5.809***	3.933**
	(1.071)	(1.362)
Observations	709	709

Note: Robust standard errors are in parentheses.
^$p < .10$; *$p < .05$; **$p < .01$; ***$p < .001$.

likely to watch Fox News. This possibility is, in part, accounted for by controlling for correlates of ex ante preferences for conservative versus liberal news, such as political and social ideology, attitudes regarding President Obama's policy agenda, income, and education. However, to further address this possibility, as well as to determine the extent to which attitudes toward healthcare reform are mediated by attitudes regarding the proper role of government, in Model 2 I add the aforementioned interaction terms.

Beginning with Fox News, the results indicate that among Republicans who believe the Republican Party has placed too much emphasis on federal spending (that is, among individuals who are relatively less concerned about the size of government), a maximum increase in Fox News consumption is associated with a 55 percentage point drop in support for healthcare reform, from 78 percent among non–Fox News consumers to 22 percent among regular Fox News consumers ($p < .01$). The corresponding effect among their counterparts who believe the Republican Party has placed too little emphasis on federal spending (that is, among individuals who are especially concerned about the size of government) is far smaller and only marginally significant: a decline of about 8 percentage points, from 17 percent for non–Fox News consumers to 9 percent for regular consumers ($p < .10$).

Turning to MSNBC, here, as anticipated, the results are stronger among respondents who believe the Republican Party has placed too little emphasis on federal spending. Among these individuals (again, Republicans all), a maximum increase in MSNBC consumption is associated with a 28 percentage point increase in support for healthcare reform, from 17 to 46 percent ($p < .01$). The corresponding effect for Republicans who believe the party has placed too much emphasis on federal spending is a statistically insignificant 8-point increase in support for healthcare reform (from 86 to 94 percent). Taken together, these results complement those from the Pew Center study. In this instance, the data suggest that after accounting for a Republican's degree of social and political conservatism, as well as their income, education, and attitudes toward President Obama's policy initiatives, their specific attitudes toward healthcare reform are heavily influenced by their decision to consume liberal or conservative news. Moreover, the effects of news consumption are strongly mediated by attitudes toward federal spending. This suggests that many respondents see the healthcare reform debate as directly related to broader questions about the role of government in society and that information consumption has a larger effect on individuals who are likely to be located closer to the threshold of changing their opinions and who expose themselves to counterideological news (that is, those relatively less worried about federal spending who consume Fox News become more worried, while those relatively more worried about it who consume MSNBC become less worried).

Conclusion

It remains true that some Democrats, some of the time, consume conservative media, while some Republicans consume liberal media. Political messages, in turn, sometimes cross the ideological boundaries of partisan media. For instance, at halftime of the 2011 Super Bowl, Fox aired an interview of President Obama conducted by conservative Fox News personality Bill O'Reilly. O'Reilly complimented the president and his State Department for their handling of an attack on two Fox

News journalists in Egypt, ultimately leading to their safe rescue. This afforded President Obama an opportunity to praise his administration's policies in the Middle East in a context likely to be unusually credible to Republican Fox viewers. Hence, the media commons, and the common civic space for public affairs dialogue it created, has not entirely disappeared, nor has the capacity of presidents to use the media as a tool for building broader support constituencies by reaching out to the "other side" via its media outlets.

That said, current trends toward ever more consumer self-selection and increasingly sophisticated information filtering and media targeting of consumer preferences all appear to portend a trend toward greater audience fragmentation and hence continued shrinking of the media commons. It seems inevitable that news providers will increasingly apply to news and public affairs content the same filtering technologies that allow media content distributors such as Netflix and iTunes to determine the types of movies or music a customer is likely to prefer and suggest to them precisely that. The end result may be what Cass Sunstein (2007) terms "cyberbalkanization," where the media commons is largely supplanted by a "daily me" in which consumers encounter only the news and information they want, most of which tends to confirm rather than challenge their preexisting attitudes. Whether or not the media commons disappears entirely, there is little question that technological innovations and shifts in audience behavior are changing the way citizens consume news, with content growing increasingly personalized and subject to individual preferences regarding what, when, and where they entertain themselves or expose themselves to politically themed information. All of these patterns appear likely to enhance, rather than reduce, attitude polarization in the electorate. This, in turn, seems likely to complicate the efforts of future presidents to forge bipartisan consensus on many of the critical challenges facing the nation.

Of course, effective presidential leadership requires both exciting the base and building coalitions across partisan lines—and there is no reason to suppose that future presidents will succeed, at least over the longer term, by emphasizing one over the other. Politics in America are at a crossroads. Traditional communications channels are increasingly foreclosed, even as new ones emerge. Different channels, in turn, reach different audiences and so privilege different communication strategies, different forms of leadership, and ultimately different policies. The proper role of the government in regulating the economy and society represents one likely arena where SSIS seems likely to enhance attitude polarization and hence make it harder for presidents to overcome partisan gridlock. The pitched battle over moving the nation toward universal health coverage is a particularly stark case in point. President Obama worked tirelessly for nearly a year to forge a bipartisan compromise. Yet in the end not a single Republican in either the House or Senate voted in favor of the policy. The Republican-controlled House of Representatives subsequently voted—in one of its first official acts upon assuming control of the House—to repeal the healthcare law, though the legislation died in the Democratic-controlled Senate.

Of course, healthcare reform proved to be an unusually polarizing policy initiative, even by contemporary standards, and hence perhaps was more likely to be influenced by qualitatively differing media coverage across news outlets than many other areas of regulatory policy. Still, it is not difficult to imagine similarly polarized outcomes in other important regulatory policy areas, ranging from finance to consumer protection to the environment. Already we have witnessed efforts by Republicans—with thus far unclear outcomes—to weaken or reverse Obama administration policies in all three areas. Partisan media, in turn, have offered starkly different descriptions of the debates surrounding the role of government.

One means of discerning such differences is simply to compare the usage frequency of combinations of keywords that carry with them implicit normative frames. Table 6.5 provides such a comparison, replicating the content analysis approach presented earlier with respect to the healthcare debate summarized in Table 6.1.

In this instance, I investigated combinations of keywords relating to tax policy in the context of stories addressing one or more of three topics: employment, infrastructure, and regulation. The results show that within story segments mentioning taxes, Fox News is substantially more likely than MSNBC or CNN to also include either (1) "small businesses" and "uncertainty" or (2) "regulations" and "uncertainty." In contrast, CNN and MSNBC are substantially more likely than Fox to pair story segments mentioning taxes with any of the following combinations of terms: (1) "invest" and "infrastructure," (2) "unemployed" and "workers" and "middle class," or (3) "unemployed" and "middle class" and *either* "wealthy" or "rich" or "millionaire" or "billionaire." This suggests that on CNN and MSNBC, tax policy is more likely to be associated with questions of fairness, public investment, or implications for workers and the middle class, while on Fox News it is more likely to be discussed in terms of its implications for small businesses and creation of an uncertain regulatory environment.

These quite different frames seem likely to influence the attitudes of consumers of these different networks, thereby helping sharpen partisan polarization across a range of policy areas involving the size and scope

Table 6.5. Frequency of Using Combinations of Terms, by Network (January 20, 2009–October 11, 2011)

Media outlet	Taxes + Small Businesses + Uncertainty		Taxes + Small Businesses + Uncertainty + Regulations		Taxes[a] + Invest + Infrastructure		Taxes + Unemployed + Middle Class + Wealthy (or Rich or Millionaire or Billionaire)		Taxes + Unemployed + Workers + Middle Class		Total no. of story segments
	No. of mentions	As proportion of total story segments	No. of mentions	As proportion of total story segments	No. of mentions	As proportion of total story segments	No. of mentions	As proportion of total story segments	No. of mentions	As proportion of total story segments	
CNN	252	.019	45	.004	959	.076	12,661	.057	571	.045	12,661
MSNBC	265	.051	72	.014	927	.187	5,224	.278	966	.185	5,224
Fox News	676	.083	190	.023	404	.049	8,160	.050	307	.037	8,160

[a] If "taxes" (plural) is changed to "tax" (singular), the corresponding percentages for CNN, MSNBC, and Fox News become .169, .400, and .115, respectively.

Source: UCLA Television News Archive.

of government, including a variety of regulatory policy issues. Indeed, given the enormity and speed of the changes in the media marketplace, the potential consequences for democratic participation and the strategic landscape for politicians, the evolution of the communication environment in which politics are contested seems likely to play a central role in shaping the future course of U.S. democracy.

Notes

1. These data represent aggregate results from over 100,000 interviews for each period (Kernell and Rice 2011; Feltus 2009).
2. For additional data on partisan filtering of cable news audiences, see Baum (2011).
3. I coded responses of "don't know" or "refused" as missing.

References

All, David (2007) "Is Yahoo!'s Online Debate Going to Be Fair and Balanced?," April 26. http://techpresident.com/blog-entry/yahoo's-online-debate-going -be-fair-and-balanced, accessed September 30, 2010.

Baum, Matthew A. (2002) "Sex, Lies and War: How Soft News Brings Foreign Policy to the Inattentive Public." *American Political Science Review* 96 (March): 91–109.

—— (2003) *Soft News Goes to War: Public Opinion and American Foreign Policy in the New Media Age.* Princeton, N.J.: Princeton University Press.

—— (2011) "Preaching to the Choir or Converting the Flock: Presidential Communication Strategies in the Age of Three Medias." In R. Fox and J. Ramos, eds., *iPolitics: Citizens, Elections, and Governing in the New Media Era.* Cambridge: Cambridge University Press.

Baum, Matthew A., and Tim Groeling (2008) "New Media and the Polarization of American Political Discourse." *Political Communication* 25: 345–65.

—— (2010) *War Stories: The Causes and Consequences of Citizen Views of War.* Princeton, N.J.: Princeton University Press.

Baum, Matthew A., and Samuel Kernell (1999) "Has Cable Ended the Golden Age of Presidential Television?" *American Political Science Review* 93: 1–16.

—— (2001) "Economic Class and Popular Support for Franklin Roosevelt in War and Peace." *Public Opinion Quarterly* 65: 198–229.

—— (2007) "How Cable Ended the Golden Age of Presidential Television: 1969–2006." In S. Kernell and S. Smith, eds., *The Principles and Practice of American Politics.* Washington, D.C.: Congressional Quarterly Press.

Campbell, Angus et al. (1960) *The American Voter.* New York: Wiley.

Cantril, Hadley (1940) "America Faces the War: A Study in Public Opinion." *Public Opinion Quarterly* 4: 387–407.

comScore.com (2008) "Huffington Post and Politico Lead Wave of Explosive Growth at Independent Political Blogs and News Sites this Election Season." http://www.comscore.com/Press_Events/Press_Releases/2008/10/Huffing ton_Post_and_Politico_Lead_Political_Blogs, accessed July 25, 2011.

Della Vigna, Stefano, and Ethan Kaplan (2007) "The Fox News Effect: Media Bias and Voting." *Quarterly Journal of Economics* 122: 1187–234.

Feltus, Will (2009) "Cable News Bias? Audiences Say 'Yes!'" *National Media Research, Planning, and Placement*, October 29. http://nmrpp.com/CableNews BiasAudiences.pdf.

Gentzkow, Matthew, and Jesse M. Shapiro (2010) "Ideological Segregation Online and Offline." NBER Working Paper 15916, April. http://www.nber.org /papers/w15916.pdf, accessed December 2, 2011.

Hamilton, James T. (2003) *All the News That's Fit to Sell: How the Market Transforms Information into News*. Princeton, N.J.: Princeton University Press.

Hindman, Matthew (2007) *The Myth of Digital Democracy*. Princeton, N.J.: Princeton University Press.

Jacobson, Gary C. (2006) *A Divider, Not a Uniter: George W. Bush and the American People*. New York: Pearson Longman.

———— (2007) "The War, the President, and the 2006 Midterm Congressional Elections." Presented to the annual meeting of the Midwest Political Science Association, the Palmer House Hilton, Chicago, April 12–15.

Kernell, Samuel, and Laurie L. Rice (2011) "Cable and Partisan Polarization of the President's Audience." *Presidential Studies Quarterly* 41: 693–711.

King, Gary et al. (2000) "Making the Most of Statistical Analyses." *American Journal of Political Science* 44: 341–65.

Kull, Steven et al. (2003–4) "Misperceptions, the Media, and the Iraq War." *Political Science Quarterly* 118: 569–98.

Pew Research Center for the People and the Press (2008) *Biennial Media Survey*, April 30–June 1. http://www.people-press.org/2008/08/17/april-2008-media -survey/.

———— (2009a) *December 2009 Political Survey*, December 9–13. http://www.people -press.org/2009/12/16/december-2009-political-survey/.

———— (2009b) *July 2009 Political-Media Survey*, July 22–26. http://www.people -press.org/2009/07/30/july-2009-political-media-survey/.

———— (2010a) *Distrust, Discontent, Anger, and Partisan Rancor: The People and Their Government*, April 18. http://www.people-press.org/2010/04/18/distrust -discontent-anger-and-partisan-rancor/.

———— (2010b) *Earmarks Could Help Candidates in Midterms: Palin and Tea Party Connections Could Hurt*, August 2. http://www.people-press.org/2010/08/02 /earmarks-could-help-candidates-in-midterms-palin-and-tea-party-connec tions-could-hurt/.

———— (2010c) *June 2010 Media Consumption Survey* (8–28 Jun.), http://www .people-press.org/2010/09/12/june-2010-media-consumption-survey/.

———— (2010d) *Little Change in Opinions About Global Warming*. http://www.people -press.org/2010/10/27/little-change-in-opinions-about-global-warming/.

———— (2010e) *Public's Priorities, Financial Regs*, May 18. http://www.people -press.org/2010/05/18/publics-priorities-financial-regs/.

Pew Research Center's Project for Excellence in Journalism (2010) *The State of News Media: Talk Radio*, March 15. http://stateofthemedia.org/2010/audio -summary-essay/talk-radio/.

Prior, Markus (2007) *Post-Broadcast Democracy: How Media Choice Increases Inequality in Political Involvement and Polarizes Elections*. Cambridge: Cambridge University Press.

Sunstein, Cass R. (2007) *Republic.com 2.0*. Princeton, N.J.: Princeton University Press.

Washington Post (2009) *Washington Post Poll*, November 19–23. http://washington post.com/wp-srv/politics/polls/postpoll_113009.html.

Chapter 7

Citizens' Perceptions and the Disconnect Between Economics and Regulatory Policy

Jonathan Baron, William T. McEnroe, and Christopher Poliquin

The political problems surrounding regulation that have inspired this book reflect a battle over the amount of regulation. Does the United States have too much, so that regulation stifles beneficial enterprises? Or does it have too little, so that the lack of regulation permits too many disasters? We shall not address this question directly in this chapter except to point out that, other things being equal, both sides could be correct. Excessive regulation imposes costs (on someone) that exceed its benefits, and insufficient regulation allows harm that is more costly than the cost of preventing it. Each social and economic problem has some optimal amount of regulation as its solution. In the United States, it is possible that some problems are overregulated and others underregulated, relative to the optimum amount of regulation for each.

The issue we address here is the possibility that both sides of the current regulatory debate could be correct at the same time and for the same regulatory problem. That is, individual regulations can be inefficient, and there may be some way to lower their costs while increasing their benefits. We want to suggest that public perceptions—which affect policy through legislation, public pressure, and other ways—often hinder the adoption of more efficient regulations. Public attitudes actually prevent improvements that should make both sides a little less unhappy.

Governments have several ways of controlling harmful side effects of economic behavior, which is the concern of most regulation. The typical example of a side effect that justifies regulation is pollution, but the same rationale applies elsewhere, to varying degrees. Egg farms, for instance, do not intend for their eggs to be infected with salmonella; this is a harmful side effect. Although varied side effects like these abound with many economic activities, we shall focus our analysis here mainly on regulation addressing pollution.

The main methods of controlling pollution are direct regulation (command and control), taxation, subsidies for reducing emissions, tort law (lawsuits), property rights combined with injunctions as a means of enforcement, cap and trade (in which rights to emit are given out and then traded in a market), and enforcement of contracts. Contracts are difficult to make when an act of polluting increases the risk of multitudes of other people by a small amount and are rarely used, so we leave them aside here.[1] However, they may be useful in situations where the potential victim is easily identified. Thus, the government will enforce contracts between the buyer and seller of a house when the contract specifies that the seller take certain safety precautions. This, too, is a form of regulation.

The choice to be made among these several methods of regulation can be analyzed in terms of costs and benefits (e.g., Shavell 2004:ch. 5). In general, there is an "optimal amount of pollution"—an idea that sounds strange to everyone except those trained in economics. As the effort to reduce pollution increases, the cost also increases of reducing a given amount of pollution (e.g., reducing CO_2 emissions). Some methods of pollution control are inexpensive, but additional reductions must rely on more expensive methods. We can further suppose that the reduction of pollution by a fixed amount has a fixed benefit. As increased efforts are made to reduce pollution, at some point the cost of further reductions exceeds their benefit. That process leads to an optimal amount of reduction; what remains is the optimal amount of pollution.

Given this basic assumption of an optimum, we can compare various methods for achieving it through a very simple analysis (Shavell 2004). Much of the analysis depends on information. In particular, the government may have more or less information about the effects of pollution or about the cost of reduction. Similarly, those affected may have more or less information about the harm, and those regulated may have more or less information about the harm and cost of control.

In the simple case of perfect information, all methods can yield the optimum. Through regulation, the government would tell polluters what to do in order to reduce pollution by the optimal amount. Through taxation, the government would tax pollution at an amount equal to the value of the harm it causes. This way, polluters would have an incentive to pollute only when the cost of reducing the pollution is greater than the harm it causes. Similarly, the subsidy is just the reverse of the tax: the government would pay for reduction an amount equal to the harm caused. The cap-and-trade mechanism would set the cap at the total amount of optimal pollution. By trading, each potential polluter would end up paying the optimal cost to reduce pollution. Those with higher costs would buy the right to pollute from those with lower costs. A successful lawsuit would require a polluter to pay for the cost of harm, thus providing an incentive to pay for pollution reduction if that costs less than the harm.[2]

A lack of information changes the optimum, however. Regulation could miss the optimum, either way, if the government is poorly informed about either harm or cost of control. If polluters know the cost of control, but the government knows only the cost of the harm, then a tax or subsidy should work well, as the government needs to know only the cost of the harm to set the level of these controlling factors. The polluters would then be able to reach the optimum amount. Tort law with strict liability would also work, if the government knew only the harm. For torts under negligence, the government (the court, in this case) would need to know the cost of control as well as the cost of the harm in order to determine whether the polluter was negligent. Tort law requires that the victim know the harm. If the harm is a risk of some disease in the future, victims may know very little.

Another relevant factor is the ability to adjust to variations in cost. Regulation is inferior to taxes, subsidies, and cap and trade because it is a "one size fits all" strategy. Polluters may differ considerably in their costs of control, and the other methods allow them to adjust individually so that each polluter is at the optimum.

Although taxes and subsidies are equivalent from the perspective of achieving the optimum, they have very different effects elsewhere. Taxes gain revenue for the government, arguably in a way that is unusually efficient compared with other taxes because they penalize (i.e., provide incentives against) harmful behavior, whereas income or payroll taxes, for example, penalize investment or work. Subsidies have the opposite effect, forcing governments to raise taxes elsewhere (or borrow) to cover them.

Most of these methods have been used or tried. Gasoline taxes have been partially justified as pollution taxes (e.g., in the increase passed early in President Clinton's first term in the United States, which arose because a more general tax on energy had been considered and rejected). Cap and trade has been used with various forms of industrial pollution in both the United States and Europe. Subsidies for "green energy," such as solar energy in homes, are available in the form of tax credits from various U.S. states. Class-action lawsuits against polluters have sometimes succeeded. And, of course, direct regulation is the approach of most environmental regulation, which sometimes specifies exactly the methods that must be used for pollution control.

Economists often make recommendations based on this sort of analysis (T. Anderson and Leal 2001). For example, Mankiw (2007) advocates a tax both on the basis of the simple theory and after considering problems of international implementation. Stavins (2008) advocates a cap-and-trade system with a decreasing cap, a system that has many of the same advantages as a tax (except for immediate revenue). Others have advocated a tax for the United States as being a solution to the budget deficit, thus killing two birds with one stone.[3]

But public policy seems not to heed these economic arguments nearly as much as it could. The United States is now beginning to regulate CO_2 emissions largely through basic regulation, such as mileage standards for vehicles, and the U.S. Environmental Protection Agency is considering direct regulation on coal-burning power plants. The usual excuse for ignoring economic theory is "politics." Taxes or even cap and trade are not sufficiently popular among legislators.

Presumably, though, legislators are somewhat responsive to the citizens who elect them. It is thus possible that citizens (and perhaps legislators as well) do not understand the economic arguments. Given that these arguments are somewhat abstract, it would be surprising if people understood them spontaneously, without training. Yet it is possible to understand them, as most of the arguments are based on simple assumptions about human motivation. Some evidence suggests, however, that people are particularly unwilling to think about incentives in the same way that economists do. For example, McCaffery and Baron (2006) found that people often ignored secondary effects of policies. Many of these effects involved incentives.

Here we report four experiments on people's understanding of the economics of pollution control. The subjects for these experiments were mostly Americans, typical on average in age, income, and education of the U.S. population, although there were a greater number of women than men. They completed questionnaires on the World Wide Web for pay. They were not selected to be representative, but they did include a variety of people with different political views and different levels of education.[4]

Experiment 1: Opposition to Emissions Trading

Despite sentiment from economists in favor of alternatives like emissions trading, such a "market-based" approach to environmental protection faces continued opposition by some environmental groups. Emissions trading can be seen by some as a moral issue (Ott and Sachs 2000; Keohane et al. 1998:354–55). Those who hold this view believe that allowing companies to acquire unused credits from other companies is like individuals paying for organs—they are buying something for which no value can be determined (Belliveau 1998), or, worse, it is like paying for the right to commit a crime. Such critics object to the commodification of environmental resources.

In Experiment 1, we attempted to determine whether an understanding of economic efficiency would increase people's preference for efficient pollution policies. We asked subjects to evaluate two types of pollution policies for a two-company economy. One policy was a simplified command-and-control policy, while the other was an emissions-trading policy. The costs associated with each policy were presented in a table. The subjects were asked to indicate personal preference and to indicate which option they believed cost less. We then trained the subjects on economic efficiency. Half of the subjects had efficiency explained in terms of pollution regulation (experimental group), while the other half were instructed in terms of purchasing apples (control group). We expected the experimental group to exhibit greater preference for efficient regulation than the control group after the training.

Method

Eighty-four subjects completed a questionnaire on the World Wide Web in February 2005. The sample was 25 percent male and had a mean age of 39 (range = 20–62). As in all the other studies reported here, subjects were drawn from a panel of about 1,200 individuals who had agree to participate in studies for pay. Typically the pay was $4 for a study that took about 20 minutes. The panel was divided into groups, and e-mail messages requesting participation in the survey were sent to the individuals in one group. (This allowed us to give similar studies to different groups.) A study was stopped when about eighty responses were received.

The questionnaire had three parts: ten regulation pages, each with a different scenario; a lesson on economic efficiency; and a repeat of the previous ten pages. The first section presented the costs associated with pollution reduction policies for two companies, A and B. Subjects were asked, "Which option would you choose?" The options were the current policy, the alternative policy, or no difference. The current policy and the alternative policy alternated between tradable credits to produce X units of pollution and a command-and-control policy control that allowed a maximum level of X units to be produced by each company. The total amount of available pollution was held constant for each policy. An example of a page is shown in Figure 7.1.

Under emissions trading policies, companies would be able to trade credits so that the costs associated with pollution reduction changed as

> Current Policy: The maximum level of pollution is set at 4 units per company.
>
> Alternative Policy: Each company is given "credits" to produce 4 units of pollution and can sell these rights as they see fit.
>
> | *Cost of pollution control for each company* | | |
> | --- | --- | --- |
> | *Total units of pollution produced by each company* | *Company A* | *Company B* |
> | 1 | $200 | $100 |
> | 2 | $180 | $90 |
> | 3 | $160 | $80 |
> | 4 | $140 | $70 |
> | 5 | $120 | $60 |
> | 6 | $100 | $50 |
> | 7 | $80 | $40 |
>
> Which option would you choose?
>
> Current Policy   Alternative Policy   No Difference.
>
> If the total pollution produced by both companies together is the most it can be, which option costs less?
>
> Current Policy   Alternative Policy   No Difference.

Figure 7.1. Questionnaire Page

a function of credits traded. For the command-and-control policies, each company would produce the maximum allowable level of pollution. Using this table, subjects could determine the relative efficiency of each plan. In the scenario that follows, emissions trading is more efficient because eight total units of pollution can be achieved at a cost of $180, while command and control would cost $210. The efficient solution is achieved when Company A produces seven units of pollution for $80 and Company B produces one unit of pollution for $100. This table is one of the ten scenarios presented to subjects.[5]

Emissions trading was the default policy for five of the ten scenarios. There was no difference in efficiency for four of the scenarios; emissions trading was the most efficient for four scenarios; and command and control was most efficient for the remaining two. The efficiency was changed from scenario to scenario to prevent one option from always being correct. This was to ensure that subjects considered the relative costs of each program and used these costs to judge efficiency.

The second part of the experiment divided subjects randomly into two groups. The first group (experimental) read an explanation of economic efficiency shown in the Appendix to this chapter. These subjects were then presented with a quiz to check comprehension. The control group was presented with the same explanation of economic efficiency, but the example given was in terms of purchasing apples.

The final part of the questionnaire repeated the same ten scenarios that had been presented in the first round for both groups. The most efficient option (greatest benefit with respect to cost) varied between command and control and emissions trading, or there was no difference. Questions in each section were presented in the same random order, chosen for each subject.

Results

Subjects in the experimental group exhibited greater change in preference for efficient regulation ($t_{87} = 3.15$, $p = .0022$). The percent preferences were, for the control group, 33 and 33 percent for the two halves and, for the experimental group, 27 and 38 percent. Note that the chance of choosing efficient regulation by responding at random was 33 percent.

The experimental group also showed significantly greater change in correct efficiency judgment (the question about which would cost less) ($t_{87} = 1.81$, $p = .0368$). The control group changed from 38 to 39 percent, and the experimental group from 33 to 41 percent. As before, there was a 33 percent chance of guessing correctly.

In sum, although initial responses were close to the result that could be achieved at random, instruction in efficiency had an effect. This outcome suggests that people in general could benefit from instruction in economic efficiency.

We replicated this experiment with one additional question given to half of the subjects: "One plan allows companies to pay more to pollute more. The other does not. Which option is more permissible morally?" The same three options were used as in the choice question. We thought that this question would cause subjects to pay more attention to moral issues and choose command and control more often, but this did not happen. What did happen was that the answer to the morality question (i.e., saying that command and control was more moral than emissions trading) predicted the discrepancy between choice and efficiency (i.e., preferring command and control despite saying that trading was more efficient). Across subjects, the mean morality response had a correlation of 0.52 with this discrepancy score (41 subjects; $p = .0005$). This finding indicates that moral judgments lead people to go against economic efficiency.

Experiment 2: The Role of Information

Experiment 2 examined subjects' understanding of the role of information in the choice of regulatory policies.

Method

In November 2009, eighty-two subjects answered a questionnaire that began as follows, using the same method as the first experiment:

> The following scenarios ask you about government regulation of harmful pollution. The details of each scenario and the method of regulation may be different in each case so read each scenario carefully.
>   The possible methods of regulation are:
>
> • tax the pollution;
> • regulate the amount of pollution by law;
> • provide a government subsidy to the polluter for not polluting;
> • permit the polluter to be sued for pollution.
>
> There are 12 scenarios, with 4 questions after each.

The twelve scenarios, each presented on a page, consisted of three groups of four pages each. The groups differed in terms of information: perfect information for both government and victims (*Perfect*), imperfect government information (*Imperfect-govt*), and imperfect victim information (*Imperfect-vict*). The page in the perfect-information tax condition read as follows:

> Acme Steel has a plant that pollutes the water of a nearby town. The pollution is expected to cause $25,000 of damage annually to pipes and septic systems, but is not otherwise harmful. The government is considering whether to regulate the pollution.

> Imagine that the government has decided to tax pollution. The company can therefore pay a tax for polluting or reduce or eliminate the pollution it creates in order to avoid the tax.

> How much should the company have to pay annually in taxes for every $1,000 worth of expected damage it causes?

> Much less than $1,000
> Less than $1,000

Exactly $1,000
More than $1,000
Much more than $1,000

For the following questions, assume that the middle answer to the first question is in effect ("Exactly $1,000").

Compared to other ways of regulating pollution, how good is this policy on the whole? (1 = worst or as bad as the worst, 4 = average, 7 = best or as good as the best)

1   2   3   4   5   6   7

Compared to other ways of regulating pollution, how good is this policy for companies? (1 = worst or as bad as the worst, 4 = average, 7 = best or as good as the best)

1   2   3   4   5   6   7

Compared to other ways of regulating pollution, how good is this policy at reducing pollution? (1 = worst or as bad as the worst, 4 = average, 7 = best or as good as the best)

1   2   3   4   5   6   7

The descriptions for the other three methods of pollution control were as follows: "Imagine that the government is considering directly regulating the pollution by forcing the company to install a scrubber (a machine that successfully filters all the pollution)"; "Imagine that the government has decided to pay a subsidy to the company for not polluting. For every $1,000 worth of expected damages that the company can prevent by reducing pollution, the government will pay some amount"; and "Imagine that the government has decided to not regulate the pollution, but instead make the company liable for the harm the pollution causes. The company must therefore pay some amount for any damage it causes."

The valuation question about how much the company should have to pay was replaced with similar questions for the other methods—for example, questions asking about "the maximum price for a scrubber at which the government should pass this regulation," how much government should "pay the company for reducing $1,000 worth of damage," or how much "the company [should] have to pay for every $1,000 worth of damage it causes." Under the simplest assumptions, we took the normatively correct answer to be the one stated, for example, $1,000. This was always the middle of the five response options, so we looked at deviations from this middle option. This was also what the subject was asked to assume in answering the last three questions.

For the two information conditions, imperfect government information and imperfect polluter information, the relevant passages were,
respectively:

- The ABC Rubber manufactures tires using a process that pollutes
  groundwater with chemical D. The government does not know how
  much damage the pollution is expected to cause each year, but is considering various regulations.
- Acme Textile and ABC Chemical dye fabric using a process that pollutes a nearby river which serves as a town's water supply. The pollution is harmless except for the $60,000 in expected damage it causes
  to pipes annually. Both companies use the same chemicals in their
  dyes, so it is difficult, if not impossible, to prove which company is responsible for particular pollution.

Results

Table 7.1 shows the mean ratings of the four policies as a function of the
type of regulation and the type of information, and the difference between the ratings for companies and for pollution control. The asterisks
in the top panel show the theoretically optimal policies. In general, subjects preferred Regulation the most and Subsidy the least, regardless
of the information condition. The differences among methods were
significant.[6]

The main result of these questions about methods is that subjects
seemed completely insensitive to the theoretical arguments for one
method or another as a function of information.

This is not because they were responding randomly. They clearly understood, for example, that companies would benefit more from subsidies than from taxes. They also favored regulation and liability over
taxation and subsidies. An interpretation of all these responses is that
the respondents view regulatory methods as punishments that should be
invoked only when a polluter behaved badly. Taxes thus suffered because
they were invoked even for small amounts of pollution, as a kind of strict
liability. (Experiment 1 suggested that people need to be taught to think
of the benefits of pricing pollution rather than setting the same standard
for everyone.) And subsidies may be disfavored because they amounted
to paying people not to behave badly.

Further evidence of subjects' sensitivity comes from their responses
to the pricing question. As shown in Table 7.2, they thought liability
should be higher than simply the cost of the harm from the pollution.
Such a response could be justified by the assumption that the probability of a lawsuit for excessive pollution was less than 1, so the penalty had

Table 7.1. Results for Experiment 2: Judgments as Function of
Information Type and Method of Control

Condition	Liability	Regulation	Subsidy	Tax
Good on the Whole				
Imperfect-govt	4.60*	4.71	4.29	4.59
Imperfect-vict	4.65	5.05	4.21*	4.50*
Perfect	4.76*	5.20*	4.38*	4.71*
Good for Companies				
Imperfect-govt	4.38	4.23	4.94	4.34
Imperfect-vict	4.30	4.48	4.91	4.33
Perfect	4.29	4.59	5.00	4.41
Good for Reducing Pollution				
Imperfect-govt	4.29	4.55	4.38	4.40
Imperfect-vict	4.48	5.01	4.15	4.22
Perfect	4.43	5.23	4.30	4.37
Difference: Companies—Pollution				
Imperfect-govt	0.09	−0.32	0.56	−0.06
Imperfect-vict	−0.17	−0.54	0.77	0.11
Perfect	−0.13	−0.65	0.70	0.05

Note: Asterisks denote the theoretically optimal policies. Imperfect-govt =
imperfect government; Imperfect-vict = imperfect victim.

Table 7.2. Results for Experiment 2: Pricing Responses (Penalty
Relative to Cost)

Condition	Liability	Regulation	Subsidy	Tax
Imperfect-govt	0.73	0.05	0.11	−0.15
Imperfect-vict	0.63	0.12	−0.33	0.68
Perfect	0.68	0.29	−0.32	0.70

to be higher in order to provide sufficient deterrence. But subjects might
also have thought in terms of punitive damages, with the idea that bad
behavior should be punished.

Experiment 3: Role of Knowledge

Experiment 3 attempted to test in another way whether subjects could
think of the effects of government knowledge of harm and prevention
and the effects of victim knowledge on the suitability of various regulatory schemes. The study was a 3 × 3 × 2 design with eighteen pages, one
scenario per page. The three variables were government knowledge

about harm (high, medium, low), government knowledge about the cost of prevention (high, medium, low), and victim knowledge about harm (high, low). As manipulation checks, subjects were asked about how much knowledge government and potential victims have. Then they were asked about their confidence in four methods of control: taxes, subsidies, command-and-control regulation, and lawsuits.

If subjects are sensitive to the relevance of different kinds of knowledge, their confidence in taxes and subsidies should correlate positively with government knowledge about harm, as only such knowledge is needed to establish a tax or subsidy rate. Regulation should be high when government has knowledge of both harms and costs of prevention. Finally, confidence in litigation should correlate positively with victim knowledge of harm, as victims must be able to demonstrate they were harmed in order to sue.

Method

The general design was similar to that of Experiment 2: eighty-six subjects completed the questionnaire in December 2009. A typical scenario was as follows:

> Acme Bearings and Steel manufactures ball bearings and metal joints used in heavy machinery. The company uses a greasing agent that contaminates a residential water supply. Although some private studies suggest the chemical is a carcinogen, the government has not confirmed these assertions and has not studied ways the company could reduce the pollution.

This was "low" in all knowledge conditions: government harm, government cost of prevention, victim harm. The high government-harm-knowledge condition gave a monetary amount, for example,"$60,000 in damage it causes to pipes annually." The medium government-harm-knowledge condition involved certainty about the harm but no mention of its monetary value. Likewise, the government-cost-knowledge condition involved a price for high knowledge, but specific knowledge of the method of prevention without a price for medium knowledge. The high victim-knowledge cases involved immediate and obvious effects, for example, "damages pipes and stains glassware, sinks, and tiles."

The manipulation check and confidence questions were as follows:

How much information do you think the government has about the harm caused by the pollution? (1 = none, 4 = a fair amount, 7 = complete knowledge)

1   2   3   4   5   6   7

How much information do you think the government has about the cost to companies of eliminating the pollution? (1 = none, 4 = a fair amount, 7 = complete knowledge)

1   2   3   4   5   6   7

How much information do you think people affected by the pollution have about its effects? (1 = none, 4 = a fair amount, 7 = complete knowledge)

1   2   3   4   5   6   7

Please rate your confidence in the following methods of regulation for achieving the best outcome. (1 = no confidence, 7 = complete confidence)

Tax on pollution

1   2   3   4   5   6   7

Subsidy for not polluting

1   2   3   4   5   6   7

Enforce legal limits on the amount of pollution

1   2   3   4   5   6   7

Allow people harmed by pollution to sue companies

1   2   3   4   5   6   7

The confidence questions (the last group of questions) did not appear until the subject had answered the first three questions.

Results

In analyzing the data, we used the manipulation checks—the subjects' individual judgments of knowledge—as predictors of the confidence judgments. For GovCost (government cost) the manipulation check worked well, but it worked less well for GovHarm (government harm) and not at all for VicHarm (victim harm). Table 7.3 shows the regression coefficients predicting the confidence judgments from the knowledge judgments.[7] The asterisks in the table indicate the coefficients that should be high if subjects are sensitive to economically relevant factors. All coefficients were statistically significant (all $ts > 2.3$) except for the last two (0.024 and 0.053) for Lawsuit; the 0.053 is the one predictor in its row and column that should have been particularly high.

In sum, although subjects were sensitive to the idea that methods of regulation work better with more knowledge, they did not distinguish

Table 7.3. Results for Experiment 3: Regression Coefficients

Method	Knowledge type		
	GovHarm	*GovCost*	*VicHarm*
Tax	0.064*	0.069	0.080
Subsidy	0.071*	0.064	0.089
Regulation	0.075*	0.053*	0.099
Lawsuit	0.088	0.024	0.053*

Note: Asterisks indicate coefficients that should be high if subjects are sensitive to economically relevant factors. GovHarm = government knowledge about harm; GovCost = government knowledge about cost; VicHarm = victim knowledge about harm.

which methods require which kinds of knowledge. Other analyses of our data also supported this general conclusion.

Experiment 4: Taxes Versus Subsidies

Taxes and subsidies are roughly equivalent, but in Experiment 2 subjects showed a preference for more pollution reduction with taxes than with subsidies. Experiment 4 examines this preference further. The idea is to test whether people have different preferences for pollution reduction with taxes and subsidies. In all cases, the optimal answer is to pay a subsidy or collect a tax equal to the expected damages from the pollution.

Method

This study was completed by seventy-nine subjects, in December 2009, using the same methods as the other experiments. The introduction to the study read:

> Most products can only be produced if companies pollute. Electricity, plastics, rubber, etc. are created by processes that necessarily create some pollution.
> This study asks about regulating pollution using *taxes and subsidies.* With a tax, companies that pollute pay the government some amount for polluting. The tax is usually paid at the time raw materials are purchased (e.g., a company that makes plastic pays a sales tax on petroleum inputs). With subsidy policies, the government pays companies to abate pollution. Both taxes and subsidies give companies a financial incentive to not pollute as much as they otherwise would.

The study used eight cases, four involving subsidies and four involving taxes. The cases differed in the amount and type of damage. One tax case was as follows:

Acme Plastics creates plastics used by medical device manufactures. The production of the plastic produces water pollution that causes $2 million worth of annual damages. For every ton of plastic Acme produces, the pollution causes $500 worth of damage.

Imagine the government has decided to regulate the pollution using a tax. Acme Plastics will therefore have to pay the government some amount for the pollution it creates.

How much should Acme have to pay in taxes for every ton of plastic it manufactures?

An example of a subsidy item is as follows:

Acme Paper creates paper and cardboard that is sold by office supply companies. The production of the paper produces water pollution that causes $2 million worth of annual damages. For every ton of paper Acme produces, the pollution causes $500 worth of damage.

Imagine the government has decided to regulate the pollution using a subsidy. The government will therefore pay Acme some amount to reduce pollution.

How much should the government pay Acme in subsidies for eliminating $500 worth of damage?

The questions on each page were as follows. The last three questions appeared only after the subject answered the first two questions.

How much should Acme have to pay in taxes for every ton of plastic it manufactures?

Much less than $500
Less than $500
Exactly $500
More than $500
Much more than $500

How much damage do you think will be prevented with the tax you selected?

None
Less than the optimal amount
The optimal amount
More than the optimal amount
All

How good do you think this policy is at reducing pollution compared to a subsidy of the same amount? (1 = much worse, 4 = the same, 7 = much better)

1   2   3   4   5   6   7

How do you think this policy affects a company's profits?

Reduces profits
Does not affect profits
Increases profits

How do you think this policy would affect a government deficit?

Reduces the deficit
Does not affect the deficit
Increases the deficit

The "optimal amount," as defined by simple economic theory, was always the middle value in the first question. The order of cases was randomized for each subject.

Results

All analyses reported are based on a mixed model with random effects for subjects and cases. Tax versus subsidy was one of the predictors. The questions about effects on profits and on the deficit were included as manipulation checks, and they showed that, in general, subjects answered in the appropriate way.[8]

Overall, subjects did not significantly prefer taxes over subsidies. For the question about how good the policy was, the mean difference in rating (on the five-point scale provided) was 0.024. However, respondents did distinguish taxes and subsidies in the question about amount of the tax or subsidy, rating the tax penalty higher than the subsidy on the five-point scale (0.367 for tax, where 0 is the theoretically optimal amount that was the same as the harm cause, −0.082 for subsidy). Again, this result suggests that subjects saw the tax as a kind of punishment, so that additional penalty was required over the economic value of the harm. The subsidy, conversely, seems to have been interpreted as a simple transaction.

The amount of damages prevented by what the subject selected did not differ for taxes and subsidies; the mean was −0.684 for taxes and −0.614 for subsidies, on the five-point scale where 0 was the optimal amount. Subjects evidently thought that both mechanisms would be less than perfect.

General Discussion

In general, the results suggest that, without education in economic theory, citizens do not spontaneously understand the advantages of more efficient methods of pollution control. Instead, they seem to think of control in moral terms: if pollution is bad, then polluters must be punished.[9] Philosophers have also made moral arguments against cost-benefit analysis itself (e.g., E. Anderson 1993; Sagoff 1998).

All surveys had spaces for comments, and some of the comments illustrated this moral approach, which overlapped with ideological beliefs about government or corporations:

> "I know that it often saves money to allow companies to sell pollution credits, but I just cannot abide the practice. The heavier polluters should be forced to seek less offensive means of production. We destroy enough of the environment as it is without encouraging some companies to avoid trying to help it."
>
> "I picked the higher figures, because I figured they would at least be paying more for creating pollution."
>
> "Am I supposed to think saving companies' money is good? Subsidizing companies to stop what is wrong is wrong too."
>
> "Companies should be limited to the amount of pollution produced and not be allowed to sell their 'extra' allotments to other pollution producing companies."
>
> "I don't feel subsidies help, but taxes as a punishment hit home."
>
> "I would use fines for violations. Taxes and subsidies are negative words to me. Taxes and subsidies are not appropriate government actions. Prefer mandates."
>
> "SUBSIDY IS JUST ANOTHER GIVE AWAY TO BIG BUSINESS."

However, some subjects did indicate an understanding of the economic arguments. Responses like those that follow, combined with the results of the first study, suggest that some of the public's lack of understanding is simply the result of lack of education in economic theory (as argued by Baron and Ritov 1993):

> "I chose the option to allow companies to sell their 'pollution credits' each time because at any given time, one company's economic condition may make it less or more able to absorb the cost of cutting pollution. I think it is wise to provide a choice for the overall health of the industries to allow some trading back and forth depending on the likely fluctuating economic health of the companies involved."
>
> "I always think laws are the most effective in limiting bad outcomes. And suing might not be the best method when you can't prove which company is to blame for sure."
>
> "Why would the U.S. taxpayer want to pay subsidies that cost money rather than apply taxes that increase revenue? But, what the hell do I know."
>
> "How to assign a value without that knowledge?"
>
> "How will the govt be able to tell how much is NOT released? . . . no way to enforce that."

Finally, other responses seemed related to trust in various institutions: for example, "I have very little faith in our government to protect its citizens. And I have little hope that companies will self-regulate or follow legal limits on pollutants. Therefore I promote the ability of people to sue and be awarded if harmed." In the studies reported here, such responses are "noise," but the general issue of trust is surely relevant.

More generally, subjects may have thought that some policies could not be implemented well because of factors not included in the standard economic arguments. Yet one result that seems difficult to explain away by concerns about implementation is the lack of support for taxes as a method of control. Taxes, in the United States, are easy to collect, especially taxes on goods such as fuel.

In general, our results suggest that the disconnect between economic theory concerning efficient regulation and citizens' (and possibly legislators') preferences is the result of two factors: the failure to understand secondary effects of policies and moral judgments that equate pollution with, roughly, sin. If these factors were somehow reduced, then both sides of the controversy between too-much and too-little regulation might be less unhappy than they now are.

Appendix: Training for Experiment 1

Please read the follow passage and answer the following questions to check your comprehension.

Allocative efficiency is the economic term for the intuition, "you shouldn't do something if it's not worth the effort." The basic idea is that when deciding how much money to spend on something, if you are putting in more money than the value you receive from what you're buying, too much money is being spent. In other words, the resource is being used inefficiently.

Consider the following example:

Total Units of Pollution	Cost for Company A	Cost for Company B
1	$150	$180
2	$140	$160
3	$130	$140
4	$120	$120
5	$110	$100
6	$100	$80
7	$90	$60
8	$80	$40
9	$70	$20
10	$60	$5

If a society sets the maximum level of pollution for an industry of two firms to 6 units of pollution and the costs associated with pollution reduction are given above, what is the most efficient allocation of pollution rights? The answer here is for company A to produce 1 unit of pollution, while company B produces 5 units of pollution. Why? Consider if both A and B produced 3 units each. The cost associated with this would be $130 + $140 = $270. If company A trades rights with company B so that A produces 1 unit and B produces 5 units, the associated cost would be $150 + $100 = $250. Thus, the same level of pollution is reached, but for $20 less. This allocation is more efficient, or cost effective.

What is the total cost of the efficient allocation of 8 units of pollution?

200   210   220   230   240   250   260

What is the total cost of the efficient allocation of 4 units of pollution?

240   250   260   270   280   290   300

What is the total cost of the efficient allocation of 7 units of pollution?

200   210   220   230   240   250   260

Acknowledgment

This work was supported by a grant from the U.S.-Israel Bi-national Science Foundation to Jonathan Baron and Ilana Ritov.

Notes

1. The first author has often thought of trying to pay a neighbor to forgo his monster noise-and-fume-producing lawn mower. Although this would be legal, it would be seen as crazy.

2. Negligence and strict liability would both work this way, but they would differ in their effects on activity level, as would taxes and subsidies.

3. A third bird that could be killed with any reduction in U.S. oil use is the nation's dependence on foreign oil suppliers in a way that distorts both the balance of payments and, arguably, foreign policy. Indeed, President Obama, in his campaign, emphasized reducing "dependence on foreign oil" rather than addressing global warming.

4. Experiment 1 is based on an independent study project done by the second author, supervised by the first. The rest of the experiments were designed by the third author when he was a research assistant to the first author.

5. The remaining scenarios are available at http://finzi.psych.upenn.edu/baron/ex/reg/pr1.htm.

6. The differences among information conditions were also significant, but we have no hypothesis about them.

7. These coefficients were derived from a mixed model in which the confidence of each type was the dependent variable, the knowledge judgments were fixed effects, and subject identity was a random effect (Baayen et al. 2008). Random slopes for subjects were also included, but inclusion of random effects or random slopes for scenarios accounted for almost no variance and were omitted.

8. We did not count it as an error if subjects said there would be no effect, because they might think, for example, that income from a tax would be offset by lowering other taxes. Or in the case of profits, one subject commented, "Charging companies high fees as punishments for polluting communities does not reduce the pollution nor save lives since companies typically earn far more money than they have to pay in government regulation fees!"

9. As a caveat, it seems that when our subjects were asked about subsidies, they thought about companies getting them. Our examples encouraged that. Subjects were not prompted to think about home owners getting tax credits for installing solar panels; if they had been, perhaps they might have liked subsidies better.

References

Anderson, Elizabeth (1993) *Value in Ethics and in Economics.* Cambridge, Mass.: Harvard University Press.

Anderson, Terry, and Donald R. Leal (2001) *Free Market Environmentalism.* New York: Palgrave.

Baayen, R. Harald et al. (2008) "Mixed-Effect Modeling with Crossed Random Effects for Subjects and Items." *Journal of Memory and Language* 59: 390–412.

Baron, Jonathan, and Ilana Ritov (1993) "Intuitions About Penalties and Compensation in the Context of Tort Law." *Journal of Risk and Uncertainty* 7: 17–33.

Belliveau, Michael (1998) *Smoke Mirrors: Will Global Pollution Trading Save the Climate or Promote Injustice and Fraud?* San Francisco: Transnational Research and Action Center.

Keohane, Nathaniel O. et al. (1998) "The Choice of Regulatory Instruments in Environmental Policy." *Harvard Environmental Law Review* 22: 313–67.

Mankiw, N. Gregory (2007) "One Answer to Global Warming: A New Tax." *New York Times,* September 16.

McCaffery, Edward J., and Jonathan Baron (2006) "Isolation Effects and the Neglect of Indirect Effects of Fiscal Policies." *Journal of Behavioral Decision Making* 19: 1–14.

Ott, Hermann E., and Wolfgang Sachs (2000) "Ethical Aspects of Emissions Trading." Wuppertal Institute for Climate, Environment and Energy, Wuppertal Paper No. 110, September. http://www.wupperinst.org/uploads/tx_wibeitrag/WP110.pdf.

Sagoff, Mark (1998) *The Economy of the Earth: Philosophy, Law, and the Environment.* New York: Cambridge University Press.

Shavell, Steven (2004) *Foundations of Economic Analysis of Law.* Cambridge, Mass.: Belknap Press of Harvard University Press.

Stavins, Robert N. (2008) "Addressing Climate Change with a Comprehensive U.S. Cap-and-Trade System." *Oxford Review of Economic Policy* 24: 298–321.

Chapter 8

Delay in Notice and Comment Rulemaking

Evidence of Systemic Regulatory Breakdown?

Jason Webb Yackee and Susan Webb Yackee

Is the U.S. regulatory system broken? The events of recent years would seem to provide depressing evidence that it is. Recent accounts detail a financial system out of control, a massive environmental disaster in the Gulf of Mexico, and a *Salmonella* outbreak in the nation's food supply. These prominent cases suggest cause for concern, but they are also a call for new scholarly investigation and research. Do these accounts represent a "new normal" for the U.S. regulatory system? Or are they better understood as prominent outliers within an otherwise more competent regulatory process? Stated differently, every administrative law or regulatory policymaking scholar seems to know that it took the U.S. Food and Drug Administration (FDA) more than ten years to conclude regulatory proceedings that sought to determine whether the minimum peanut content of "peanut butter" should be 90 percent or 87 percent (Samaha 2006).[1] But is this proof that regulation generally takes too long (or is "ossified"), proof of a nightmarish "undue process" that has infected our administrative state, as Samaha (2006:603) has suggested?[2]

Before concluding that the regulatory system is broken—or even that it has recently become broken—it is worth thinking about how we might measure and observe this phenomenon. In this chapter, we focus largely on delay in the notice and comment rulemaking process as it takes place under Section 553 of the Administrative Procedure Act (1946).[3] Of course, delay is not the only possible conception of regulatory failure, and it might not even be the best one. But administrative law scholars have long focused on regulatory delay as highly undesirable and one of the principal evils of modern bureaucratic reality. Additionally, delay is relatively easily operationalized, unlike more ambitious notions of regulatory failure or success that might require weighing the social costs and benefits of regulatory actions taken or avoided.

Using a large data set of all substantive Section 553 rulemaking activities between 1983 and 2006, we find little evidence of systematic regulatory delay and, by extension, little evidence of regulatory breakdown as a generalized phenomenon of the administrative state. This is not to say that individual regulatory efforts are not sometimes significantly delayed. Delays on individual matters persist, as is evidenced in a recent example of the proposed rules governing sunscreen labeling, which, as the *New York Times* reported, took thirty-three years to develop (Harris 2011), and in the recent attempts to regulate egg safety by the U.S. Department of Agriculture and the FDA. In 1999, then President Clinton proposed reforms that would aim to reduce the occurrence of *Salmonella* in the nation's egg supply. However, the final rule was not issued until 2010—a delay, as the *New York Times* reported, that may have been caused by internal agency politics and a White House focused more on deregulatory policies than on protecting the public from tainted eggs (Martin 2010). However, such extreme delay in the promulgation of specific regulations, though newsworthy, is hardly proof that regulation in toto takes too long or is "ossified."

This chapter proceeds as follows: first, we discuss the importance of notice and comment rulemaking within the larger political system in the United States. Second, we briefly review the administrative law literature that argues that delay is factually widespread and normatively bad. Third, we present our data and analysis, which expands on our earlier work on this subject (Yackee and Yackee 2010, forthcoming). Finally, we offer a brief conclusion, suggesting that our analysis does not unveil evidence of systemic regulatory failure.

Notice and Comment Rulemaking

Schoolchildren have long been taught that Congress "makes" laws and that the executive branch "implements" them. They are less likely to recognize that implementing the law requires a significant amount of lawmaking itself. Federal agencies, charged with giving practical meaning to legislative commands that are often vague, ambiguous, and gap-filled, have enormous authority to shape both the amount of "law" in the political system and its substantive content through the formulation and promulgation of rules and regulations. Indeed, these regulations affect almost every facet of modern American life. Existing rules specify standards for power plant emissions, workplace safety, and child car seats, and future rules will likely cover such timely topics as derivative trading and capital bank standards (Chan 2010). Warren (2004:282) summarizes rulemaking's importance by noting the "truth, even though it might gravely shock those who wrote the Constitution . . . that more than 90 percent of modern American laws are rules (public policies) promulgated by agency administrators."

These various rules and regulations are often as legally binding on affected parties as any law passed by Congress and signed by the president. And although in many cases agency rules may be mere "details" attached to policy decisions already made by the political branches of government, in other cases agency rules amount to important and original statements of policy that can be of enormous practical, economic, and normative importance. The stakes in the administrative rulemaking process are, in other words, often quite high (Balla 1998; Coglianese 2002; Croley 2000; Golden 1998; Kerwin and Furlong 1992, 2011; Shapiro 2002; Spence 1999; West 1995, 2005; Yackee and Yackee 2006; Yackee 2006, forthcoming).

Notice and comment rulemaking is the process by which the majority of legally binding federal agency regulations are formulated, and it represents "the most important way in which the bureaucracy creates policy" (West 2005:655). Section 553 of the Administrative Procedure Act (APA) governs federal agency rulemaking, which typically begins with agency regulators publicly announcing a draft government regulation or a "Notice of Proposed Rulemaking" (NPRM). This draft regulation is then open for public comment. After receiving public feedback, agency officials generally promulgate a "final rule," which is enforceable as law.

Delay as Regulatory Failure

For some time, observers of the federal administrative process have pointed to excessive delay in developing and promulgating regulations as a major failure. Morgan (1978:21), for example, asserts that "A remarkably diverse group of citizens and political leaders, business executives and consumer advocates, economists and lawyers seem to agree on a fundamental point—something is wrong with much of the substance and procedure of regulation. Objections vary considerably, but high on many lists is the complexity of administrative procedure and the sheer time consumed in obtaining action of authorization from an agency." Macey (1992:93) similarly suggests that the administrative process suffers from "extraordinary" delay and cites a study finding that the "most frequently mentioned problem with . . . federal regulations" highlighted by lawyers was "undue delay."

The argument that the federal regulatory process takes too long is most influentially articulated in the literature on regulatory "ossification"

(McGarity 1992, 1997; Pierce 1995; Seidenfeld 1997; Verkuil 1995). The ossification literature argues that in the early years of the APA, it was relatively easy for agencies to develop and promulgate legally binding regulations. Judicial review was deferential, and neither the Congress nor the White House imposed much in the way of procedural hoops and hurdles on agency regulatory autonomy. This state of affairs is said to have shifted in the 1970s and 1980s. Federal courts reinterpreted the APA to require agencies to more carefully consider the factual and policy bases of their regulations. The White House began requiring agencies to screen their rulemakings through the President's Office of Management and Budget (OMB), which, among other things, imposed a cost-benefit analysis requirement on major rules (Croley 2003). Additionally, Congress began to command agencies to undertake time- and resource-consuming analyses of regulatory effects prior to rule promulgation (Eisner 1989).

The basic claim is that these various intrusions on bureaucratic autonomy are now so onerous that agencies' capacity to do their jobs, and to do it quickly, has been severely weakened. Although one implication of the ossification thesis is that federal agencies often fail to give us desirable regulations at all, another implication is that even when we might eventually get desirable regulations, we will get them later rather than sooner. That possibility is routinely portrayed as a malady, and a common malady at that. As Kerwin and Furlong (2011:105) note, "the general view that the pace of rulemaking is a problem is supported by several committees of the U.S. Congress, the recently reauthorized Administrative Conference of the United States, the federal courts, and elements of the private sector." Some ossification scholars have cited the prevalence and severity of such delay to justify proposals for radical change to the federal regulatory system, portraying the system, as it currently functions, as fundamentally broken. But is that view supported by evidence? In the following section we raise several doubts.

Data and Analysis

We use data from the Unified Agenda of Regulatory and Deregulatory Actions to investigate patterns of delay in notice and comment rulemaking. The Unified Agenda is published semiannually and summarizes the expected and pending substantive rulemaking activities of all federal agencies.[4] Federal agencies have been required to compile and distribute their regulatory agendas since 1978. However, comparable data are available only from 1983 and later. Each rulemaking activity is assigned a unique Regulatory Identifier Number (RIN), which allows us to track regulatory progress over time. For instance, we can identify when a particular regulatory initiative was formally commenced at the NPRM stage and then follow the RIN through time to identify when the agency completes the regulatory action.

Figure 8.1 provides a snapshot of the Unified Agenda data. We see here the total annual number of substantive NPRMs and final rules proposed and promulgated under APA Section 553 by all federal rule-writing agencies since 1983. We will not spend much time interpreting the figure, except to note that it shows, at the least, that the federal government proposes and promulgates hundreds of rules every year. Given how many regulations are regularly proposed and promulgated, it seems a stretch to characterize the system as "failing" or "broken," at least as measured by the volume of rulemaking outputs.

A real understanding of regulatory supply, of course, must be tied to baseline expectations regarding how many rules should be produced in a given year. We do not claim to know (nor do others purport to know) what the proper level of overall rulemaking activity should be. We are thus unable to say whether the levels illustrated in Figure 8.1 are "high" or "low" in an objective sense. However, one admittedly crude way of addressing the baseline expectations problem is to estimate congressional demand for rules. Agencies often initiate rulemaking activity in response to demands from Congress; as a result, we might expect the annual number of public laws passed by Congress to serve as a rough proxy for the amount of rulemaking that Congress expects from agencies. We

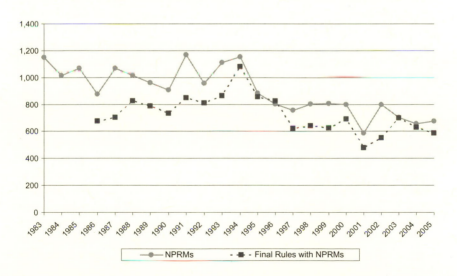

Figure 8.1. Volume of Rulemaking Activity. *Source:* Data come from the Unified Agenda.

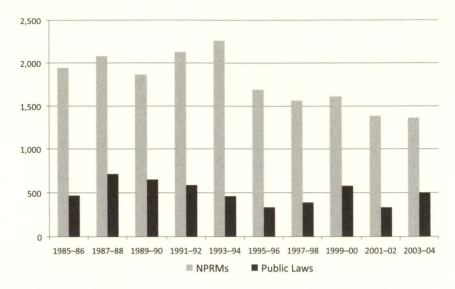

Figure 8.2. The Supply and Demand of Regulation. *Source:* Data come from the Unified Agenda and the Library of Congress.

might, in other words, reasonably anticipate the overall volume of agency rules to roughly track the number of public laws. Figure 8.2 plots the demand for rules, measured as the biannual number of public laws passed by Congress, with the biannual number of NPRMs. Figure 8.2 suggests, but certainly does not confirm, such a connection.

We can also use the Unified Agenda data to calculate average regulatory times to completion, measured from the date of NPRM publication to the date of publication of a final rule.[5] This allows us to examine the incidence of severe regulatory delay as an indicator of systemic regulatory failure. Tables 8.1 and 8.2 provide different visualizations of the data. In Table 8.1, we list the annual median and mean times to regulatory completion for all federal notice and comment rules from 1987 to 2006. We see that, on average, most NPRMs become final rules in remarkably little time. The median NPRM becomes a final rule in a year or less; the mean NPRM becomes a final rule in about one and a half years. The second table shows Kaplan-Meier estimates of rule time to completion. Here we show the number of months that it takes to promulgate 25 percent, 50 percent, and 75 percent of the NPRMs in the data set. For all rules promulgated from 1983 to 2006, we see that 50 percent are promulgated within thirteen months. The vast majority (75 percent) are promulgated within forty-one months. Those numbers are stable if we restrict our analysis to more recently promulgated rules

(1993–2006). They are also stable if we look only at "important" rules, proxied by whether the rule was subject to OMB review. In fact, rules subject to OMB review actually take less time to promulgate than non-reviewed rules. The vast majority (75 percent) of OMB-reviewed rules are finalized within thirty months; half of all OMB-reviewed rules are finalized in just one year.

We can sharpen our focus by examining the median time to completion for all finalized rules across the most prolific regulatory agencies.[6] Table 8.3 shows the top fifteen final rule-writing agencies in our data. Independent agencies (those that exist outside of the federal executive departments and hold greater independence from presidential influence) are italicized. This disaggregated view presents more variation in the numbers. We see that the U.S. Fish and Wildlife Service (FWS), the National Oceanic and Atmospheric Administration (NOAA), and the Internal Revenue Service (IRS) are far and away the most important sources of new regulations and that those three agencies differ markedly in their ability to finalize rules quickly. The median FWS rule takes a year; the median NOAA rule takes a mere three months; the IRS, meanwhile, needs eighteen months to promulgate a regulation. While

Table 8.1. Time to Rule Finalization in Months

	All Agencies	
Year	*Median*	*Mean*
1987	10	14
1988	10	15
1989	10	16
1990	13	19
1991	12	17
1992	12	18
1993	12	18
1994	12	18
1995	10	18
1996	10	19
1997	10	17
1998	10	17
1999	10	17
2000	10	16
2001	9	16
2002	11	20
2003	10	18
2004	10	19
2005	11	18
2006	12	18

Source: Data come from the Unified Agenda.

Table 8.2. Time to Rule Finalization

Period analyzed	Kaplan-Meier time estimates in months		
	25%	*50%*	*75%*
From 1983 to 2006			
All rules	6	13	41
From 1993 to 2006			
All rules	6	12	41
From 1983 to 2006			
Rules not reviewed by OMB	6	13	53
Rules reviewed by OMB	6	12	30

Source: Data come from the Unified Agenda.

the variability is interesting, and certainly might aid efforts to distinguish broken agencies from their well-functioning counterparts, it nonetheless seems striking that for almost all of the top fifteen, median time to finalization is well under two years. And we have to say "almost" only because the FDA needs twenty-four months—exactly two years—to push its median rule through the regulatory process.

Table 8.3 also lists the percentage of each agency's NPRMs that are abandoned prior to final promulgation. We might be tempted to view this column as an indicator of regulatory failure. We would caution, however, that high NPRM abandonment rates might not necessarily be a reliable sign of regulatory failure or breakdown. Although the ossification literature can certainly be read to suggest that more regulation is necessarily better, and that our regulatory system is in crisis because we are not getting the regulations that we collectively need, want, or deserve, we can safely assume that, depending on the survey language used, many Americans would prefer (wisely or foolishly) that the Federal Communications Commission (FCC) or the IRS did not regulate much of anything. Indeed, Newport (2010) reports Gallup polling data showing that 57 percent of Americans worry that government regulates business too much, while only 37 percent believe that there is not enough regulation of business.

Table 8.3 illustrates agency-level heterogeneity. While a simple average of all fifteen agencies' indicators finds a mean NPRM abandonment rate of 20 percent (or a completion rate of 80 percent), some agencies, such as NOAA, see barely any of their NPRMs fail to reach completion (approximately 7 percent). Other agencies—the IRS, the FDA, and above all the FCC—have abandonment rates that are much higher (34

Table 8.3. Finalization Rates for Top Fifteen Rule-Writing Agencies

Rank	Agency name	Acronym	Final rules	Median time to finalization in months	Mean time to finalization in months	Percentage of agency's NPRMs not finalized
1	U.S. Fish and Wildlife Service	FWS	1,297	12	16	11.02
2	National Oceanic and Atmospheric Administration	NOAA	1,005	3	7	6.79
3	Internal Revenue Service	IRS	973	18	28	34.07
4	Air and Radiation	OAR	487	14	19	16.60
5	National Highway Traffic Safety Administration	NHTSA	385	13	19	13.43
6	*Securities and Exchange Commission*	SEC	365	8	14	21.58
7	Federal Aviation Administration	FAA	349	17	27	18.92
8	*Office of Personnel Management*	OPM	336	7	12	12.68
9	*Nuclear Regulatory Commission*	NRC	314	12	17	9.67
10	Centers for Medicare and Medicaid Services	CMS	275	13	20	29.41
11	U.S. Coast Guard	USCG	266	10	20	22.55
12	Farm Service Agency	FSA	248	7	10	7.87
13	*Federal Communications Commission*	FCC	204	18	26	59.67
14	Social Security Administration	SSA	203	14	19	9.71
15	Food and Drug Administration	FDA	198	24	42	27.31

Note: Independent agencies are italicized.
Source: Data are from the Unified Agenda.

percent, 27 percent, and 60 percent, respectively). It is beyond the scope of this chapter to explain these agency-level differences, but we can imagine a few possibilities deserving of testing. One possibility is that agencies have different regulatory styles, customs, or norms, with some agencies preferring to invest significant pre-NPRM time and effort in crafting high-quality NPRMs that would attract little unwanted or unanticipated scientific, political, or legal controversy. Other agencies may prefer to use the NPRM process to float regulatory trial balloons, withdrawing unwise or underdeveloped proposals as their shortcomings are revealed during the notice and comment process. Another possibility is that increased abandonment rates are linked to the extent to which an agency's regulatory portfolio is inherently important, controversial, or both. For instance, the FCC's proposed rules are abandoned before final promulgation at a relatively high rate, but the FCC regulates one of America's favorite hobbies, TV watching, and its activities routinely invite intense congressional and media scrutiny. Perhaps the same cannot be said for the Farm Service Agency. We can get a sense of this by looking at how often the Congressional Record mentions either of these agencies. In 2002 alone, we find, according to *GPOAccess*, 137 hits for "Federal Communications Commission" and just 42 for "Farm Service Agency." Hits for 1995 were 141 and 22, respectively.

What about instances of severely delayed rules? After all, the demonstrable fact that the median rule takes only twelve or so months to complete does not contradict the suspicion that some rules take much longer to finish. We operationalize "severely delayed rules" as rules taking three years or more to move from NPRM to a final rule. In the data, approximately 10 percent of final rules are severely delayed, so the phenomenon is relatively rare. The disaggregated statistics are more interesting, however. Table 8.4 shows the top fifteen agencies ranked by their share of all severely delayed rules. The table also lists the percentage of each agency's own final rules that are "severely delayed."

In some ways, the list is not terribly surprising. Agencies with notoriously controversial regulatory histories and mandates see relatively larger percentages of their NPRMs severely delayed. The courts, for instance, have lambasted the Occupational Safety and Health Administration (OSHA) in the past for its dilatory regulatory practices; such litigation may result from, as OSHA claims, the agency's need to "juggle competing rulemaking demands on its limited scientific and legal staff." (*In re International Chemical Workers Union* 1992:1150). It is also probably relevant that OSHA's regulatory agenda is driven in part neither by its political masters nor by its exercise of bureaucratic expertise, but by petitions from interested parties for agency action. Note also that four U.S. Environmental Protection Agency (EPA) subunits or offices (OAR,

Table 8.4. Severely Delayed Rules, by Agency

Rank	Agency name	Acronym	Percentage of all severely delayed rules	Percentage of agency's final rules that were severely delayed
1	Internal Revenue Service	IRS	12.37	21.17
2	U.S. Fish and Wildlife Service	FWS	4.92	6.32
3	Federal Aviation Administration	FAA	4.38	20.92
4	Food and Drug Administration	FDA	3.96	33.33
5	Air and Radiation	OAR	3.24	11.09
6	*Federal Communications Commission*	FCC	2.76	22.55
7	Centers for Medicare and Medicaid Services	CMS	2.58	15.64
8	National Highway Traffic Safety Administration	NHTSA	2.58	11.17
9	Office of Prevention, Pesticides and Toxic Substances	OPPTS	2.52	22.58
10	Solid Waste and Emergency Response	SWER	2.40	20.51
11	Water	WATER	2.16	21.56
12	National Oceanic and Atmospheric Administration	NOAA	1.98	3.28
13	Occupational Safety and Health Administration	OSHA	1.98	48.53
14	U.S. Coast Guard	USCG	1.92	12.03
15	*Nuclear Regulatory Commission*	NRC	1.62	8.60

Note: Independent agencies are italicized.
Source: Data come from the Unified Agenda.

OPPTS, SWER, and WATER) make the list, each contributing between about 2 and 3 percent of all severely delayed rules. For three of those subunits, severely delayed rules make up over 20 percent of their promulgated rules. Perhaps not surprisingly, the EPA also experiences a good deal of petitioner demand for agency action, and when it refuses to perform as demanded, it suffers lawsuits alleging excessive regulatory delay and inaction.[7]

The FDA also contributes a large percentage of delayed rules (nearly 4 percent) and sees about one-third of its own final rules severely delayed. Perhaps the one surprise is that the IRS tops the list; of the nearly one thousand rules that it promulgated in the underlying sample, 206, or 21 percent, took three years or longer to promulgate. We can only speculate here as to the determinants of IRS regulatory practice, but we can conjecture that the reason that some IRS rulemakings take so long is not an ossification-like fear within the Service that their rules will be overturned by "hard look" courts strictly policing procedural compliance with an enhanced APA. We know this because IRS regulations are hardly ever challenged—or challengeable—for APA violations (Hickman 2011). The reason for IRS delay in rulemaking may be even less than what it seems once we recognize that the Treasury has a habit of issuing legally binding "temporary" regulations, often getting around to issuing a proper NPRM only after the fact (Hickman 2011). The incentive for an agency to push an NPRM through to finalization may decline markedly where a final rule is not necessary to legally bind regulatory targets. Thus, although these data may appear to suggest that the IRS's rulemaking operations are highly protracted, in fact they may be anything but.

Our speculative explanations for IRS practice reflect sensitivity to the fact that "administrative law" is not necessarily one of universal content or experience. As Hickman (2011) points out, at least since the 1960s agencies have differed greatly in the procedures that they follow when regulating, in the contours of the statutes that authorize and guide their behavior, and even in the doctrines that courts apply when, for example, deciding whether an agency action is an abuse of discretion. But useful explanations for regulatory delay (or failure) do not necessarily have to be fully particularized. We can use the Unified Agenda data to look for the determinants of delay, as we did in Yackee and Yackee (2010). For instance, there we presented results from Cox proportional hazards models that showed that several key procedural constraints actually speed up most agency rulemakings—a finding contrary to the ossification thesis. Additionally, our forthcoming article employed data on all notice and comment regulations promulgated by the U.S. Department of the Interior (DOI) from 1950 to 1990 (Yackee and Yackee, forthcoming). We examined whether DOI agencies promulgated fewer rules in the supposedly ossified era of 1976–90 than they did in earlier years; whether there is evidence of a movement away from rules toward ostensibly illegal regulation via more informal policy devices; and whether notice and comment regulations took significantly longer to complete in the allegedly ossified era. We found that the federal agencies in our study remained able to promulgate large volumes of rules and did not appear to be substituting informal policy devices for notice and comment regulations. Additionally, although rules did take longer to complete in the ossified era than before it, the majority of supposedly ossified regulations were promulgated within one year of proposal and the vast majority were promulgated within two years.

In this chapter we perform a simpler analysis, using t tests to identify statistically significant differences in theoretically interesting rule-level variables across groups of severely delayed and non-severely delayed rules. For example, a t test indicates that congressional deadlines for agency action might help prevent severe delay; at the least, severely delayed rules are less likely to have been promulgated under a congressional deadline. Conversely, severely delayed rules are more likely to be subject to court deadlines, implying either that court deadlines paradoxically contribute to severe delay or that courts tend to be asked to issue deadlines where a given regulatory effort is already severely delayed, as Gersen and Connell (2008) have suggested. Significantly delayed rules tend to have statistically significantly longer NPRM abstracts (arguably a proxy for rule complexity), but we find no statistically significant difference in the issuing department's number of employees or budget when comparing the two groups of rules. In other words, department resources do not seem to be related to severe rule delay. Severely delayed rules are, surprisingly, no more likely to be economically significant, that is, having an annual impact of $100 million or more. Perhaps less surprising, severe delay is more likely to occur when an NPRM is issued under a Republican rather than a Democratic presidential administration.

Discussion

Neither hazards models nor more simplistic t tests can provide definitive evidence of or explanations for regulatory failure. Our basic aim in this chapter has instead been to suggest some ways in which scholars interested in regulatory failure might begin to operationalize and test their intuition that too often regulatory efforts drag on if not quite forever, then certainly for "too long." Large-n data on the regulatory state have become increasingly available in recent years, a bounty that has enabled the emergence of what might be called the "new empirical administrative law" (e.g., Coglianese 2002; Croley 2003; Gersen and O'Connell 2008; O'Connell 2008; Yackee and Yackee 2010, forthcoming). These data begin to allow us to examine whether regulatory failure is a systemic characteristic of our modern U.S. administrative state. They also allow us to judge the performance of different agencies and different rules on a comparative basis, letting us move more confidently from systemic to particularistic judgments. Only once we have identified the problem with reasonable empirical certainty and conceptual clarity can or should we begin to talk about useful potential reforms. If we find evidence of systemic problems, then reform ideas may be properly systemic in focus. But where problems appear isolated to particular circumstances and situations, the best reform ideas will probably be narrower in their scope and ambition, less concerned with what Mashaw (2010:978) calls "transsubstantive statutes and ubiquitous judicial review"—for example, drafting a "new APA" or formulating a "new Chevron"—and more concerned with the internal and often agency-specific procedures and practices that shape and influence individual agency processes in important ways.

Our analysis here, and the fuller discussion contained in our larger research project on ossification, provides suggestive evidence against the notion that our administrative state is systemically broken or prone to failure, if the reader agrees with us that delay in rulemaking is a relevant place to look. Most federal agencies seem able to promulgate a good number of regulations when they want to, and to do so relatively quickly. Agencies operating in complex and contentious policy environments may have more difficulty doing things that reasonable people think they should do, and there may be costs to such agency inaction. Agency-specific or regulation-specific delay is a potentially serious concern, and explaining it and preventing it ought to be a focus of future scholarship. But even if such delay occurs, and even if it is severe enough to be evidence of a "failure" of some sort, the failure may be a political failure rather than a regulatory failure. We ask agencies such as OSHA to tackle enormously complicated social problems, and we ask them to do it quickly. Moreover, we often suggest that we are asking agencies to provide nothing but "expert" decisions in the instrumental pursuit of politically settled value choices, and that the agencies are capable of providing them, when in fact we may be simply transferring the task of making hard and eminently contestable political choices from one branch of government to another. That agencies sometimes fail to act, or sometimes take a very long time to act, is probably at least in part an inevitable consequence of what we ask them to do. And given the contestable nature of what they often are asked to do (or decide to attempt to do), their failure to do it, or to do it quickly, may not always be a bad thing.

Notes

1. Although the regulatory question may seem substantively silly, in fact a 90 percent standard would have forced two of the most popular brands of peanut butter at the time, Skippy and Peter Pan, to change their formulas (*Corn Products Co. v. Dep't of Health, Education and Welfare, Food and Drug Administration* 1970).

2. For Samaha, "undue process" means "the point at which government decision making becomes too tardy, or too inclusive, or too careful as a matter of law" (Samaha 2006:603).

3. Section 553 rulemaking does not encompass the sum total of the modern administrative state. It is undoubtedly true, however, that Section 553 provides a critical arena in which regulatory battles are won or lost.

4. The Unified Agenda, like all data sources, is not without its flaws. For example, it relies on agencies to self-report information on their rulemaking activities; however, there are few incentives for agencies to systematically misrepresent the dates of NPRMs and final rules, which are also published in the *Federal Register.*

5. Because NPRMs are the first publicly available evidence of the beginning of a given regulatory process, it is logical to rely on them as the official start of that process. In fact, however, agencies begin working on regulations prior to the issuance of an NPRM, though systematically identifying that actual start date for a large sample of rules across multiple agencies is currently not feasible.

6. The distribution for the time-to-completion variable is single-peaked (i.e., it is a unimodal distribution), and the distribution also suggests that the majority of completed rules are finalized relatively quickly. There is also a relatively thin yet long right-side tail, indicating that a small percentage of rules take many months, indeed multiple years, to finalize.

7. For examples of such litigation, see *Raymond Proffitt Foundation v. U.S. Environmental Protection Agency* and *National Resources Defense Council v. U.S. Environmental Protection Agency.* It may be possible that many severely delayed rules, and perhaps the lawsuits they sometimes engender, involve rules that the agency does not itself support and that it is pursuing halfheartedly at best.

References

Balla, Steven J. (1998) "Administrative Procedures and Political Control of the Bureaucracy." *American Political Science Review* 92: 663–73.

Chan, Sewell (2010) "Regulators to Write New Financial Rules in the Open." *New York Times*, August 14.

Coglianese, Cary (2002) "Empirical Analysis and Administrative Law." *University of Illinois Law Review* 2002: 1111–38.

Croley, Stephen P. (2000) "Public Interested Regulation." *Florida State University Law Review* 28: 7–107.

——— (2003) "White House Review of Agency Rulemaking: An Empirical Investigation." *University of Chicago Law Review* 70: 820–85.

Eisner, Neil (1989) "Agency Delay in Informal Rulemaking." *Administrative Law Journal* 3: 7–52.

Gersen, Jacob E., and Anne Joseph O'Connell (2008) "Deadlines in Administrative Law." *University of Pennsylvania Law Review* 156: 923–90.

Golden, Marissa Martino (1998) "Interest Groups in the Rule-Making Process: Who Participates? Whose Voices Get Heard?" *Journal of Public Administration and Theory* 8: 245–70.

Harris, Gardiner (2011) "F.D.A. Unveils New Rules About Sunscreen Claims." *New York Times*, June 14.

Hickman, Kristin E. (2011) "Response: Agency-Specific Precedents: Rational Ignorance or Deliberate Strategy." *Texas Law Review* 89: 89–112.

Kerwin, Cornelius M., and Scott R. Furlong (1992) "Time and Rulemaking: An Empirical Test of Theory." *Journal of Public Administration and Theory* 2: 113–38.

——— (2011) *Rulemaking: How Government Agencies Write Law and Make Policy*, 4th ed. Washington, D.C.: CQ Press.

Macey, Jonathan R. (1992) "Organizational Design and Political Control of Administrative Agencies." *Journal of Law, Economics, and Organization* 8: 93–110.

Martin, Andrew (2010) "Egg Recall Exposes Flaws in Nation's Food Safety System." *New York Times*, August 24.

Mashaw, Jerry L. (2010) "The American Model of Federal Administrative Law: Remembering the First One Hundred Years." *George Washington Law Review* 78: 975–92.

McGarity, Thomas O. (1992) "Some Thoughts on 'Deossifying' the Rulemaking Process." *Duke Law Journal* 41: 1384–462.

———— (1997) "The Courts and the Ossification of Rulemaking: A Response to Professor Seidenfeld." *Texas Law Review* 75: 525–58.

Morgan, Thomas D. (1978) "Toward a Revised Strategy for Ratemaking." *University of Illinois Law Forum*, 1978: 21–50.

Newport, Frank (2010) "Americans Leery of Too Much Gov't Regulation of Business." *Gallup*, http://www.gallup.com/poll/125468/Americans-Leery-Govt-Regulation-Business.aspx.

O'Connell, Anne Joseph (2008) "Political Cycles of Rulemaking: An Empirical Portrait of the Modern Administrative State." *Virginia Law Review* 94: 889–986.

Pierce, Richard J. (1995) "Seven Ways to Deossify Agency Rulemaking." *Administrative Law Review* 47: 59–95.

Samaha, Adam (2006) "Undue Process." *Stanford Law Review* 59: 601–72.

Seidenfeld, Mark (1997) "Demystifying Deossification: Rethinking Recent Proposals to Modify Judicial Review of Notice and Comment Rulemaking." *Texas Law Review* 75: 483–524.

Shapiro, Stuart (2002) "Speed Bumps and Roadblocks: Procedural Controls and Regulatory Change." *Journal of Public Administration Research and Theory* 12: 29–58.

Spence, David B. (1999) "Agency Discretion and the Dynamics of Procedural Reform." *Public Administration Review* 59: 425–42.

Verkuil, Paul R. (1995) "Comment: Rulemaking Ossification—A Modest Proposal." *Administrative Law Review* 47: 453–59.

Warren, Kenneth F. (2004) *Administrative Law in the Political System*, 4th ed. Boulder, Colo.: Westview Press.

West, William F. (1995) *Controlling the Bureaucracy: Institutional Constraints in Theory and Practice.* New York: M. E. Sharpe.

———— (2005) "Administrative Rule-Making: An Old and Emerging Literature." *Public Administration Review* 65: 655–68.

Yackee, Jason Webb, and Susan Webb Yackee (2006) "A Bias Toward Business? Assessing Interest Group Influence on the Bureaucracy." *Journal of Politics* 68: 128–39.

———— (2010) "Administrative Procedures and Bureaucratic Performance: Is Federal Rule-making 'Ossified'?" *Journal of Public Administration Research and Theory* 20: 261–82.

———— (forthcoming) "Testing the Ossification Thesis: An Empirical Examination of Federal Regulatory Volume and Speed, 1950–1990." *George Washington Law Review.*

Yackee, Susan Webb (2006) "Sweet-Talking the Fourth Branch: Assessing the Influence of Interest Group Comments on Federal Agency Rulemaking." *Journal of Public Administration Research and Theory* 26: 103–24.

———— (forthcoming) "The Politics of *Ex Parte* Lobbying: Pre-Proposal Agenda Building and Blocking During Agency Rulemaking." *Journal of Public Administration Research and Theory.*

Cases Cited

Corn Products Co. v. Dep't of Health, Education and Welfare, Food and Drug Administration, 427 F.2d 511, 513 (3rd Cir. 1970).
In re International Chemical Workers Union, 958 F.2d 1144 (D.C. Cir. 1992).
Natural Resources Defense Council v. U.S. Environmental Protection Agency, 93 F. Supp. 531 (S.D. N.Y. 2000).
Raymond Proffitt Foundation v. U.S. Environmental Protection Agency, 930 F.Supp. 1088 (E.D. Pa. 1996).

Statute Cited

Administrative Procedure Act of 1946, 5 U.S.C. §551 et seq.

Chapter 9
The Policy Impact of Public Advice
The Effects of Advisory Committee Transparency on Regulatory Performance

Susan L. Moffitt

The influence of the Food and Drug Administration (FDA) reaches beyond its formal authority and into global pharmaceutical research, development, and marketing (Carpenter 2010:1–2). Despite this image of domestic and international prominence, a series of food and drug recalls over the past decade have exposed weaknesses in the FDA's regulatory processes and in the public's confidence in its work. Although public opinion about the FDA varies, one widely reported 2009 poll suggests that 52 percent of respondents gave the FDA negative ratings for "ensuring the safety of imported prescription drugs" (Harris 2009:1). Respondents were evenly split—47 percent positive to 47 percent negative—on the FDA's overall ability to ensure prescription drug safety and efficacy, which stands in contrast to the 56 percent positive rating the agency enjoyed in 2004 (Harris 2009:3).[1]

Although agency approval ratings reflect predictable, albeit sometimes temporary, declines in public support following a scandal, systematic reviews of the FDA have revealed underlying structural weaknesses in the agency's drug review and post-marketing monitoring processes. These weaknesses include insufficient opportunities for staff from the Office of Surveillance and Epidemiology to participate in the drug review process, an ineffective system for reporting and monitoring drug adverse events, and insufficient in-house expertise (Institute of Medicine 2007:6–9). As the final chapter in this volume reminds us, the FDA continues to lack regulatory authority over some key domains, such as off-label drug use and drug pricing (see Ruger this volume).

A perceived lack of transparency in the FDA's regulatory processes and concerns about the agency's relationship to the firms it regulates accompany some of these structural challenges and figure prominently in calls for agency reform. "The FDA has a relationship with drug companies that is far too cozy," Senator Charles Grassley alleged in 2004 at Senate hearings convened to investigate the withdrawal of the blockbuster arthritis drug Vioxx from the market in response to concerns that it increased heart attacks and strokes. The remedy for the FDA's coziness with industry, the senator asserted, would entail "changes inside the FDA that [would] result in greater transparency and greater openness" (U.S. Senate Committee on Finance 2004). In its subsequent review of U.S. drug safety, the Institute of Medicine (IOM) similarly claimed that "the FDA's reputation has been hurt by a perceived lack of transparency and accountability to the public" (IOM 2007:17). As part of its package of proposals to improve the agency's impaired reputation, the IOM called on the FDA to make greater use of its public advisory committees, to limit committee members' financial conflicts of interest, and to enhance transparency in the drug approval process (IOM 2007:9–10).

The FDA, however, had publicly reviewed and discussed Vioxx long before Senator Grassley's admonishment and before the IOM's charge: the agency consulted with its Arthritis Drugs Advisory Committee to review Vioxx's safety and efficacy both in 1999 and again in 2001. Both meetings invited nonbinding advice from technical experts and consumer representatives in front of large public audiences. However, critics charged that the public meetings had not been "public" enough, either in the sense of visibility or accessibility. Committee deliberations can shine light on agencies' regulatory decisions and bring policy issues into visible, permeable venues. They can also offer individuals and groups a seat at government agencies' policymaking tables that excluded interests may not otherwise enjoy. Reports surfaced, however, that the FDA had failed to reveal all of its information at its public meetings and that some members of the public committees had financial ties to Merck and other pharmaceutical companies. As the IOM argued, "[The] FDA's credibility is its most crucial asset and recent concerns about the independence of advisory committee members . . . along with broader concerns about scientific independence in the biomedical research establishment, have cast a shadow on the trustworthiness of the scientific advice received by the agency" (IOM 2007: 9). The policy narrative that has emerged following Vioxx's withdrawal points to a broader puzzle confronting transparency policies in regulatory politics. To what extent can a lack of policymaking transparency be linked with evidence of impaired product quality and regulatory failure?

This chapter uses the case of the drug regulation to build on recent scholarship on the impact of procedures on regulatory performance (Carpenter et al. 2012). Analyzing new molecular entities (NMEs) that have been approved between 1986 and 2009, the evidence presented in this chapter suggests that FDA consultation with an advisory committee reduces the likelihood of post-marketing drug safety problems when the advisory committee consists of members with few or no conflicts of interests. Advisory committee consultation overall, however, does not appear to be systematically associated with measures of improved product safety. These results suggest a nuanced story for the policy impact of public advice. Transparency through public advice may promote the flow of information into and out of government agencies, possibly informing agency policymaking and possibly assisting regulatory performance. But its contribution ultimately depends on the quality of the information it helps distribute.

Transparency Through Public Advice

The U.S. public advisory committee system is vast, consisting of over one thousand committees—ranging from the Federal Advisory Council on Occupational Safety and Health and the National Drinking Water Advisory Council to the Advisory Committee on Nuclear Reactor Safeguards—and filled with over sixty thousand appointed members (General Services Administration 2011). Scholars and policymakers habitually look to public advisory committees to bring both greater expertise—especially in the context of policies that involve evolving technologies and knowledge—and greater transparency and access to agency policymaking (IOM 2007; National Academies 2005; Rettig et al. 1992; Weimer 2007).

Yet, for well over half a century, critics of U.S. federal advisory committees have worried about the committees' potential to privilege dominant group interests, especially large firms; to exclude general public interest groups and other organizations; to compromise agency expertise; and to promote secrecy rather than transparency in agency work. Allegations in the 1950s that the antitrust division of the Department of Justice (DOJ) used its public committees to benefit the firms it was charged to oversee led to DOJ directives, which in turn informed subsequent executive orders and ultimately the Federal Advisory Committee Act of 1972 (Croley and Funk 1997). These guidelines and directives sought to make public meetings more transparent and to give agencies explicit authority over committee operations—including over committee agendas and meeting times—to help ensure that government agencies, not firms or other interests, were setting the terms of transparency (Croley and Funk 1997:459).

Concerns about federal advisory committees have persisted nonetheless (Karty 2002; Petracca 1986). Some scholars raise doubts that expert public advice has a meaningful effect on agency policymaking or that agencies "hear anything [at advisory committee meetings] they could not have anticipated" (Heimann 1997:154; Kaufman 1981:40). Other research documents incentives for firms to enlist the same experts the agency consults (Glodé 2002), and some suggests that committee members are pressured to come to a consensus and recommend product approval despite safety concerns (Zuckerman 2006). A review of conflicts of interest in FDA drug advisory committees between 2001 and 2004 found some association between committee members with conflicts of interest and product-approval voting patterns. However, the study also found that excluding members with conflicts would not have changed the outcome of the advisory committee vote (Lurie et al. 2006).[2] The FDA argues that granting waivers that allow advisory committee members with some types of potential conflicts of interest to participate in committee meetings enables the agency to receive vital expertise from eminent scholars in the field; and the agency commissioned a study documenting that members with more expertise are more likely to receive conflict-of-interest waivers (Ackerley et al. 2007).

Despite sustained interest in the effects of conflicts of interest on regulatory performance, scholarship has been unable to detect a meaningful association between those conflicts of interest and the ultimate quality of regulatory decisions. Policymakers and scholars continue to claim that expert advice should cultivate product quality and that conflicts of interest at a minimum tarnish agency reputations (IOM 2007). Yet it remains unclear both whether and how committee reviews or conflicts of interests bear on the product quality that regulatory oversight is supposed to ensure. This chapter considers two sets of questions to advance this debate. The first set involves frequency and access: are agencies able to use public advice for policy tasks when uncertainty is high and when the agency stands to benefit from external expertise? The second set considers quality: does public expert advice bear on ultimate policy outcomes? What are the characteristics of advice that matter to product safety, and what are possible mechanisms of influence?

Conditions for Public Advice

As part of its package of proposals to improve drug safety, the IOM proposed that the FDA send all NMEs to one of the agency's public advisory committees for review either before the agency approves the drug or shortly afterward (IOM 2007:133). This proposal arose partly as a response to the claim of some FDA staffers that deadlines created as part of the Prescription Drug User Fee Act of 1992 discourage the FDA from consulting with public advisors: the deadlines make it more difficult for the FDA to consult with advisors and satisfy deadline requirements (U. S. Department of Health and Human Services 2003; U. S. Government Accountability Office 2006; IOM 2007). The FDA did not adopt this recommendation and presently consults with its advisors for fewer than half of the NMEs that it approves.[3] The IOM recommendation implies the FDA's crisis of confidence may stem partly from matters of insufficient public meeting frequency and access.

With a primary sample consisting of NMEs approved between 1986 and 2009, the following analyses use generalized linear models for panel data and mixed effects models (McCullagh and Nelder 1989) to assess the conditions of FDA advisory committee consultations before the approval of NMEs.[4] The unit of analysis is the drug, and committee consultation is a dichotomous measure of whether the drug was reviewed by one of the FDA's advisory committees before the agency reached its approval decision.[5] Of the 565 approved drugs in the primary sample, 224 went to an advisory committee for review before the FDA reached its approval decision.

Given the FDA's assertion that it consults with its advisors for its "close calls" or its most uncertain cases, we expect a drug's priority status to be positively associated with advisory committee consultations. A drug's designation as a priority review reflects its innovation: its potential contributions to effectiveness, compliance, and safety. Along with innovation, however, comes potential uncertainty: the drug formulation is new and has not been tested in practice, outside of experimental conditions, in unrestricted patient populations who take multiple therapies. Priority drugs represent the potential for greater drug safety and greater drug efficacy, and yet they also represent the potential for greater risk as they are introduced into the market. A drug's priority status is a dichotomous measure, coded as 1 if the drug was a priority review.

Scholarship suggests that firms and groups may use public participation to obtain a place in agency policymaking they would not otherwise enjoy; or that firms and groups that already enjoy privileged access to agency policymaking may induce agencies to keep tasks sensitive to those interests away from broader, more inclusive public participation. If firms or groups influence public advisory committee agendas, systematic patterns could emerge in either direction. To measure potential firm prominence, the models include a count of the number of drugs each firm previously submitted to the FDA. To assess group demand for new therapies, the models include measures of the drug's novelty. Novelty is measured as the log of the number of drugs previously approved to treat the disease represented in each drug's primary indication, with a higher count representing lower drug novelty.

The models add measures for the year of the drug's submission. Consistent with Carpenter et al. (2012), the models include an index of the drugs' primary indications. This allows the models to consider significant but potentially unobservable differences between diseases the drugs are indicated to treat as well as to help account for FDA division characteristics.[6]

As predicted and consistent with the FDA's claims, priority drugs are 3.7 times more likely than standard drugs to be sent to an advisory committee for a pre-approval review. Neither the measure of drug novelty (reflecting demand for the drug) nor the measure of firm experience achieves conventional levels of statistical significance. The measure of time suggests a decreasing likelihood of advisory committee consultations in more recent years. A second set of models introduces a dichotomous measure of whether the drugs were submitted to the FDA before or after the introduction of deadlines under the Prescription Drug User Fee Act. Results from Table 9.1 suggest that drugs reviewed after the

Table 9.1. Pre-Approval Advisory Committee Consultations (NMEs Approved 1986–2009, Random Effects Logistic Regression)

Variable	Advisory Committee Yearly Controls Model		Advisory Committee Deadline Model	
	Coefficient (SE)	Odds ratio (SE)	Coefficient (SE)	Odds ratio (SE)
Priority review	**1.321**	**3.745**	**1.270**	**3.562**
	(0.238)	(0.892)	(0.241)	(0.860)
Firms' prior approvals	0.007	1.007	0.006	1.006
	(0.009)	(0.009)	(0.009)	(0.009)
Drug novelty	0.015	1.015	−0.013	0.987
	(0.122)	(0.124)	(0.127)	(0.125)
Year of submission	**−0.082**	**0.922**		
	(0.018)	(0.017)		
Deadline			**−1.088**	**0.337**
			(0.248)	(0.083)
Constant	161.829		−0.416	
	(36.523)		(0.327)	
# of primary indications	180		180	
# of NME observations	565		565	
Log likelihood	−336.739		−337.038	

Note: Boldface denotes statistical significance at the $p < .05$ level (all tests are two-tailed). NME = new molecular entities.

introduction of deadlines are significantly less likely to receive pre-market advisory committee consultation than drugs reviewed before the deadline regimes began at the FDA. Carpenter et al. (2012) extend this finding to suggest that drugs approved right before the deadline elapses are also significantly less likely to receive an advisory committee review.

Although the FDA appears to target its priority drugs for advisory committee reviews, these results also lend support to FDA staffers' concerns that deadlines may impair the agency's ability to consult with advisors before reaching an approval decision. Drug review deadlines have been associated with greater post-marketing safety problems for drugs that are approved right before their deadlines (Carpenter et al. 2008, Carpenter et. al., 2012). What effects emerge from potentially limiting the use of advisory committees? Do public committees hold promise of ensuring drug safety?

Policy Impact of Public Advice

Prevailing scholarship predicts that expert public advice should promote regulatory quality (IOM 2007) and speculates that reductions in advisory committee consultation may help account for the negative effects that drug review deadlines have on drugs' safety portfolios (Carpenter et al. 2012), but it also finds that advisory committee consultation does not yield safer drug portfolios in general (Moffitt 2010). This analysis goes further by assessing the conditions under which expert public advice may support product safety, using two measures of a drug's post-marketing safety. One is a dichotomous indicator of whether an approved drug later received a new, post-market boxed warning on its label for a significant new adverse drug reaction (Lasser et al. 2002). A second indicator measures FDA drug-specific safety alerts—such as safety-related letters, press releases, and health advisories released by the FDA and by pharmaceutical firms from 1996 through 2011—for NMEs approved from 1996 to 2009.[7] Each of the following generalized linear models examines the overall relationship between advisory committee consultation and drug safety. Each model then looks within the subset of drugs that went to advisory committees to assess differential effects of drugs that were reviewed by committees that did or did not have committee members who received waivers to participate in the meetings, despite their financial conflicts of interest.

The models include an index of drugs' primary indications to account for unobserved drug and agency characteristics. Nevertheless, we might worry that the riskiest drugs—those with the greatest chance of future post-marketing problems—are the most likely to receive advisory committee reviews and warrant waivers. Supplemental models reported in the technical appendix to this chapter offer both coarsened exact matching models (Iacus et al. 2011) and treatment-effects models to reduce the likelihood further that these results stem from unobserved differences between drugs that did and did not receive advisory committee reviews, or between drugs that did and did not have committee members with conflicts of interest.

Consistent with the advisory committee agenda-setting models in the previous section, each model contains a dichotomous measure of the drug's priority status, a measure of the drug's novelty, a count of the number of drugs previously submitted by the sponsoring firm, a control for time, and an index of the drugs' primary indications. The FDA can allow individuals with possible financial conflicts of interest to participate in committee deliberations by granting the individual a waiver or "conflict of interest determination" (US Government Accountability Office 2008). Conflict of interest measures are based on reports of waivers granted to members of the advisory committee, recorded in advisory committee meeting transcripts from 1990 to 2009.[8] Conflicts of interest are measured both as the total count of waivers granted at the committee meeting and as an indicator of whether any waiver was granted at a committee meeting for a particular drug.[9]

The results suggest that, even when controlling for underlying drug risks, drugs that receive an advisory committee consultation are 2.5 times more likely to have a boxed warning added to their label after reaching the market than drugs that do not go to an advisory committee for a pre-market review. In the subsample of drugs that went to a pre-market advisory committee meeting, however, those that were reviewed by committees without any financial conflict of interest waivers were significantly less likely to receive subsequent boxed warnings. The results similarly suggest that advisory committee reviews are associated with higher counts of safety alerts.[10] This implies some limits to the promise of public advice: public consultations alone may be insufficient to ensure product safety. Yet, when considering only the pool of drugs that received advisory committee reviews, results suggest that drugs reviewed by committees with no conflict of interest waivers were associated with significantly fewer subsequent drug safety alerts. The quality or nature of the advice, this suggests, may matter to regulatory performance.

Analysis using observational data cannot fully account for potential problems of nonrandom assignment and selection bias. To reduce the likelihood that these results arise from underlying and unmeasured differences between treatment and control groups, I employ both coarsened exact matching models and treatment-effects models, which offer additional nuance and urge some caution. Although all six supplemental models reported in the appendix confirm the direction of the results

Table 9.2. Post-Marketing Safety Problems: New Boxed Warnings (NMEs Approved 1986–2009, Random Effects Logistic Regression)

Variable	Boxed Warning Model 1		Boxed Warning Model 2		Boxed Warning Model 3	
	Coefficient (SE)	Odds ratio (SE)	Coefficient (SE)	Odds ratio (SE)	Coefficient (SE)	Odds ratio (SE)
Pre-approval advisory committee	0.900† (0.462)	2.459† (1.137)				
Count of waivers			**0.407** (0.151)	**1.502** (0.227)		
No waivers					**−2.251** (1.147)	**0.105** (0.121)
Firms' prior approvals	**0.029** (0.015)	**1.03** (0.015)	−0.009 (0.025)	0.992 (0.025)	0.001 (0.023)	1.001 (0.023)
Drug novelty	0.140 (0.185)	1.150 (0.213)	0.144 (0.339)	1.155 (0.391)	0.231 (0.294)	1.260 (0.370)
Priority review	0.357 (0.478)	1.43 (0.684)	1.55† (0.874)	4.689† (4.098)	1.452† (0.832)	4.270† (3.553)
Year of submission	**0.082** (0.035)	**1.085** (0.038)	0.085 (.066)	1.089 (0.071)	**0.136** (0.066)	**1.146** (.075)
Constant	**−167.572** (70.372)		−175.616 (131.064)		**−275.915** (131.556)	
# of primary indications	180		94		94	
# of NME observations	561		196		196	
Log likelihood	−91.814		−41.662		−43.723	

Note: Boldface denotes statistical significance at the $p < .05$ level (all tests are two-tailed); † indicates significance at the $p < .1$ level.

Table 9.3. Post-Marketing Safety Problems: Safety Alerts (NMEs Approved 1996–2009, Random Effects Negative Binomial Regression)

Variable	Safety Alerts Model 1 Coefficient (SE)	Safety Alerts Model 2 Coefficient (SE)	Safety Alerts Model 3 Coefficient (SE)
Pre-approval advisory committee	0.422[†] (0.223)		
Count of waivers		**0.141** (0.068)	
No waivers			**–2.014** (0.832)
Firms' prior drug approvals	**0.020** (0.007)	–0.001 (0.013)	0.005 (0.013)
Drug novelty	**0.241** (0.087)	0.140 (0.154)	0.167 (0.147)
Priority review	0.054 (0.222)	0.370 (0.372)	0.247 (0.374)
Year of submission	**–0.140** (0.032)	–0.087 (0.055)	–0.016 (0.064)
Constant	**278.953** (63.368)	172.971 (110.461)	30.813 (128.468)
# of primary indications	118	56	56
# of NME observations	264	78	78
Log likelihood	–296.093	–105.136	–102.972

Note: Boldface denotes statistical significance at the $p < .05$ level (all tests are two-tailed); [†] indicates significance at the $p < .1$ level.

presented in Tables 9.2 and 9.3, only four achieve standard levels of statistical significance. Implementing these models reduces the drug sample sizes considerably, yielding higher levels of uncertainty. Each of these models approaches the selection issue differently: generalized linear models through the index of primary indications; treatment-effects models through instrumental variables; and coarsened exact matching models by creating multivariate bins with different dimensions, by placing covariates in those bins, and then by matching observations in the same bin. Together, these three classes of model represent a rigorous effort to address potential selection bias as much as possible.

Scholarship suggests that preventing individuals with financial conflicts of interest from serving on public committees would not change the overall outcome of an FDA advisory committee vote (Lurie et al. 2006). However, there is much more to an advisory committee meeting than votes on product approval. Advisory committees serve both internal and external audiences (Hilgartner 2000; Jasanoff 1990; Carpenter 2010). Committees can facilitate the flow of expert information into an agency, assisting the agency's policymaking process and ultimate regulatory decision. Committees also facilitate the flow of information out of an agency, sending signals and providing expertise that may support ultimate drug regulation (Moffitt 2010). Public advisory committees can provide the first opportunity for the agency to communicate publicly with various audiences about a drug's risk. Might the presence of conflicts affect the strength of the signal a committee sends to the agency, external observers, and implementers? While advisory committee votes matter to firms' asset prices, the substance of advisory committee deliberation may be crucial to ultimate drug safety.

Public Deliberation and Risk Communication

Returning to Vioxx's narrative provides an illustrative example and suggests a possible pathway through which conflicts of interest may bear on risk communication. The Arthritis Drugs Advisory Committee convened in February 2001 to review and discuss the implications of Merck's VIGOR study, which had been designed primarily to assess Vioxx's gastrointestinal effects compared with those of the drug naproxen. Five of the committee members at the February 2001 meeting had interests that required them to receive full waivers in order to participate in the meeting. Three of those five members, along with another committee member, had "interests which do not constitute a financial interest . . . but which could create the appearance of a conflict." Five additional members had neither financial nor other interests that posed potential conflicts.

Though designed to assess gastrointestinal events, the VIGOR study also found a higher risk of cardiovascular events in the Vioxx group than in the naproxen group. Merck argued that the higher rate among Vioxx users arose not from Vioxx's risk but from the cardio-protective benefits associated with naproxen. The advisory committee agreed that some mention of cardiovascular events should be added to the Vioxx label, and the committee agreed that Merck should be required to conduct more studies to assess Vioxx's safety. Committee members differed, however, in how narrow they thought that label language should be.[11]

Several members who received waivers offered arguments consistent with Merck, stating that "these data suggest . . . that at least some of the difference between rofecoxib and naproxen is due to naproxen benefit." Rather than report on Vioxx's cardiovascular risks, these committee members instead emphasized the lack of cardiovascular benefit:

"the consumer must be warned very, very carefully by physicians that these drugs are not replacements for aspirin for cardiac prophylaxis" and that "the absence of a cardioprotective effect for both COX-2 inhibitors should be emphasized in the product literature." Their cautiousness had scientific grounds: "We don't have the data we need to actually make a final determination . . . [that] what we saw was cardioprotective effect of naproxen or excess risk for rofecoxib, and I just think we can't go beyond what the data actually tells us."

However, some members without conflicts used bolder language and recommended that "something stronger than just saying there is a lack of cardioprotective events is warranted." The justification for a stronger statement was also grounded in science: "I think while one doesn't want to claim that something has been proven at this point, there is more than just one piece of evidence and they all kind of tie together." While a member who received a waiver emphasized Vioxx's gastrointestinal benefits and called for labeling to reflect those benefits, a member who took a stronger stand on cardiovascular risks warned, "one certainly wants to avoid a sentence which implies that you get a lot of advantage in GI and only a little extra worry in cardiovascular or something like that, which would hide the overall total rise in adverse events."

The revised Vioxx label that appeared in April 2002 reported results of the VIGOR study, allowed Merck to claim that Vioxx was associated with fewer gastrointestinal events than naproxen, noted "a higher incidence of adjudicated serious cardiovascular thrombotic events in patients treated with VIOXX 50 mg once daily as compared to patients treated with naproxen 500 mg twice daily," and stated that "VIOXX is not a substitute for aspirin for cardiovascular prophylaxis." The FDA's accompanying statement maintained that "the relationship of the cardiovascular findings in the VIGOR study to use of Vioxx is not known."

The revised label largely reflected the more narrow, cautious recommendations that members with waivers advanced. Would fewer conflicts have promoted more aggressive risk communication from the onset—when the drug first emerged on the market—and subsequently fewer safety alerts and boxed warning additions later? Further systematic reviews are necessary to produce evidence on differences in committee members' deliberations and their impact on both internal agency policymaking and external risk communication.[12] This example, however, suggests that advisory committees' potential contributions extend beyond the official votes that the committee takes. Although voting patterns (Lurie et al. 2006) and ultimate votes may help predict a drug's likelihood of subsequent approval, committees also represent potentially important venues for sending signals to the FDA and the broader community about drug characteristics.

While members' conflicts of interest may shape the substance and tone of deliberation on drug risks, this narrative underscores the fundamental problem of knowledge—and its absence—for product safety. Addressing the knowledge problem is not limited to the agency and its advisors but reaches into the broader system of medical and pharmaceutical research, training, and practice. Nevertheless, committee deliberations ultimately shed some light on the cardiovascular risk associated with Vioxx: it was in the course of reporting on the February 8, 2001, Vioxx advisory committee meeting that the popular press first mentioned the possibility of cardiovascular risks associated with that drug.[13] Along with that transparency came additional studies from outside of Merck and some measure of heightened public awareness of Vioxx's potential risks.

Discussion and Implications

As the IOM noted, the crisis of confidence in the FDA consists of many facets, one of which is concern about "the trustworthiness of the scientific advice received by the agency" (IOM 2007:9). The results presented here provide some empirical foundation for those perceptions and concerns. The results confirm claims that deadlines for drug reviews are associated with declines in FDA advisory committee use. They also suggest that, although overall committee use may not improve product safety, public committee reviews with fewer conflicts of interest are associated with fewer safety-related problems when drugs reach the market. Results from the supplemental models included in the Appendix confirm the direction of these results but not always their magnitude or certainty. In the words of the advisory committee member reviewing Vioxx in 2001, who noted that "there is more than just one piece of evidence and they all kind of tie together," here too we see a discernible pattern of results suggesting fewer post-marketing safety problems when drugs are reviewed by committees with few conflicts of interest.

As Machiavelli observed in 1514, "A prince who is not himself wise cannot be well advised." Expert advice will assist internal agency decision making only if the agency itself is receptive and well equipped to put that knowledge to use. Expert advice will help external agency risk communication only if the ultimate implementers—doctors, patients, pharmacists—are aware and able to act on that knowledge (Fung et al. 2007). The crisis of confidence facing the FDA has its roots in agency structure, institutional designs, and guiding policy (IOM 2007). Public advice is only a partial antidote for the systemic challenges facing the agency.

Ultimately, advisory committee members' financial ties to pharmaceutical companies reflect a broader fundamental dilemma facing the medical community (Lo and Field 2009). Limits on the number of members who may receive waivers to participate in FDA meetings in which they may have a financial stake touch only lightly on the intricate ties among industry funding, physician education, and medical research. The FDA depends on knowledge and practice far outside the scope of its regulatory reach, and factors fueling the crisis of confidence facing the FDA are only partly under the agency's jurisdiction.

Though advisory committees play only one part in perceptions of crisis, they remain crucial venues for facilitating the flow of information in and out of the FDA. They provide an accessible forum through which disease sufferers can call publicly on the agency to make therapies available more quickly, as the case of AIDS suggests (Epstein 1996). They can mark the start of public and scholarly attention to drug risks that would otherwise receive less media attention, and the publicity they generate can induce firms to reveal information they would otherwise not reveal publicly.[14] They offer potential transparency and deliberation in an otherwise closed regulatory process. The transparency and deliberation that public committees may offer invite us to look beyond formal committee votes and product approval recommendations to the information exchange that committees facilitate. A former FDA staff member made the following observation:

> Do the committee members often offer insights that the agency people would not have thought of if they really thought about it in that context? Probably not very often. Is it a good forum for exposure of data, for exposure of issues, for making the decision-making process more transparent? Sure, absolutely. Because don't forget, the FDA is prohibited from releasing any data in a new drug application . . . that's a trade secret, and so the advisory committee basically provides an override . . . in that it enables them to disclose data publicly and to release those data, and I think that's an enormous public health benefit.[15]

The FDA has taken a series of steps in recent years both to enhance transparency in the regulatory process and to reduce potential conflicts of interest on its public committees. The agency has launched a Transparency Initiative aimed, in part, at enhancing access to "the information the agency has in its possession." The FDA now restricts the percentage of committee members on public committees who may receive waivers. In 2010, this cap was 13 percent of members, and the agency reports that it granted waivers for less than 5 percent of committee members during that year (Hamburg 2010). Both of these efforts represent steps to attend to some of the recommended reforms proposed in the IOM's 2007 report.

Enhanced transparency and a reduction in conflicts of interest both come with potential costs. More stringent conflict-of-interest provisions on public advisory committees risk limiting the pool of experts the agency may consult, especially for narrow topics, and may account for current vacancy rates on FDA committees. Communicating drug risk carries risks of its own. Negative reports—including those from advisory committees—may dampen drug innovation or induce patients to inappropriately abandon needed therapies.[16] Rigorous scientific debate, moreover, may better thrive behind closed doors.

Although the FDA has taken significant steps toward limiting conflicts of interest on public committees, the time pressures facing the agency remain robust. There is little evidence suggesting that the agency has made significant steps toward reaching the IOM's recommendation to review all NMEs before they receive approval or shortly after they reach the market. As the IOM suggests, committee reviews—coupled with fewer conflicts of interest—have the potential to reduce the "perceived lack of transparency and accountability to the public" (IOM 2007), a perception that fuels at least part of the crisis of confidence facing the FDA. The study reported in this chapter pushes beyond the IOM report to suggest that committee reviews coupled with fewer conflicts of interest may contribute to improved regulatory safety.

Appendix

The following treatment-effects model assesses the effect of binary treatment z_j (advisory committee review) on variable y_j (drug safety) conditional on independent variables x_j and w_j:

$$y_j = x_j\beta + \delta z_j + \varepsilon_j \, ,$$

where z^* is a linear function of exogenous covariates w_j and random component u_j,

$$z^*_j = w_j\gamma + u_j,$$

and

$$z_j = 1, \text{ if } z^*_j > 0$$
$$z_j = 0, \text{ otherwise.}$$

The w_j instrument is identified through measures of the density of committee workload and committee chair position vacancy. Vacancy was measured as "1" for a report of chair vacancy listed on the committee roster or when no information was available from the FDA website about the committee chair, when a roster was not publicly available. While this identification strategy works for the boxed warning models, it does not identify the safety alert models.

Table A9.1 presents the results for new boxed warnings, obtained with the treatment-effects models; Tables A9.2 and A9.3 show results for both new boxed warnings and safety alerts obtained with the coarsened exact matching models.

Table A9.1 Treatment-Effects Models: Advisory Committee Use, Conflicts of Interest, and Safety Outcomes

Variable	Boxed warning, Model 1 Coefficient (SE)	Boxed warning Model 2 Coefficient (SE)
Pre-approval advisory committee	**0.200** (0.056)	
No waivers at committee meeting		**−0.198** (0.091)
Firms' prior approvals	0.001[†] (.001)	0.0006 (0.002)
Drug novelty	0.007 (0.007)	0.024 (0.017)
Priority review	−0.030 (0.025)	**0.089** (0.040)
Year of submission	**0.004** (0.001)	**0.007** (0.003)
Constant	**−7.648** (2.996)	**−14.772** (6.354)
Selection models		
Committee chair vacant	**−0.496** (0.248)	0.492 (0.487)
Committee workload	−0.023 (0.032)	**−0.169** (0.056)
Priority review	**0.766** (0.118)	−0.026 (0.204)
Firms' prior drug approvals	0.004 (0.005)	−0.004 (0.008)
Drug novelty	−0.007 (0.046)	−0.059 (0.085)
Constant	**−0.546** 0.165	0.034 (0.285)
	N = 543	N = 196

Note: Boldface denotes statistical significance at the $p < .05$ level (all tests are two-tailed); [†] indicates significance at the $p < .1$ level.

Table A9.2 Advisory Committee Consultation and Post-Marketing Safety: Coarsened Exact Matching

Variable	New boxed warnings Coefficient (SE)	Safety alerts Coefficient (SE)
Pre-approval advisory committee	**1.480** (0.589)	0.221 (0.249)
Firms' prior drug approvals	0.026 (0.019)	**0.022** (0.010)
Drug novelty	0.164 (0.242)	0.180 (0.123)
Priority review	0.220 (0.568)	−0.129 (0.262)
Year of submission	**0.106** (0.042)	**−0.132** (0.034)
Constant	**−217.093** (83.123)	**264.962** (68.980)
NMEs (number of observations)	463	178

Note: Boldface denotes statistical significance at the $p < .05$ level (all tests are two-tailed).

Table A9.3 Conflicts of Interest and Post-Marketing Safety: Coarsened Exact Matching

Variable	New boxed warnings Coefficient (SE)	Safety alerts Coefficient (SE)
No waivers at committee meetings	−0.864 (1.168)	**−1.221** (0.412)
Firms' prior drug approvals	−0.002 (0.043)	−0.006 (0.018)
Drug novelty	0.293 (0.457)	0.143 (0.203)
Priority review	0.426 (1.183)	0.907[†] (0.516)
Year of submission	0.118[†] (0.700)	0.032 (0.057)
Constant	−239.519[†] (139.067)	−63.815 (114.166)
NMEs (number of observations)	169	38

Note: Boldface denotes statistical significance at the $p < .05$ level (all tests are two-tailed); [†] indicates significance at the $p < .1$ level.

Acknowledgments

I am grateful to Daniel P. Carpenter for his helpful advice and for very generously sharing drug safety data. Mark Bouchard, Jennifer Cassidy, and Rob Kantner provided excellent research assistance. This research was supported by the Robert Wood Johnson Foundation's Scholars in Health Policy Research Program. All errors are my responsibility.

Notes

1. The 2009 Harris survey was conducted online and did not represent a random sample of adults. Instead, "Respondents . . . were selected from among those who have agreed to participate in Harris Interactive survey," and the data were "weighted to reflect the composition of the U.S. adult population" (Harris Interactive/HealthDay 2009:4).

2. Lurie et al. (2006) also found that members with ties to competitors were weakly but significantly associated with voting for product approval.

3. Committee meetings follow a predictable format, with time allotted for an FDA presentation, a firm presentation, a period of open public comment when members of the audience may address the committee, and committee deliberations. Topics include whether to approve a drug, how the drug should be labeled, and what subsequent studies the firm should perform.

4. The primary sample was restricted to NMEs in order to limit the scope of the inquiry to a comparable group of policy tasks, consistent with prevailing scholarship (Carpenter 2002; Carpenter et al. 2012). Moreover, this sample is restricted to drugs that were eventually approved, consistent with industry observers' claim that the FDA primarily brings drugs it wants to approve to committees for review (Pines and Cotton 1997:36).

5. The sample in this chapter thus differs from that of Lurie et al. (2006), who considered all FDA advisory committee meetings between 2001 and 2004, not only those meetings related to the approval of an NME.

6. Each of these measures is consistent with and builds on Moffitt (2010) and Carpenter et al. (2012).

7. Each of these measures is consistent with and builds on Carpenter et al. (2012).

8. Meetings that did not contain a conflict-of-interest report were excluded. This measure does not distinguish the amount of the conflict or the source of the conflict.

9. This study does not distinguish between conflicts of interest with drug sponsors and with drug competitors. It does not do so in part because other scholarship has established that financial conflicts with competitors are associated with "approval" votes (Lurie et al. 2006). The authors of that study note several possible explanations for the "paradox of competitor conflicts" including the possibility that conflicts of interest "might be a proxy for an attitude relatively favorable to industry (Lurie et al. 2006:1927).

10. This finding is consistent with Moffitt (2010).

11. Data for this narrative come from the author's field notes from the February 8, 2001, meeting; from the Arthritis Drugs Advisory Committee transcript from February 8, 2001 (Food and Drug Administration 2001); and from the FDA's document "Sequence of Events with VIOXX, since opening of IND," posted at http://www.fda.gov/ohrms/dockets/ac/05/briefing/2005-4090B1 _04_E-FDA-TAB-C.htm.

12. The Vioxx case also underscores the need for more systematic analysis of committee deliberation. A committee member who received a conflict of interest waiver to participate in the 2001 Vioxx meeting went on to publish an important article that demonstrated associations between Cox-2 inhibitors and cardiovascular events, and recommended that doctors prescribing Vioxx or other drugs in its class do so cautiously.

13. This claim is based on the author's search of LexisNexis newspaper articles.

14. Some accounts point to the threat of an advisory committee review as a factor contributing to Johnson and Johnson's decision to withdraw the drug cisapride from the market. "Do we want to stand in front of world and admit that we were never able to prove efficacy!" a Johnson and Johnson executive wrote in internal company documents (Harris and Koli 2005).

15. Interview with author.

16. Studies of drug development abandonment and studies of patient prescription abandonment are currently under way by Daniel Carpenter and several colleagues, including this chapter's author.

References

Ackerley, Nyssa et al. (2007) *Measuring Conflict of Interest and Expertise on FDA Advisory Committees*. Final report submitted to Food and Drug Administration Office of Policy, Planning and Preparedness.

Carpenter, Daniel P. (2002) "Groups, the Media, Agency Waiting Costs and FDA Drug Approval." *American Journal of Political Science* 46: 490–505.

Carpenter, Daniel (2010) *Reputation and Power: Organizational Image and Pharmaceutical Regulation at the FDA*. Princeton, N.J.: Princeton University Press.

Carpenter, Daniel P. et al. (2008) "Drug-Review Deadlines and Safety Problems." *New England Journal of Medicine* 358: 1354–61.

Carpenter Daniel P. et al. (2012) "The Complications of Controlling Agency Time Discretion: FDA Review Deadlines and Postmarket Drug Safety." *American Journal of Political Science* 56: 98–114.

Croley, Steven P., and William F. Funk (1997) "The Federal Advisory Committee Act and Good Government." *Yale Journal on Regulation* 14: 451.

Epstein, Steven (1996) *Impure Science: AIDS, Activism, and the Politics of Knowledge*. Berkeley: University of California Press.

Food and Drug Administration (2001) "Arthritis Advisory Committee Meeting Transcript: Vioxx, February 8." Rockville, MD: Food and Drug Administration.

Fung, Archon et al. (2007) *Full Disclosure: The Perils and Promise of Transparency*. New York: Cambridge University Press.

General Services Administration (2011) "Federal Advisory Committee Act (FACA) Management Overview." http://www.gsa.gov/portal/content/104514, accessed December 14, 2011.

Glodé, Elizabeth R. (2002) "Advising Under the Influence? Conflicts of Interest Among FDA Advisory Committee Members." *Food and Drug Law Journal* 57: 293–322.

Hamburg, Margaret A. (2010) "Commissioner's Letter to FDA Staff on Disclosure of Financial Conflicts of Interest," April 21. http://www.fda.gov/Advisory Committees/AboutAdvisoryCommittees/ucm209001.htm, accessed October 18, 2011.

Harris, Gardiner, and Eric Koli (2005) "Lucrative Drug, Danger Signals and the FDA." *New York Times*, June 10, 2005.

Harris Interactive/HealthDay (2009) "Public's Opinion of FDA Shows Room for Improvement." http://www.harrisinteractive.com/news/pubs/Harris_In teractive_HealthDay_News_2009_04_30.pdf, accessed October 24, 2011.

Heimann, C. F. Larry (1997) *Acceptable Risks: Politics, Policy and Risky Technologies*. Ann Arbor: University of Michigan Press.

Hilgartner, Stephen (2000) *Science on Stage: Expert Advice as Public Drama*. Stanford, Calif.: Stanford University Press.

Iacus, Stefano et al. (2011) "Multivariate Matching Methods That Are Monotonic Imbalance Bounding." *Journal of the American Statistical Association* 106: 345–61.

Institute of Medicine (2007) *The Future of Drug Safety: Promoting and Protecting the Health of the Public*. Washington, D.C.: National Academy Press.

Jasanoff, Sheila (1990) *The Fifth Branch: Science Advisors as Policy Makers.* Cambridge, Mass.: Harvard University Press.

Karty, Kevin D. (2002) "Closure and Capture in Federal Advisory Committees." *Business and Politics* 4: 213–38.

Kaufman, Herbert (1981) *The Administrative Behavior of Federal Bureau Chiefs.* Washington, D.C.: Brookings Institution.

Lasser, Karen E. et al. (2002) "Timing of New Black Box Warnings and Withdrawals for Prescription Medications." *Journal of the American Medical Association* 287: 2215–20.

Lo, Bernard, and Marilyn J. Field (2009) *Conflict of Interest in Medical Research, Education and Practice.* Washington, D.C.: Institute of Medicine.

Lurie, Peter et al. (2006) "Financial Conflicts of Interest Disclosure and Voting Patterns at Food and Drug Administration Advisory Committee Meetings." *Journal of the American Medical Association* 295: 1921–28.

McCullagh, Peter, and John A. Nelder (1989) *Generalized Linear Models.* London: Chapman and Hall.

Moffitt, Susan L. (2010) "Promoting Agency Reputation Through Public Advice: Advisory Committee Use in the FDA." *Journal of Politics* 72: 880–93.

National Academies (2005) *Science and Technology in the National Interest: Ensuring the Best Presidential and Federal Advisory Committee Science and Technology Appointments.* Washington, D.C.: National Academies Press.

Petracca, Mark P. (1986) "Federal Advisory Committees, Interest Groups and the Administrative State." *Congress and the Presidency* 13: 83–114.

Pines, Wayne L., and Mary Ann N. Cotton (1997) "Preparing for an FDA Advisory Committee Meeting." *Drug Information Journal* 31: 35–41.

Rettig, Richard et al., eds. (1992) *Food and Drug Administration Advisory Committees.* Washington, D.C.: National Academy Press.

U. S. Department of Health and Human Services, Office of the Inspector General (2003) *FDA Review Process for New Drug Applications.* OEI-01-01-00590. Washington, D.C.: Department of Health and Human Services.

U. S. Government Accountability Office (2006) *Drug Safety: Improvement Needed in FDA's Postmarket Decision-Making and Oversight Process.* GAO 06-402. Washington, D.C.: U.S. Government Accountability Office.

——— (2008) *FDA Advisory Committees: Process for Recruiting Members and Evaluating Potential Conflicts of Interest.* GAO 08-640. Washington, D.C.: U.S. Government Accountability Office.

U.S. Senate Committee on Finance (2004) *Hearing on the Withdrawal from the Market of Vioxx Arthritis Pain Medication, Part 1.* Washington, D.C.: Government Printing Office.

Weimer, David L. (2007) "Medical Governance: Are We Ready to Prescribe?" *Journal of Policy Analysis and Management* 26: 217–29.

Zuckerman, Diana M. (2006) *FDA Advisory Committees: Does Approval Mean Safety?* Washington, D.C.: National Research Center for Women and Families.

Statutes Cited

Federal Advisory Committee Act of 1972, 5 U.S.C. App. 2.
Prescription Drug User Fee Act of 1992, 21 U.S.C. § 379.

Chapter 10
Reforming Securities Law Enforcement
Politics and Money at the Public/Private Divide

William W. Bratton and Michael L. Wachter

The United States system of securities regulation has come under sustained criticism in recent years in the wake of both the unraveling of Bernie Madoff's multibillion-dollar Ponzi scheme as well as the national economic crisis triggered by mortgage securitization and the collapse in the housing market. This chapter looks at one aspect of the U.S. system of securities regulation: private class action enforcement of the antifraud provisions of the federal securities laws. To the casual observer, the issue of private fraud enforcement is settled ground occupied by litigation specialists, the lawyers and judges who attend to a long-established cause of action known as "fraud on the market" (FOTM). Closer attention reveals a long-unsolved policy problem—namely, that FOTM, the primary federal antifraud class action vehicle, just does not work.

Private enforcement of FOTM claims nonetheless persists as a billion-dollar litigation industry thanks to agency lassitude, lawyerly rent seeking, and political stasis. In this chapter, we survey the politics and track the money to see whether anything can be done to solve the problems with the FOTM system. We propose a radical redirection of enforcement resources—all of which are dollars drawn from shareholder pockets—from the private to the public sector. But we tack against the political winds in so doing. Although financial disasters have historically led to stepped-up public antifraud enforcement as well as new financial regulation (as has occurred in response to the most recent crisis), financial disaster simultaneously enhances the prestige of private antifraud enforcement. FOTM's moments of vulnerability occur during bull markets, when congressional sympathies tend toward the interests of management. We are left for now, in the immediate aftermath of disaster, to remit our proposal to a hypothetical federal regulator pursuing the goal of sound public policymaking.

The Fraud on the Market Problem

FOTM follows from two notions, both bound up in securities laws' concept of "investor protection." The first notion dates from the 1960s and 1970s and holds that investor protection under the securities laws' antifraud provisions, in particular section 10(b) of the Securities and Exchange Act of 1934, as well as Rule 10b-5 thereunder (Securities and Exchange Commission 1948), needs private enforcement as an assist and that the class action is the only suitable procedural mode for private enforcement. The second notion emerged as the courts, having implied a private right of action, filled in its terms by reference to the common law of fraud. The common law fraudster pays the victim her out-of-pocket losses, compensating her. It followed that the securities fraud defendant should pay the out-of-pocket losses of those who buy (or sell) a stock that is over- (or under-) priced due to a misrepresentation (or omission). The common law template also threw up substantive hurdles. The tort of fraud presupposes parties dealing face to face and requires a showing of reliance on the misrepresentation (American Law Institute 1965:§310), a showing that cannot be made as a practical matter in a class action. FOTM, adopted by the Supreme Court in *Basic Inc. v. Levinson* (1988), patched over the problem by relaxing the reliance requirement. With a famous cite to the "efficient capital market hypothesis," the Court ruled that a showing of reliance on the integrity of the market price would suffice. That seemed like a good idea at the time, but, as we explain, things went wrong when it was acted out in practice.

At its conception, FOTM came forth making two promises: it would, first, compensate present victims of fraud and, second, operate as a deterrent against future fraud. It is now generally seen to have altogether failed to deliver on the first promise. Plaintiffs' lawyers calculate out-of-pocket damages that support multibillion-dollar claims, claims that if ever pursued to judgment against actual fraudsters would import both hit-the-jackpot compensation and crushing deterrence. Unfortunately, or perhaps fortunately, attorneys in real-world class actions look for settlement value, and human beings facing financial destruction are either disinclined to settle or already judgment proof. Thus do the corporate issuers of securities, hauled into court along with their employees on an enterprise liability theory, pick up the settlement tab in FOTM cases. With the corporation paying the settlement, the cost of compensating the shareholders in the plaintiff class befalls those holding the company's shares at the time of settlement. The shareholders in the class and the successful plaintiffs' attorney thus pick the pockets of the payor shareholders, and by definition, the company's longer-term shareholders fall into the payor group. Moreover, to the extent that the paying and receiving shareholders are fully diversified, cash inflows and outflows due to FOTM settlements even out over time, making FOTM a wash rather than a source of compensation, a wash that ripens into a net loss once we account for attorneys' fees, liability insurance premiums, and other costs.

As to the second, deterrent, promise, FOTM is thought to deliver some value but only a little. Enterprise liability causes the problem once again: if FOTM were to be used seriously to promote deterrence, the funding for damage settlements would come from individual miscreants. Instead, the corporation and its insurance company rather than the corporation's culpable agents make the payments. At the same time, fraud is widely thought to be underdeterred.

FOTM, in short, does not work. Such is the consensus view that has emerged among academics (Jackson and Roe 2009:209). The consensus is notable in itself, for big-ticket causes of action normally tend to have squads of academic cheerleaders. But the consensus about FOTM's failure has fostered only a limited menu of alternative policy solutions.

Some of FOTM's opponents bring out the blunderbuss. They argue that FOTM should be abolished along with the entire mandatory disclosure regime (Choi 2000:283; Mahoney 1997:1454). We think disclosure mandates are necessary and so reject the opponents' all-or-nothing connection between FOTM and mandatory disclosure. How best to enforce disclosure mandates is a separate question.

FOTM's proponents strenuously try to make it work, even as they acknowledge the failure critique's power. They take two routes in this pursuit. Proponents' first approach is to treat FOTM as a misunderstood cause of action in need of fresh policy justification: even if FOTM makes no sense as a compensatory tort, it can be made to make sense if recast as a corporate governance device that reduces agency costs. But the conceptual switch in the end fails to break FOTM free of its original conceptual framework and attendant shortcomings. If FOTM were to help the governance system, it would do so as a deterrent—and yet FOTM does little to deter wrongdoing.

FOTM's proponents' second approach focuses on practice and politics. We are counseled to stick with FOTM as a needed enforcement supplement even as the attendant conceptual problems are conceded (Langevoort 2007b: 656; Langevoort 1996). More particularly, an individual liability system that held out penalties of sufficient magnitude to attract private enforcers would be draconian and likely would impair recruitment of talented corporate executive officers. Contrariwise, a system of individual liability lacking that draconian aspect would have insufficient salience, removing the deep pocket from the settlement table and reducing the incidence of private enforcement. As a consequence, fraud, already underdeterred, would be deterred even less. Finally, we are told that the public enforcement provides no substitute. It is hampered by incentive problems—private actors pursuing profits perform better than public servants. It also remains subject to political constraints. The public enforcement commitment just is not there and would be transient even if it suddenly coalesced (Coffee 2006:1557; Booth 2008:8; Fox 2009:285).

Once the layers of defense have been worked through, there remains only a negative justification: although FOTM does not work, it is the best enforcement we are going to get. We are, as it were, stuck. This joins the issue, challenging any FOTM opponent to make an affirmative case for disrupting the status quo.

The issue, thus joined, is more political and practical than it is theoretical. The remaining parts of this chapter address it with a political economy of FOTM. Our analysis comes in two segments. The first is explanatory and shows how a cause of action that does not work still continues to enjoy political legitimacy. The second challenges a central piece of the policy defense. We are told that we have to live with a flawed tort because public enforcement resources are inadequate, a point that has been repeated like a mantra since the Supreme Court first implied a private right of action under the 1934 Act in *J. I. Case Co. v. Borak* (1964). We inquire into this assumption's continued viability, tracing the sources and amounts of funding supporting securities law enforcement and showing that today's Securities and Exchange Commission (SEC) deploys enforcement resources of materially greater magnitude than those available when the courts first started implying private rights of action decades ago. Damage dollars yielded by private enforcement once dwarfed those brought in by SEC enforcers, but that no longer is the case. Furthermore, enforcement money in both public and private spheres comes out of shareholder pockets. There is reason to think that the SEC offers shareholders a more effective use of their money.

Our analysis leads to a suggestion for getting antifraud enforcement unstuck. We acknowledge that directing enforcement against individual perpetrators will deter fraud more effectively than a system based on enterprise liability, but, conversely, taking enforcement actions against individuals could also create a risk of overdeterrence. To address this tension, our recommendation is simply to reinstate the reliance requirement. Specifically, FOTM should be abolished except in cases where the issuer is trading in its own securities, including selling a new issue. An actual reliance requirement tailored to the circumstances of investors who do fundamental analysis should be substituted, these being the investors who actually rely on false disclosures.

We expect that little in the way of a reduction in deterrence would result, since FOTM as it stands does not provide a credible deterrence weapon. That said, we agree that eliminating FOTM altogether would reduce the flow of private enforcement litigation; however, we argue that public enforcers should and can pick up the slack. A public enforcer can pursue individuals unencumbered by an economic imperative to settle quickly. At the same time, an enforcer constrained by an administrative intelligence can pull back if overdeterrence becomes a problem. We accordingly recommend that FOTM reform be accompanied by an increase in support for the enforcement division of the SEC. We look to the SEC, rather than Congress or the courts, to initiate the reform. The SEC might have taken the initiative to shape antifraud law by rulemaking decades ago. Instead, it left matters to the courts. Looking forward, however, the SEC remains the institution best equipped to fix things.

The Politics of FOTM

Policy vacuity does not necessarily imply political vulnerability. Indeed, FOTM came up on the congressional chopping block in the run-up to the Private Securities Litigation Reform Act (1995) (PSLRA), only to be spared when Arthur Levitt, then the chairman of the SEC, raised objections (Avery 1996:348). An inference arises: FOTM enjoys the protection of a shield of legitimacy even in adverse political climates. We here look into the sources of FOTM's political credibility.

Management Accountability

Management accountability is the first of a two-piece puzzle. The management story goes way back. Berle and Means (1933) long ago depicted managers as private actors who wield considerable social and economic power without being subject to accountability constraints comparable to those imposed on public actors (Bratton and Wachter 2008:118–22). Ever since, policy debates have focused on appropriate modes of constraint, public and private.

These debates wax and wane with the economy. When the economy grows, so does management's legitimacy. Thus did a buoyant stock market clear the way for the PSLRA, which imposed constraints on the scope of private antifraud litigation and the zone of discretion of the plaintiffs' lawyers who conduct it. Contrariwise, economic reverses trigger new demands for accountability, and managers' legitimacy wanes. Each of the Foreign Corrupt Practices Act (1977) (FCPA), the Sarbanes-Oxley Act

(2002) (SOX), and, just recently, the Dodd-Frank Act (2010) addressed such downside demands. So did the federal securities laws themselves. According to a creation story told and retold at the SEC, the 1933 and 1934 Acts responded to market failure and the need to defuse public resentment of economic privilege in the midst of the Depression (Langevoort 1999:1329).

The SEC creation story, with its overtones of class warfare, nicely suits the plaintiffs' bar. Securities class actions create a field in which upstart lawyers get to pursue the social structure's top dogs. The class warfare story of the 1930s is dated, of course. But it still resonates, for private economic and social empowerment generates demands for rectitude and accountability even in our market-oriented, deregulatory age (Coglianese 2007:160–61). Private antifraud litigation addresses the demand, a demand periodically stoked when corporate actors abuse their positions, lining their own pockets as they perpetrate fraud (160). That the upstart private attack dogs never go for the top dogs' jugulars does not seem to matter; the performative value is there.

All this teaches an important lesson: it is corporate managers themselves who keep the game going for FOTM. They do so partly by virtue of their economic and social position; they are, after all, at the top of society's power pyramid. To this extent, they are not to blame. But they also do so partly by virtue of the actions of the subset of miscreant managers—the faithless fiduciaries who require an active enforcement agent to deter their abuse of power. To this extent, FOTM is their own fault.

Shareholder Solicitude

Shareholder solicitude is the other piece of FOTM's political coin. It is wrought into the structure of antifraud litigation as the "right to compensation" in the private right of action—the "right" is not merely the means to the end of a policy goal but a substantive entitlement of recompense for pecuniary loss.

Shareholder solicitude, thus embedded in the tort, began imparting political traction only relatively recently. The shareholder interest used to be seen as distinct from that of the public. Another look back at Adolf Berle illustrates this. Although Berle spent a career arguing for stronger fiduciary protections for shareholders (Berle and Means 1932:247–76), he drew a sharp distinction between the shareholder interest and the public interest: shareholder welfare would proxy for social welfare only when shares were equitably distributed among the public as a whole (Bratton and Wachter 2008:142–43). Such was not the case then, nor is it the case now.

The FCPA, enacted in 1977, holds out a legislative (and political) example of separation between shareholder and public interests. The FCPA, like SOX, responded to political demands for management accountability in the wake of scandals. In the FCPA's case, the scandals involved "questionable foreign payments" made by corporations to actors abroad in connection with the sale of big-ticket American products, payments incidentally discovered in the course of the Watergate investigation (Karmel 2005:87). The public response cast managers as irresponsible public actors. Corporate corruption was unacceptable, even if it was corruption abroad in pursuit of shareholder value at home.

SOX admits of a similar reading. Although nominally investor protective, it accorded shareholders no new powers. Instead, it imposed good governance constraints on businesses toward the end of dulling overly sharp incentives and keeping corporate risk taking within socially acceptable limits (Langevoort 2007a:1828–29). Viewed this way, SOX was no more about shareholder value maximization than was the FCPA. Like the FCPA, it imposed public accountability on large corporations toward the end of public legitimacy (Langevoort 2007a:1820).

But unlike the FCPA, SOX was prompted by scandals without immediate ties to elected officials, scandals tied instead to spectacular losses at a number of large enterprises. The shareholder losses figured into the political motivation. Shareholding had become more widespread between 1977 and 2002, albeit collectivized in the form of pension and mutual fund interests. Politicians, moreover, had begun to promote an "ownership society" in which individually vested pension savings figured importantly. So when Congress enacted SOX, even though retail investors, viewed as an interest group, continued to have little influence (Langevoort 2004:10–11), the shareholder qua shareholder had edged much closer to the median voter and loomed large politically. An "investor class" had come into political existence. Shareholder empowerment, missing in SOX, would follow in the next round, as the Dodd-Frank Act of 2010 enables the placement of shareholder board nominees in management proxy statements and accords the shareholders "say on pay," among other things (Dodd-Frank Act 2010:§§951, 953–55, 971).

The Congress that enacted SOX, while granting no new powers to shareholders, found other innovative ways to show solicitude of their interests. Consider in this regard the Investor and Capital Markets Fee Relief Act (2002), a tax relief measure for the investor class. The fees in question were those that fund the SEC, fees collected from exchange transactions and in connection with SEC registrations. Fee revenues had been much in excess of the SEC's annual budget for many years, and the excess had disappeared into the Treasury. Congress enacted the Fee Relief Act to align revenue with the cost of running the SEC. The "Fair

Funds" provision in SOX (2002:§7246) was similarly motivated. Historically, the SEC had endeavored to return profits disgorged by its enforcement defendants to victimized investors. In contrast, when defendants
paid penalties, the monies were remitted to the Treasury. The Fair
Funds provision charges the SEC also to endeavor to return penalty
monies to injured investors,[1] elevating the interests of shareholder "victims" over those of the public treasury.

Significantly, Fair Funds disbursements mimic the economics of
FOTM. SEC penalties tend to be paid by corporate defendants, just as
are FOTM settlements. A Fair Funds distribution to a subset of shareholders is every bit as much an exercise in pocket shifting as is payment
of a FOTM settlement. Fair Funds, by tracking the structure of FOTM
so closely, holds out at least an implicit political endorsement.

This shareholder-based account of the support for FOTM opens up a
contradiction. A more sustained consideration of the shareholder interest shows that shareholders are harmed by FOTM since they get neither
deterrence nor compensation. Indeed, they are net losers since they pay
the plaintiffs' bar its fees through enterprise liability.

What is the political economy story for the shareholders? The answer
is that they are not actors, at least at this point. The "investor class" is still
more a political term than an organized interest group. Individual investors are rationally apathetic. Institutional shareholders are organized,
but they are a diverse group with differing views on the importance of
the matter and thus have no incentive to foot the entire bill for organizing against FOTM. Moreover, since the plaintiffs' bar does not target
institutional shareholders, institutional shareholders have no reason to
target it in return. This may change, but change will require political
assistance. The new political solicitude toward the investor class could
be the motivating factor, but only if FOTM's elimination comes to be
seen as shareholder friendly.

So long as catering to the shareholder interest appears advantageous
to members of Congress and FOTM is seen to be in their interest, it is difficult to imagine a political coalition forming to eliminate it. Meanwhile,
Dodd-Frank, although it does nothing to enhance the present position of
securities plaintiffs, signals a tilt in FOTM's direction. Among the many
studies commissioned by the statute, two concern private securities litigation and look into the possibility of overruling Supreme Court decisions
that restrict the scope of FOTM actions (Dodd-Frank Act 2010:§929Z).

Agency Problems

Two different groups of private agents populate the FOTM fact pattern—
plaintiffs' attorneys and corporate managers. This section brings these

groups into our political economy account. They stare at each other across a field of combat. Plaintiffs' lawyers favor FOTM as it is (or, better, was), while managers would like to pick up where the PSLRA left off and constrain it still further. At the same time, there is a point of commonality: neither group of agents, each for its own reasons, would want Congress to eliminate FOTM completely.

We start with the plaintiffs' bar, which has its own legitimacy problem. Those in charge of an enforcement institution founded on concerns about management accountability must be accountable in turn. Unfortunately, the class action lawsuit is not an institution well suited to this end. Plaintiffs' attorneys, in theory the agents of the shareholders, in practice make litigation decisions in a zone of discretion. When they are seen to abuse their discretion and impose deadweight costs on defendant companies without corresponding benefits to shareholders, constraining legislation can follow in the right political climate. Thus did a bull stock market and a class of favored companies in the technology sector combine in 1995 to focus congressional attention on abusive practices of securities plaintiffs, in particular the strike suit (Thompson and Sale 2003:884–85).

The PSLRA resulted and with it an experiment in attorney agency cost control in the form of the lead plaintiff provision (PSLRA 1995:§78u-4(a)(3)). This takes the selection of a class action's named plaintiff out of the plaintiffs' lawyers' hip pockets, making it contestable, and vests the decision in a court charged to presume that good litigation governance follows from "the largest financial interest in the relief sought" (PSLRA 1995:§78u-4(a)(3)(B)(iii)). Thus constructed, the PSLRA operates on the assumption that a financial interest in the stock by itself imports incentives to control litigation agency costs (Weiss and Beckerman 1995:2055–56).

Experience has taught a different lesson, namely, that shareholders are not likely to be activists in reforming FOTM, even in their own interests. Mutual funds have competitive reasons to avoid investing time and resources in shareholder activism and business reasons to keep friendly channels open to the corporate sector (Rock 1991:474). They accordingly refrain from stepping forward as lead plaintiffs (Choi and Thompson 2006:1504). Public pension funds, in contrast, are managed by public servants who have incentives to build reputations as governance activists (Bratton and McCahery 1995:1914–18). Unsurprisingly, lead plaintiffs come from this sector (Choi and Fisch 2008:330), a sector populated by actors lacking the pure financial incentives contemplated by the PSLRA.

Even so, an element of "public" control, even one of marginal effectiveness, can have a legitimacy-enhancing effect. FOTM may be emerging with more political strength than ever as an effect of congressional containment. Strike suits do not appear to be as salient a problem in the wake of the PSLRA (Choi 2007:601–2). Without a basis for credible allegations of corruption, anti-plaintiff politics could lose impetus, falling back into the more nebulous politics of deregulation. There it takes a place on long legislative agendas, litigation being only one of a number of regulatory costs business would prefer to do without.

This prediction's accuracy will be tested in a future political cycle. Current corporate legislative wish lists contain proposals addressed to securities litigation. National competitiveness, particularly with respect to international securities listings, is the across-the-board policy imperative of choice. A string of proposals respecting securities litigation awaits the light of day, sitting in the drawer, ready for enactment in a favorable political environment. If the past is any guide, such an environment presupposes an expanding economy and a rising stock market. It follows that the proposals may be gathering dust for some time.

Interestingly, outright abolition of FOTM is not on any of the current management lists. No doubt political expediency has something to do with this. But there also may be a juncture at which management's interest intersects with that of the plaintiffs' bar.

When fraud and misuse of corporate authority trigger policy issues, progressives look for ex ante regulatory responses that disempower managers generally, constraining business judgments and reducing rents (Coglianese 2007:161–62; Langevoort 2003:1142). Conservative politicians and administrators, in contrast, prefer to redirect political demands against management to tough enforcement of existing regulation against miscreant individual managers. Thus has criminal antifraud enforcement come to the fore in the years since Enron. The redirection averts substantive regulation that constrains discretion in business policymaking (Langevoort 2003:1141–42). FOTM plays a background role here. It contributes to the deregulatory equilibrium by making a show of enforcement and providing management with "regulatory burden" to target. At the same time, it holds out only a limited threat of disruption.

Indeed, the preference of the plaintiffs' bar for enterprise liability fits well with the preferences of managers who fear individual liability. The implicit agreement is that the plaintiffs' bar gets to collect from the enterprise and the managers get the discretion to run the corporation without additional regulatory oversight. It follows that management could actually prefer FOTM constraint to FOTM termination. Suppose that FOTM termination was a possibility but could give rise to a perception of an enforcement gap, leading to pressure for stepped-up public enforcement. As between a private action safely nested in enterprise liability and a public enforcement resource that could move in the direction of direct action against individuals, the management interest could very well gravitate to the former. More generally, FOTM, by disempowering managers, makes them more legitimate, even as it holds out little threat to individual malefactors.

Summary

We emerge in a political equipoise that holds out a narrow stretch of contestable territory. The plaintiffs' bar has had the upper hand recently, with the management interest lying back in the reeds, looking for opportunities to reduce FOTM's scope and salience without otherwise exciting any new public enforcement initiatives. Initiatives that might actually improve antifraud enforcement somehow get lost in the balance.

Our political economy account has not yet included an important actor, the SEC, the agency responsible for enforcing the securities laws. We turn to it in the next two sections, first taking a historical look at its funding and then considering its role as a political actor in the battle over FOTM.

Public Enforcement Resources

We have seen that FOTM survives and prospers even though it does not work from a public policy perspective. Few law reform discussants mention the simple expedient of doing away with FOTM's reliance presumption. The hesitancy follows from the assumption that public enforcement resources are inadequate to the task of containing fraud, a situation deemed natural and inevitable. Given a limited public apparatus, it follows that any private enforcement is better than none.

The inadequate resources claim sounds as loudly as ever in 2011. The Dodd-Frank Act directed the engagement of a consultant to review the SEC's structure and operations (Dodd-Frank Act 2010:§967(a)(1)). The consultant reported back, confirming the inadequacy of the agency's resources and posing a stark choice to Congress: either provide the agency with funds sufficient to support its required capabilities or cut back on its responsibilities to fit the funds made available (Boston Consulting Group 2011:165–69). Any hopes that Congress would choose the former option were dashed during the budget fracas of 2011.

We here reconsider the inadequate resources assertion, despite the consultant's recent confirmation. The objective is not to controvert the assertion but to reframe the question it answers, inquiring into the degree of resource deficiency instead of putting forward a "yes-or-no" question. The policy literature on antifraud takes the yes-or-no approach and makes in strong form an inadequacy assertion—the public glass is empty, period. Such was indeed the situation when the Supreme Court first implied a private right of action under the federal securities laws in 1964. But public resources have increased greatly since then (particularly during the last decade),[2] so much so as to rejoin the question respecting relative reliance on public and private enforcement. Here is that question: Is it plausible to suggest that the SEC could pick up any enforcement slack occasioned by the removal of the FOTM presumption? We answer in the affirmative, suggesting that FOTM's elimination could be paired with a step up in public enforcement funding for a net improvement in deterrence at no added cost to shareholders.

Before proceeding, we pause to note what we do not contend. We are not claiming that public enforcement is categorically superior to private enforcement, whether as regards to securities law or any other legal regime. Nor are we arguing for across-the-board withdrawal of private rights of action. We address only the shortcomings of FOTM.

The SEC Budget

In 1964, the SEC's budget was $13,900,000; in 2010 its budget was $1,119,000,000. Adjusting the 1964 number for inflation yields a directly comparable 1964 budget figure of $99,232,000.[3] This in turn yields a multiple of increase of 11.4 times. Figure 10.1 shows the SEC's budgets in 2011 dollars. Although large increases by no means occur annually, there is only one extended period of real decline, from 1976 to 1985, during which high inflation was succeeded by political disfavor in the first Reagan administration. At no time has an anti-enforcement Congress or executive used budget cuts to eviscerate the agency.[4]

There are three instances of notable increases, all coincident with high-profile enforcement activity—the first in the mid-1970s, coincident with the foreign payment scandals; the second in the early 1990s, after the Drexel Burnham action and the savings and loan crisis; and the third after Enron in 2001. Of the three, the post-Enron budget increase is the most notable, amounting to a historic upward jump in the amount of public resources devoted to securities law enforcement.

It has been said that whatever budget increases the SEC has received, its available staff always lags behind market growth (Cox and Thomas 2004:758). There is something to this but not as much as once was the case. Figure 10.2 takes the SEC budget, expressed in real terms, and compares it with the number of personnel employed by the agency and the number of publicly traded stocks. In 1964 the SEC had lines for

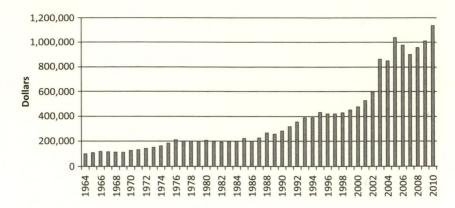

Figure 10.1. SEC Budget (inflation adjusted), 1964–2010. *Source:* SEC Annual Reports.

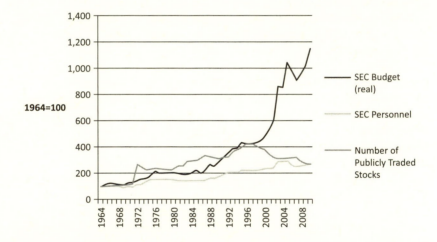

Figure 10.2. SEC Resources to Publicly Traded Stocks, 1964–2010. Number of publicly traded stocks as of the last business day of each year. *Source:* SEC Annual Reports and the Center for Research in Security Prices (CRSP).

1,379 personnel; in 2010 it had lines for 3,748 personnel. In 1964 there were 2,127 publicly traded stocks; in 2010 the number was 5,701. Prior to Enron, the three figures proceed in a band, with the SEC personnel figure lagging. Personnel finally return to parity with the number of stocks traded in 2009. In contrast, the budget, once stoked in the wake of Enron, breaks out of the band.

Figure 10.3 tracks annual SEC personnel and budget figures (here expressed in nominal terms) across the same period against the market value of publicly traded equities (which increased from $490 billion to $17 trillion), also expressed in nominal terms. The budget roughly tracks increases in equity market capitalization until the mid-1990s, when the stock market's sudden rise outstripped that of the budget. The pattern is reversed after 2000, when the market entered a period of backing and filling while the SEC enjoyed budget increases in the wake of Enron and SOX.

Figure 10.4 fleshes out the picture, using enforcement actions initiated by the SEC as a yardstick for agency productivity. These increased from 43 in 1964 to 681 in 2010. The numbers impress when compared with the personnel numbers, and they stay ahead of inflation-adjusted budget increases. At the same time, numbers of enforcement actions per dollar of resources never return to the level achieved in the early 1970s—the complexity and magnitude of the cases doubtless has something to do with this. The numbers show a burst of activity in the wake of the collapse of the 1960s bull market, followed by more moderate and steady increases, with notable upticks after 1990 and again after Enron.[5]

Figure 10.5 offers another view of enforcement, beginning in 1981, when the SEC first included in its annual report the penalties and profit disgorgements ordered in connection with its enforcement actions. The sequence begins at $30 million in 1980 and ends at $2.85 billion in 2010.[6] On an inflation-adjusted basis, the average annual amount ordered during the last five years of the sequence increased 20.2 times over the average amount ordered during the first five years.

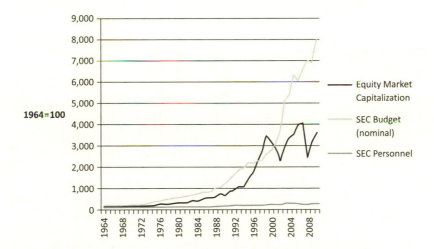

Figure 10.3. SEC Resources to Equity Market Capitalization, 1964–2010. Number of publicly traded stocks as of the last business day each year. *Source:* SEC Annual Reports and CRSP.

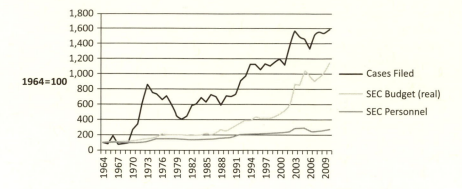

Figure 10.4. SEC Resources to Enforcement Activity, 1964–2010. *Source:* SEC Annual Reports.

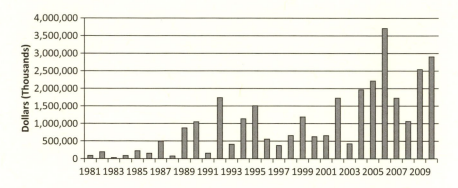

Figure 10.5. Fines and Disgorgements Ordered in SEC Enforcement Actions (inflation adjusted), 1981–2010. *Source:* SEC Annual Reports.

Comparing the Public and Private Sectors

The figures tell us that the SEC's enforcement reach has been extended materially since 1964. But they tell us nothing about the "adequacy" of the resulting enforcement operation.

Figure 10.6 offers some information respecting magnitude and salience, comparing annual amounts of penalties and disgorgements reported by the SEC with total annual class action settlement dollars. The private sector extracts larger sums, especially given big ticket cases like those settled in the wake of Enron and WorldCom. Contrariwise, in recent years the SEC has pulled itself up to parity. Indeed, if one lops off the mega returns in private settlements in 2006 as an outlier, the divergence between the lines is surprisingly small. Figure 10.7 offers a contrasting view, comparing annual numbers of class actions initiated with annual SEC enforcement actions initiated. By this case-by-case measure, the SEC has the larger volume.

Too much should not be made of either comparison. The larger private-sector dollar amounts reflect different incentives and objectives. Lawyers in the private sector have the high-powered motivation of financial gain, while those working at the agency pursue reputational gain in

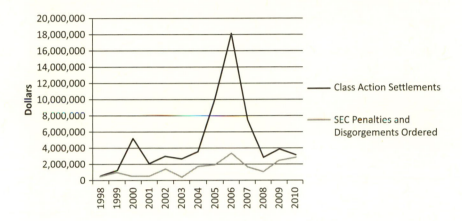

Figure 10.6. SEC vs. Private Actions, Dollar Amounts, 1998–2010. *Source:* SEC Annual Reports and Cornerstone Research.

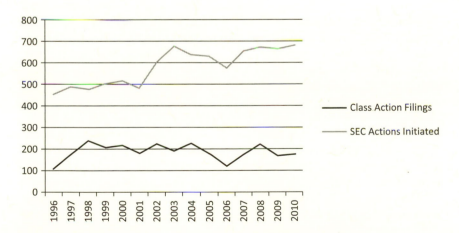

Figure 10.7. SEC vs. Private Actions, Numbers Initiated, 1996–2010. *Source:* SEC Annual Reports and Cornerstone Research.

addition to whatever motivation public service imparts. Plaintiffs' attorneys evaluate potential class actions by settlement value. The SEC is interested more in the magnitude and character of the violation and the proceeding's deterrent payoff (Hillman and Yager 2002:6; Cox and Thomas 2004:760). It also seeks to innovate, bringing new fact patterns within the ambit of the antifraud regime (Cox and Thomas 2004:752). Finally, its enforcers cover a much broader range of subject matter dealing with the defalcations of broker-dealers, investment companies, and investment advisors in addition to the antifraud subject matter covered by private class actions (SEC 2010:9–11). The antifraud overlap segment makes up 50 percent of the enforcement volume at the SEC.[7] The SEC still emerges as the higher volume enforcer, but not by as much as Figure 10.7 indicates.

Finally, we compare numbers of lawyers deployed in the public and private sectors. In 2009–10, five law firms were responsible for 61 percent of the amounts yielded in class action settlements (Ryan and Simmons 2011:14).[8] The law firms in question employed a total of 453 lawyers in mid-2010.[9] Extrapolating, it took around 743 attorneys to produce the 2009–10 settlement yield. In 2009, the SEC enforcement division had a total of 1,223 personnel. Based on a rough estimation, 782 of those were attorneys.[10] The SEC thus matches the private sector in per-capita human resources.

But there are significant differences in focus as well as subject matter coverage. The SEC spends most of its enforcement resources on primary investigation.[11] If there is a front line in fraud enforcement, it is here: in recent years, numbers of investigations initiated by the Enforcement Division have ranged between 3,500 and 4,000 annually (GAO 2009:22). Eighty percent of the division's nonsupervisory lawyers work on the investigative side, while only 20 percent are trial lawyers. This investigative investment spills over to the private sector, where law firms (for the defense as well as for classes of plaintiffs) collect rents once class actions are filed against companies already subjected to SEC investigations. Thirty percent of the class actions settled in 2010 followed the settlement of an SEC action in the same case. The average class action settlement in this SEC overlap subset was $13 million during the period 1996 to 2010; the average settlement in cases without the overlap was $5.8 million (Ryan and Simmons 2011:11).

Finally, we note that the Enforcement Division is reputed to be a troubled operation. It suffers problems of morale and a high personnel turnover rate (although improvements have been noted in recent years; GAO 2009:19–20). The personnel also operate under cumbersome internal review and approval procedures (GAO 2009:27–30). Overall enforcement capacity, moreover, is subject to political controls. The division can grow only to the extent that Congress allocates the necessary funds.

Sources of Funds

If Congress decided to make a stronger commitment to enforcement, the necessary monies would be available at no cost to the taxpayers. As noted above, the SEC is funded by fees it collects from exchange transactions and registrations. Figure 10.8 compares the agency's fee revenues with its operating costs from 1964 to 2010. Fee revenues have exceeded costs since 1983. The sharp decrease in revenues that begins in 2007 results less from decreased market volume than from Congress's enactment of the Fee Relief Act (2002), which achieved in 2008 its objective of aligning the agency's revenues and costs. Previously, excess revenues were remitted to the Treasury; under the Fee Relief Act, they are saved in a separate account for the SEC's future use. The bottom line is that funding for stepped-up enforcement can be procured simply by resetting the fees.

There is yet another potential source of funds. As noted above, SOX's Fair Funds provision charges the SEC with endeavoring to return penalty monies to injured investors. Although the decision to remit is left to the agency's discretion in any given case (SOX 2002:§7246(a)), the agency has followed the course indicated by the statute and remits the funds to investors. Indeed, it has created a new Office of Collections and Distributions to administer the funds (GAO 2009:14–16).[12] The SEC distributed $6.6 billion from 2002 to 2009, of which $2.1 billion flowed out in 2009 (SEC 2010:11).

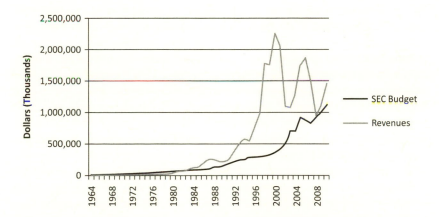

Figure 10.8. SEC Budget and Revenues, 1964–2010. *Source:* SEC Annual Reports.

Congress, having elevated the shareholders' interest in these monies in 2002, redirected a portion to stepped-up enforcement in section 922 of the Dodd-Frank Act (2010). This section provides that between 10 percent and 30 percent of penalties and disgorgements ordered in SEC proceedings be made available to pay a bounty to any whistleblowers who provided the agency with essential information in the case. The SEC is directed to set aside a fund for this purpose, drawing on disgorgement and penalty monies. The SEC duly set aside $452 million in 2010 (SEC 2011:21).

The whistleblower fund is a step in the right direction. From a policy point of view, it correctly elevates the deterrence objective over shareholders' interest in compensation. From a practical point of view, it confirms our fiscal point—should a future Congress again decide to invest in stepped-up antifraud deterrence, funding does not present a barrier.

Recall that FOTM fails as a compensatory mechanism because shareholders ultimately pay the settlements. We now add a countervailing point: it makes no difference who does the enforcing, as the shareholders always end up picking up the tab. The costs, however, do fall differentially within the shareholder class. Private costs fall hardest on undiversified long-term holders; public costs, in contrast, fall hardest on those who do the most trading.

Bang for the Buck

Given that the shareholders pay, there arises a question about comparative costs and results, as between the two sectors. Figure 10.9 sets out the results of an eleven-year comparison between class action attorneys fees, calculated on the assumption of a payout of 23 percent of the settlement,[13] and the cost of the SEC Enforcement Division, calculated on the assumption that the division receives 34 percent of the agency's annual budget.[14] A 23 percent average class action attorneys' fee award implies a damage payout of $4.35 per enforcement dollar invested. The SEC enforcement payout, taken as the average annual quotient of announced disgorgements and penalties divided by the cost of running the Enforcement Division, is $6.20 per dollar invested for the period 1999 to 2009. On this comparison, then, private enforcement emerges as relatively less cost-effective than public enforcement.[15]

Standard policy analysis in corporate law has strongly favored the private sector. Private enforcement benefits from the sharp prod of financial incentives, whereas public enforcers are civil servants working within burdensome administrative contexts. The numbers here, though, suggest that the case for the public side is stronger than generally assumed. High-powered private incentives come at a cash price, and the

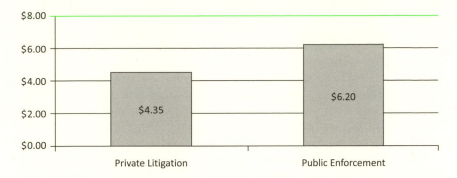

Figure 10.9. Judgment or Settlement Amounts per Dollar Invested in Litigation. *Source:* SEC Annual Reports and Cornerstone Research.

maintenance of the cash machine builds in dependence on enterprise liability, a suboptimal result from an enforcement point of view. An administrative framework could work better here, given the chance. An adequately funded agency could redirect its efforts to individual perpetrators as a matter of policy choice, where the private bar is locked in by its own private economics.

Suppose shareholders were offered the choice between maintaining the status quo or doubling the SEC enforcement budget and abolishing FOTM, leaving the door open for private actions against nontrading issuers where actual reliance can be shown. As we have shown, the case for doubling enforcement resources on the public side is quite plausible. So is indifference between the two choices. The one result that is precluded is the status quo preference for FOTM.

A Proposal for the SEC

Where the plaintiffs' bar looks for settlement value, the SEC is otherwise motivated and thus free to pursue law enforcement objectives. Where the plaintiffs' bar is driven by the economics of settlement and locked into enterprise liability, the SEC is limited by its budget. The SEC settles, too, and often pursues the path of least resistance in so doing, accepting a payment from the corporation rather than pursuing individual miscreants. The implication is that, given additional funds and personnel, the SEC could push harder to target individual defendants and make sure that they in fact pay for their misrepresentations, thus with added deterrent effect. Indeed, the SEC already has taken a step in this direction in its settlements with individual defendants, using the settlement agreement to block resort to directors and officers liability insurance policies.[16] A stronger push need not implicate overdeterrence. Administrative intelligence can seek out the sweet spot where a private incentive to maximize returns holds out risks.

How much additional funding would be required, and how much time would be required to build the needed organizational infrastructure— these are questions to which we have no answers at present. We point out only that the money is available, whether from increased fees or further diversion of penalty and disgorgement proceeds to deterrent use. If Congress doubled the SEC's budget and the SEC then put the entire increase into enforcement, funding for enforcement would increase 300 percent over its present level.

But why would the SEC make such a request? Although requests for large SEC budget increases have been commonplace in the wake of SOX and Dodd-Frank (Sorkin 2011), a one-time, precedent-breaking request for enforcement funding could hold out negative political implications. Langevoort describes the politics of the SEC's budget as a balancing act: on the one hand, the agency needs to depict the markets as investor friendly, for otherwise it has failed in its mission; on the other hand, it needs to depict a continuing threat from miscreant executives (Langevoort 2003:1144). Historically, both sides of the balance have signaled moderate increases in enforcement resources even as the balance has inhibited the agency from seeking a large enforcement increase.

Further dissuading the SEC from pushing for an expanded role in enforcement is its frequent emergence in the role of sacrificial goat when things go wrong. After the pillaging managers themselves, it is next best to blame the SEC in the public press. No one thinks that regulation is perfect or enforcement resources unlimited, but that does not stop anyone from blaming the SEC in the wake of high-profile regulatory breakdowns.

There also are disincentives at the individual level. Many members of the SEC's senior staff come from elite law firms. They use their agency experience to return to the private sector with enhanced prestige (Langevoort 2006:1601–2). On return, they tend to do corporate defense work, work that does not necessarily exist absent plaintiffs with plausible causes of action. Even assuming more SEC enforcement actions and hence more SEC defense work, billable hours across the sector could shrink, especially if individuals displace deep-pocketed companies as defendants. Thus might our proposal excite opposition on both the plaintiffs' and defendants' sides of the bar.

Hence, as a political actor, the SEC would at best have a mixed reaction to our proposed FOTM reform. This is a singular case in which an administrative agency has no reason to seek to maximize its own power and budget, contrary to the prediction of rational choice theory. The SEC has too many bumps and bruises to take a much-enhanced enforcement role, even leaving mixed motives aside.

Furthermore, even assuming the SEC made a request for more resources, why would Congress go along? It has often increased the SEC's budget in the past, but never by leaps and bounds; unusual increases tend to come in the wake of scandals and legislative overhauls. In addition, opposition from the business lobby safely can be predicted.

Within the present political economy of securities law enforcement, then, there is no reason for the SEC to request an extraordinary budget increase directed to enforcement nor for Congress to grant one. But political equilibriums can be disrupted.

We think Congress would view increases in the SEC enforcement budget more favorably if a political give-back came in tandem. More particularly, we propose a quid pro quo: stepped-up public enforcement in exchange for reduced reliance on private enforcement; increased funding for enforcement in exchange for the elimination of the FOTM presumption. The objective is a more effective enforcement regime, funded to facilitate enforcement against individual defendants, but without an overall increase in costs borne by shareholders.

Our proposition is simple, and its objectives have solid grounding in two decades of policy analysis. The party best situated to effectuate the proposal is the SEC, which recently has been reorganizing, reforming, and expanding its enforcement operations.

In our view, the SEC has the rulemaking power to remove the FOTM presumption. The authority follows from the words of section 10(b) of the Securities and Exchange Act of 1934, which delegates authority to make such antifraud "rules and regulations as the Commission may prescribe as necessary or appropriate in the public interest or for the protection of investors." It has been argued, plausibly in our view, that the resulting envelope of authority is capacious enough to allow the SEC to remove the implied 10b-5 private right of action (Grundfest 1994:976–79). Even if that were not the case and judicial implication of a private action somehow were deemed to limit the SEC's rulemaking authority,[17] many of the terms of the private right of action remain open to statement, modification, or reversal by rule.

The matter is not entirely clear, however. It can be argued that ex post statutory modifications of the private right of action signal congressional affirmation if not ratification of the action's basic terms, including the FOTM presumption.[18] Were this interpretation to prevail, our proposal would have to be remitted in its entirety to Congress.

Either way, we look to the SEC to take the initiative, assuming primary responsibility for antifraud enforcement, along with all accompanying management and planning problems, and stepping away from a long-standing, ad hoc public/private arrangement.

We acknowledge a risk of unintended effects. The management interest could seize the occasion to effect through political pressure a net reduction in enforcement resources. This result would follow if, say, the SEC were to present a plan to Congress and Congress then decided to eliminate the FOTM presumption legislatively without approving a compensating increase to the SEC's enforcement budget. This is possible but in our view unlikely. We have seen that the politics tilt in favor of enforcement, with the less attractive aspects of the private action providing the political point of engagement for management opposition.

Conclusion

We hold out no hopes for our reform's early adoption. Management is more concerned about individual liability and maintaining discretion in running corporations. In its current form, FOTM threatens neither. Individual shareholders are unorganized and rationally apathetic. Institutional shareholders have a standing legal agenda and are unlikely to interject themselves into this fight. The plaintiffs' bar has resources to throw into maintaining the status quo and so remains the big winner if change can be resisted. There is nothing wrong with that; private sector players are expected to act in their own interests. The SEC does not now have and may not want the mandate to fix FOTM, but we believe it is the actor best placed to fix the problem.

FOTM creates a deadweight loss to society, simultaneously generating winners and losers. In such a situation, there may be a void unless a government actor proactively enters the play, representing society's best interests. We contend that the SEC has the finances, the expertise, and the legal opening to step in and fill the void.

Notes

1. The charge is conditioned on a concomitant disgorgement order and the decision to remit is left to the agency's discretion in any given case (SOX 2002:§7246(a)).

2. Precedent inquiries into SEC enforcement resources emphasize limitations (Cox and Thomas 2004:129–31).

3. The calculation was performed using the Bureau of Labor Statistics calculator available at http://data.bls.gov to yield dollars in 2011.

4. SEC partisans recently alleged just this, when Congress rejected the agency's 2012 budget request and some in the House talked cuts (Curran and Hamilton 2011). But cuts have not been forthcoming. Under the present Continuing Resolution, the SEC comes away with a $74 million increase (Waddell 2011).

5. The early 1990s increases may reflect a legislative adjustment—Congress materially added to the SEC's stock of enforcement weapons in the Securities Enforcement and Penny Stock Reform Act (1990). Before 1990, the agency had only two choices in addressing violations of mandatory disclosure rules (outside of the public offering context)—either going to court for an injunction or proceeding administratively to request a corrective filing. The 1990 legislation added the administrative cease-and-desist order with an express possibility of profit disgorgement and opened doors for the agency to seek civil monetary penalties outside of insider trading contexts.

6. It is noted that amounts ordered are greater than amounts actually collected. The SEC has a problem collecting awards from judgment-proof defendants. The problems are unsurprising given that securities violations tend to occur at companies experiencing financial difficulty.

7. In 2008, 23 percent of SEC actions initiated concerned issuer reporting problems; adding actions concerning securities offerings and insider trading brings the total to 50 percent (GAO 2009:23). The SEC also initiated significant numbers of actions against investment advisors, broker-dealers, and market manipulators.

8. The law firms were Robbins, Rudman and Dowd; Bernstein, Litowitz, Berger and Grossman; Barroway, Topaz, Kessler, Meltzer and Check; Labaton Sucharow; and Milberg.

9. The numbers were counted on the law firms' websites on July 24, 2010.

10. We roughed out using percentages for 2008 detailed in the GAO (2009:18). According to the report, 54 percent of nonsupervisory positions in enforcement are taken by investigative attorneys and 10.3 percent by trial attorneys. Our estimate assumes that these percentages hold for supervisory personnel as well.

11. Extrapolating from the numbers reported in footnote 10, we estimate that 80 percent of the division's lawyers do investigation and 20 percent trial work.

12. The action came at the instance of a GAO recommendation (GAO 2007:24–31).

13. This is the mean percentage recovery in securities cases for the period 1993–2008 in Eisenberg and Miller (2009:15). Figures for earlier periods tend to be higher (32 percent) (Martin et al. 1999:141).

14. The 34 percent figure is derived by comparing the Enforcement Division budget for the years 2004 to 2008, as reported in GAO (2009:19), to the SEC's overall budget for each year. It is an average of the five years' figures.

15. The result reverses a conventional wisdom regarding the respective costs of public and private service provision. For an example of the conventional view, see Trebilcock and Iacobucci (2003:1429), which cites data on waste collection, electric utilities, and postal services.

16. Historically, even when individual fines are imposed, the settlements tend to permit the operation of indemnification agreements between corporations and managers (Spatt 2007). But SEC practice has changed and individual defendants now must pay themselves (Bailey Cavalieri LLC 2005).

17. We think that result unlikely. Our view would be different if the statute itself created the private right of action. For example, *Kelley v. EPA* (1994) reads an express private right of action to block administrative rulemaking power over the scope of substantive rights.

18. This occurred with the enactment of the PSLRA (1995). The theory would be that recognition implies the reception of the basic outlines of the judicially

outlined action into the statutory scheme so as to shield the action from altera-
tion by agency rulemaking. The Supreme Court brought congressional ratification to the fore in its reasoning in *Stoneridge Investment Partners LLC v.
Scientific-Atlanta, Inc.* (2008:165), concluding that congressional recognition
tied the court's hands and blocked an expansion of the action's scope.

References

American Law Institute (1965) *Restatement (Second) of Torts*. Philadelphia: American Law Institute.

Avery, John W. (1996) "Securities Litigation Reform: The Long and Winding
Road to the Private Securities Litigation Reform Act of 1995." *Business Lawyer* 51: 335–78.

Bailey Cavalieri LLC (2005) "SEC's Dim View of Indemnification Darkens."
www.baileycavalieri.com/68-SECs_View_Indemnification.pdf.

Berle, Adolf A., Jr., and Gardiner C. Means (1932) *The Modern Corporation and
Private Property*. New York: Macmillan.

Booth, Richard A. (2008) "The Paulson Report Reconsidered: How to Fix Securities Litigation by Converting Class Actions into Issuer Actions." Villanova
Law and Public Policy Research Paper No. 2008-1, http://papers.ssrn.com
/sol3/papers.cfm?abstract_id=1084040.

Boston Consulting Group (2011) *U.S. Securities and Exchange Commission: Organizational Study and Reform*. www.sec.gov/news/studies/2011/967study.pdf.

Bratton, William W., and Joseph A. McCahery (1995) "Regulatory Competition,
Regulatory Capture, and Corporate Self-Regulation." *North Carolina Law
Review* 73: 1861–47.

Bratton William W., and Michael L. Wachter (2008) "Shareholder Primacy's
Corporatist Origins: Adolf Berle and the Modern Corporation." *Journal of
Corporation Law* 34: 99–152.

Choi, Stephen J. (2000) "Regulating Investors Not Issuers: A Market Based Proposal." *California Law Review* 88: 279–334.

——(2007) "Do the Merits Matter Less After the Private Securities Litigation
Reform Act?" *Journal of Law Economics and Organizations* 23: 598–626.

Choi, Stephen J., and Jill E. Fisch (2008) "Survey Evidence on the Developing
Role of Public Pension Funds in Corporate Governance." *Vanderbilt Law Review* 61: 315–54.

Choi, Steven J., and Robert B. Thompson (2006) "Securities Litigation and Its
Lawyers: Changes During the First Decade After PSLRA." *Columbia Law Review* 106: 1489–533.

Coffee, John C., Jr. (2006) "Reforming the Securities Class Action: An Essay on
Deterrence and Its Implementation." *Columbia Law Review* 106: 1534–86.

Coglianese, Cary (2007) "Legitimacy and Corporate Governance." *Delaware
Journal of Corporate Law* 32: 159–68.

Cox, James D., and Randall Thomas (2004) "SEC Enforcement Heuristics: An
Empirical Inquiry." *Duke Law Journal* 53: 737–80.

Curran, John J., and Jesse Hamilton (2011) "Schapiro SEC Seen Ineffectual
Amid Dodd-Frank Funding Curbs." *Bloomberg Markets Magazine*, March 31.

Eisenberg, Theodore, and Geoffrey P. Miller (2009) "Attorney's Fees and Expenses in Class Action Settlements: 1993–2008." New York University School
of Law, Law and Economics Working Paper 09-50.

Fox, Merritt B. (2009) "Civil Liability and Mandatory Disclosure." *Columbia Law Review* 109: 237–308.

Government Accountability Office (2007) *Securities and Exchange Commission: Additional Actions Needed to Ensure Planned Improvements Address Limitations in Enforcement Division Operations.* http://www.gao.gov/products/GAO-07-830.

——— (2009) *Securities and Exchange Commission: Greater Attention to Enhance Communication and Utilization of Resources in the Division of Enforcement.* http://www.gao.gov/products/GAO-09-358.

Grundfest, Joseph A. (1994) "Disimplying Private Rights of Action Under the Federal Securities Laws: The Commission's Authority." *Harvard Law Review* 107: 961–1024.

Hillman, Richard J., and Loren Yager (2002) Statement: Major Human Capital Challenges at SEC and Key Trade Agencies. Hearing Before the Senate Subcommittee on Oversight of Government Management, 107th Congress.

Jackson, Howell E., and Mark. J. Roe (2009) "Public and Private Enforcement of Securities Law: Resource-Based Evidence." *Journal of Financial Economics* 93: 207–38.

Karmel, Roberta (2005) "Realizing the Dream of William O. Douglas—The Securities and Exchange Commission Takes Charge of Corporate Governance." *Delaware Journal of Corporate Law* 30: 79–144.

Langevoort, Donald C. (1996) "Capping Damages for Open Market Securities Fraud." *Arizona Law Review* 38: 639–64.

——— (1999) "Rereading *Cady, Roberts*: The Ideology and Practice of Insider Trading Regulation." *Columbia Law Review* 99: 1319–43.

——— (2003) "Managing the 'Expectations Gap' in Investor Protection: The SEC and the Post-Enron Reform Agenda." *Villanova Law Review* 48: 1139–66.

——— (2004). "Structuring Securities Regulation in the European Union: Lessons from the US Experience." Georgetown Public Law, Research Paper No. 624582, http://papers.ssrn.com/sol3/papers.cfm?abstract_id=624582.

——— (2006) "The SEC as a Lawmaker: Choices About Investor Protection in the Face of Uncertainty." *Washington University Law Review* 84: 1591–626.

——— (2007a) "On Leaving Corporate Executives 'Naked, Homeless and Without Wheels': Corporate Fraud, Equitable Remedies, and the Debate over Entity Versus Individual Liability." *Wake Forest Law Review* 42: 627–62.

——— (2007b) "The Social Construction of Sarbanes-Oxley." *Michigan Law Review* 105: 1817–56.

Mahoney, Paul G. (1997) "The Exchange as Regulator." *Virginia Law Review* 83: 1453–500.

Martin, Denise N. et al. (1999) "Recent Trends IV: What Explains Filings and Settlements in Shareholder Class Actions." *Stanford Journal of Law, Business and Finance* 5: 121–74.

Rock, Edward B. (1991) "The Logic and (Uncertain) Significance of Institutional Shareholder Activism." *Georgetown Law Journal* 79: 445–506.

Ryan, Ellen M., and Laura E. Simmons (2011) *Cornerstone Research, Securities Class Action Settlements: 2010 Review and Analysis.* http://www.cornerstone.com/news/xprNewsDetailCornerstone.aspx?xpST=NewsDetailandnews=118.

Securities and Exchange Commission (1948) "Rules and Regulations Under the Securities and Exchange Act of 1934." *Federal Register* 13: 8177, 8183, December 22, codified at 17 C.F.R. § 240.10b-5.

——— (2010) *FY2009 Performance and Accountability Report.* http://www.sec.gov/about/secpar/secpar2009.pdf.

———— (2011) *FY2010 Performance and Accountability Report.* http://www.sec.gov
/about/secpar/secpar2010.pdf.
Sorkin, Andrew Ross (2011) "Wall St. Aids S.E.C. Case for Budget." *New York
Times*, February 8, B1.
Spatt, Chester S. (2007) Address Before the American Economic Association,
January 6. http://www.sec.gov/news/speech/2007/spch010607css.htm.
Thompson, Robert B., and Hillary A. Sale (2003) "Securities Fraud as Corporate
Governance: Reflections upon Federalism." *Vanderbilt Law Review* 56: 859–910.
Trebilcock, Michael J., and Edward M. Iacobucci (2003) "Privatization and Ac-
countability." *Harvard Law Review* 116: 1422–54.
Waddell, Melanie (2011) "Congress Moves Budget Vote to Thursday; SEC, CFTC
See Budget Boost." *Advisor One*, April 12. http://www.advisorone.com/article
/congress-moves-budget-vote-thursday-sec-cftc-see-budget-boost.
Weiss, Elliott J., and John S. Beckerman (1995) "Let the Money Do the Monitor-
ing: How Institutional Investors Can Reduce Agency Costs in Securities
Class Actions." *Yale Law Journal* 104: 2053–128.

Cases Cited

Basic Inc. v. Levinson, 485 U.S. 224 (1988).
J. I. Case Co. v. Borak, 377 U.S. 426 (1964).
Kelley v. Environmental Protection Agency, 15 F.3d 1100 (D.C. Cir. 1994).
Stoneridge Investment Partners LLC v. Scientific-Atlanta, Inc., 552 U.S. 148 (2008).

Statutes Cited

Dodd-Frank Wall Street Reform and Consumer Protection Act of 2010, Pub. L.
No. 111-203, 124 Stat. 1376.
Foreign Corrupt Practices Act of 1977, Pub. L. No. 95-213, 91 Stat. 1494.
Investor and Capital Markets Fee Relief Act of 2002, Pub. L. No. 107-123, 115
Stat. 2390-2401.
Private Securities Litigation Reform Act of 1995, Pub. L. No. 104-67, 109 Stat.
737.
Sarbanes-Oxley Act of 2002, Pub. L. No. 107-204, 116 Stat. 745.
Securities and Exchange Act of 1934, 15 U.S.C. § 78j (2006)
Securities Enforcement and Penny Stock Reform Act of 1990. Pub. L. No. 101-
429, 104 Stat. 931.

Chapter 11

Why Aren't Regulation and Litigation Substitutes?

An Examination of the Capture Hypothesis

Eric Helland and Jonathan Klick

In the United States, regulatory agencies and private litigation operate parallel systems of regulation in many substantive areas. At times, these systems can generate mutually inconsistent outcomes, as complying with a regulation sometimes leads to liability exposure. Even when these systems do not directly conflict, a number of critics suggest that these overlapping mechanisms lead to too much regulation. Because of these concerns, some scholars and reformers argue that courts should be more willing to hold that regulations preempt litigation or to allow the use of a regulatory compliance defense, which is currently unavailable in most U.S. jurisdictions but is a standard option in many other countries. With relatively few (and narrow) exceptions, however, policymakers and judges in the United States have been resistant to these suggestions.

The intuitive belief that regulation should shrink the scope of litigation finds support in the more formal work of scholars. In the standard law and economics model, levels of regulation and litigation move in opposite directions. As regulations become more restrictive, there is less harm to be litigated over; more litigation leads to deterrence and a corresponding reduction in the need to regulate inefficiently risky behavior. In the production function for safety, regulation and litigation are substitute inputs on the margin. This intuition has been formalized by Steven Shavell, and it motivates most economic analyses of regulatory design (Shavell 1984a:357; 1984b:271).

Unfortunately, there is a disconnect in this case between economic theory and what actually seems to happen in the world at large. In earlier work on insurance law, we have shown that, if anything, litigation and regulation move together (Helland and Klick 2007, forthcoming). Similar claims about litigation and regulation moving together have been made with respect to securities law, products liability, consumer protection, and a host of other legal areas.

The original equipment manufacturer (OEM) parts cases (*Avery v. State Farm Mutual Auto Insurance* 1999) that we discussed in our earlier work are illustrative of a "damned if you do, damned if you don't" quality of overlapping regulatory and litigation systems (Helland and Klick, forthcoming). In the OEM class action litigation, insurers found themselves defending against a myriad of consumer protection claims that they had not used OEM parts, even though state regulations had explicitly allowed the use of non-OEM parts and, in a few states, had actually required the use of nonoriginal parts (Government Accountability Office 2001).

Given the standard economic model's implication that efficiency requires regulation and litigation to be substitutes on the margin, and the empirical observations—some anecdotal and some more systematic— that substitution does not occur, concerns about the inefficient, duplicative effects of coterminous regulatory and litigation systems may be justified. However, the standard model assumes away many issues that could reverse conclusions that the current dual system of litigation and regulation is inefficient. Perhaps, once these issues are considered, the lack of substitution is less troubling, and we may have a partial solution to the puzzle of why decision makers are hesitant to hold that regulations preempt liability or to recognize the regulatory compliance defense more broadly.

In this chapter, we investigate one of the primary alternate theories of overlapping regulations and litigation, namely, that litigation is necessary to fill gaps created due to regulatory capture. While the standard model developed by Shavell assumes that a benign social planner will choose the proper level of regulation (and that regulations will be enforced without error), this may not hold true in reality.

Litigation and Regulatory Capture

Although we find little evidence that regulation and litigation are substitutes in deterring harm, there is one possible explanation for the absence of this finding that would still preserve a role for litigation alongside the regulatory process. Specifically litigation, especially class action litigation, may serve as a method for undoing regulatory capture.

There is a large literature in economics and political science about industry co-opting regulators. One of the earliest proponents of this view was George Stigler, who argued that regulation largely worked to the benefit of industry, a state of affairs often characterized as "regulatory capture" (Stigler 1971). The potential for regulatory capture by industry would appear to recommend litigation as a backstop to regulation, as it gives injured parties a second venue in which to pursue claims necessary to generate efficient levels of deterrence.

Some suggestive evidence on the relationship between regulatory capture and the filing of lawsuits might be found in the differences between elected and unelected utility or insurance commissioners. It has been documented in several studies that states that elect their insurance commissioners also have lower utility and insurance rates (Besley and Coate 2003:1176). This difference is usually attributed to elected officials being more pro-consumer and less subject to capture.

Elections may also break the "revolving door" since many elected insurance commissioners are looking for higher office and are hence less likely to have either been drawn from or returning to industry. The basic hypothesis would be that state regulatory commissions in which commissioners must face the voters are less likely to be captured by industry because voting offers a low-cost way to punish commissioners who become too friendly with industry. If this is correct, and if capture helps drive the frequency of litigation, then states that elect their commissioners would be expected to have fewer insurance class action lawsuits. The logic is that class actions and elections would serve similar functions in providing a venue for consumers to reverse pro-industry rulings by the regulator.

To investigate this hypothesis, we use the RAND insurance class action data set that has formed the basis for other academic studies (Helland and Klick 2007, forthcoming; Pace et al. 2007). The data come from a survey of 130 insurance companies, primarily larger property-casualty, life, and health insurers, covering 748 distinct class actions filed during the period 1992 to 2002. Table 11.1 provides the distribution of insurance lines implicated by the cases.

Table 11.1. Cases in Data Set

Lines	Percentage of all cases
Automobile	67.5
Homeowners	12.8
Life	7.1
Workers' compensation	6.3
Health	2.4
Multiple lines	1.2
Annuities	1.2
Earthquake	1.2
Mobile home	0.9

States with Elected Regulators

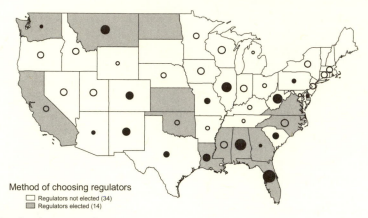

Method of choosing regulators
☐ Regulators not elected (34)
▨ Regulators elected (14)

Circles represent number of cases per capita
Solid circles denote positive deviations from the mean
Hollow circles denote negative deviations from the mean
Circle size proportional to absolute value of deviation

Figure 11.1. States with Elected Regulators and the Number of Class Actions Filed in the State per Capita.

Figure 11.1 provides some evidence relating to the capture hypothesis.[1] The shading of the maps shows which states, during the sample period, elected insurance commissioners and which appointed them. In the thirty-one appointed states and eleven of the fourteen elected states, our survey contained information on the number of class actions filed in the state. The map reveals several states that stand out for the number of class action filings, but these states appear to be similarly divided between states with elected or unelected insurance regulators.[2]

The mean number of cases and filings for both elected and unelected commissioners is presented in Table 11.2. The number of class actions and class actions per one thousand residents of the state are actually higher in states that elect their commissioners, a result inconsistent with the notion that class actions are a method by which consumers can reverse the regulatory mandate of captured regulators. Table 11.2 suggests that, in states where electoral institutions would be expected to tend to push regulators to act more favorably toward consumers, we in fact see more class actions, not fewer.

In summary, at least by one measure—namely, elections—states with regulators that are less susceptible to industry capture are in fact more likely to face more class actions. These data are inconsistent with the hypothesis that class actions are a device for reversing anticonsumer regulatory decisions by a regulatory agency that favors industry.

Table 11.2. Elected Regulators and Class Action Frequency

Selection method	Number of cases	t test	Number of cases per 1,000	t test
Unelected commissioners	12.61		2.18	
	(17.51)		(1.72)	
Number of observations	31		31	
Elected commissioners	24.45		3.29	
	(36.69)		(2.75)	
Number of observations	11	−5.996	11	−2.01

This finding, however, might be consistent with an alternative hypothesis about a deeper, if not more pernicious, theory of capture: perhaps elected regulatory commissions are more prone to capture, producing less effective regulation that allows a larger scope for litigation. Given that regulated industries have greater incentives to band together and to contribute to the election of favorable regulators, relatively dispersed consumers may be unable to counter this with their own voting behavior and contributions. Of course, we have no way to test this alternative hypothesis directly.

Judicial Capture

Left without strong support for our hypothesis regarding regulatory capture and the relationship between regulation and litigation, we seek other candidates. In this section we examine two factors that potentially could determine filing location independent of the underlying harm. We examine a specific measure of how "pro-plaintiff" the state's judiciary is: judicial elections. Several authors have provided evidence that when judges stand for election, the parties to disputes seek to influence the outcome of cases usually by contributing to judicial election funds (Hall and Bonneau 2006:50; 2008:457; Schotland 1985:57; Geyth 2003:64; Wright 1996).[3]

At first glance, the courts seem unlikely candidates for capture. Unlike insurance companies and regulators, plaintiffs and defendants are usually not repeat players in the courts. Moreover, litigants' choice of venue is limited, meaning that capturing a single judge would not be sufficient. Defendants would have to capture all judges who could possibly hear their case.

Yet there are repeat players in litigation, namely, plaintiffs' attorneys (Helland and Tabarrok 2000, 2002; Johnston and Wadfogel 2002). Class action litigation is different from other litigation in that both parties' attorneys are potentially repeat players. Admittedly, if industry is not initiating the litigation, it may be less likely to be able to capture a court. But the possibility of forum shopping by plaintiffs' attorneys increases the likelihood of judicial capture in a manner favorable to plaintiffs. Although there is relatively little systematic information on the likelihood of repeat class action litigation in the same venue, stories of forum shopping and "litigation hell holes" abound.

This suggests that although we may find no relationship between the electoral institutions used to select regulatory commissioners and class action frequency, plaintiffs' attorneys can still be expected to file cases in states where judges are more sympathetic. Helland and Tabarrok (2000, 2002) found that in states that elect judges in partisan elections, awards against out-of-state defendants in tort cases are $230,092 higher than similar cases tried in states that do not elect judges in partisan elections.

There is some evidence that class action filings are more likely in states that elect their judges. Figure 11.2 shows how states with elected judges compare against the national average in total filings per capita during the sample period.[4] Four of the above-average states have appointed judges while eight have elected judges.[5]

If we consider the ten states that elect judges in partisan elections, a similar pattern holds. As Figure 11.3 shows, states with partisan elections

States with Elected Judges

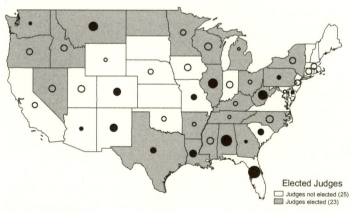

Elected Judges
☐ Judges not elected (25)
▨ Judges elected (23)

Circles represent number of cases per capita
Solid circles denote positive deviations from the mean
Hollow circles denote negative deviations from the mean
Circle size proportional to absolute value of deviation

Figure 11.2. States with Elected Judges and per Capita Class Action Filing Frequency.

States with Partisan Elected Judges

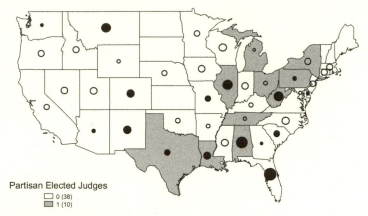

Partisan Elected Judges
☐ 0 (38)
▨ 1 (10)

Circles represent number of cases per capita
Solid circles denote positive deviations from the mean
Hollow circles denote negative deviations from the mean
Circle size proportional to absolute value of deviation

Figure 11.3. States with Judges Elected in Partisan Elections and per Capita
Number of Class Action Filings.

have a disproportionate share of above-average filing rates compared
with the rest of the country. The pattern is even more pronounced if
total filings (not adjusted for population) are examined: seven states
with partisan-elected judges have above-average levels of filings, compared with only five of the other states having above-average levels.

Tables 11.3 and 11.4 test whether the difference in means between
class action frequencies in elected and partisan elected states is statistically significant. The total number of filings is higher in states with
elected judges, although the difference is not statistically significant.

For the states that use partisan elections to select their judges, the
results are similar. States with judges elected in partisan elections have
a higher number of filings during the sample period, and the difference is statistically significant for both the total number of cases and for
per-capita cases.

The question remains of how much to make of the fact that class
action filings are similar in states that use elections to select their
regulators—but class action filings are more frequent in states using
elections, and particularly partisan elections, to select their judges. The
results do not appear consistent with class actions acting as a check on
captured insurance regulators, at least to the extent that Besley and
Coate (2003) and others are correct that elected regulators are less likely

Table 11.3. Elected Judges and Class Action Frequency

Selection method	Number of cases	t test	Number of cases per 1,000	t test
Unelected judges	14.45		2.48	
	(28.25)		(2.08)	
Number of observations	20		20	
Elected judges	16.86		2.47	
	(20.21)		(2.088)	
Number of observations	22	−1.042	22	−0.05

Table 11.4. Partisan Elected Judges and Class Action Frequency

Selection method	Number of cases	t test	Number of cases per 1,000	t test
Unelected judges	10.97		2.104	
	(22.85)		(1.93)	
Number of observations	32		32	
Elected judges	30.9		3.66	
	(22.59)		(2.09)	
Number of observations	10	−6.68	10	−5.9

to be captured by industry. The results are instead more consistent with a broader political economy story in which interest groups compete for influence with the regulator. In this case, however, the "regulator" appears to be elected judges. One explanation is the plaintiffs' attorneys are filing cases in venues they think will be more sympathetic to their cases.

Further research is clearly needed on the connections between the electoral institutions used to select judges and class actions. For the purposes of this chapter, it is sufficient to say that the evidence is not consistent with class actions being a method for consumers to undo regulatory capture by industry. Whatever else may be driving the filing decisions of plaintiffs' attorneys, it does not appear to be related to how pro- or anti-consumer the local regulators are.

Putting It All Together

The previous sections, and some of our previous work, have examined the correlations between class action litigation and regulation, as well as the related hypothesis that regulatory inattention due to capture by industry is driving class actions. We find little evidence that litigation and regulations are substitutes. It is possible, of course, that our analysis misses important interactions between the various measures of regulatory stringency.

In this section, we present the results of a regression of each of the factors mentioned in this chapter. The dependent variable, $cases_{ijt}$, is the number of cases filed in the state i, of a specific allegation j, in year t. We divide the factors into three categories. The first category includes factors related to the substitution hypothesis, which we include in x_{ijt}. The factors include those used in our earlier work: the log of the number of market conduct investigations in the state regulatory office per insurance company, the log of the number of market conduct examiners per regulated firm, the log of the regulatory budget per regulated firm, and the log of the number of fines per regulated firm. These variables are designed to capture regulatory intensity. For example, a higher enforcement budget and fines would, according to the substitution hypothesis, reduce the number of insurance-related harms and hence reduce the number of class actions.

One concern is that regulators simply may not be interested in the same types of harms that generate class actions. In the case of securities litigation, the federal Securities and Exchange Commission explicitly prosecutes cases against small firms because the recovery in these cases will be small and it leaves the litigation against larger firms to private attorneys. Something similar could result in insurance class actions. To determine the relationship between regulator interest and class actions, the RAND Institute for Civil Justice conducted a survey in 2005 of staff members of state departments of insurance. Seventeen states completed the survey. The survey asked the regulators to rank the 260 key allegations made by the plaintiffs according to their relationship to the traditional activities of the regulator. Each allegation was ranked on a five-point scale. A rating of 1 implied little or no relationship between the particular allegation and the regulators traditional activities. A rating of 5 implied a significant overlap with the regulators' activities. A more complete discussion of the results is contained in Pace et al. (2007).

The across-state average rankings ranged from 2.0 for claims alleging that the defendants "failed to have settlements reached with minors reviewed and approved by a judge," to an average of 5.0 for claims that "the defendants sold coverages in insolvent plans or with unlicensed carriers." The mean- and median-adjusted responses were about 3.6. Pace et al. (2007) classified regulatory issues with an adjusted response above the 80th percentile (i.e., those greater than 4.07) as having the "strongest" potential relationship to a state's regulatory regime. They further labeled issues in the bottom 20th percentile of all adjusted responses (3.15 and below) as having the "weakest" relationship. Those issues between the 20th and 80th percentile were ranked as having a "modest" relationship. We include the proportion of cases making a similar allegation that regulators ranked as having a strong relationship in the ICJ survey to control for regulator interest in the specific allegation.

The second category of factor, z_{ijt}, includes whether the state insurance regulators are elected, whether the state chooses its judge via elections, and whether the state chooses it judges in partisan elections.

The final set of factors, w_{ijt}, relate to the existence of previous class actions concerning a given allegation in a state. It includes the proportions of cases in the four years prior to the observation year that are remanded to federal courts (e.g., 1991–94 for a 1995 observation year), the proportions of cases in which the class was certified, the proportion of cases certified for a multistate class, the proportion of cases certified for nationwide classes, and the proportion of cases in which regulators filed a brief on behalf of the defendants. The factors are measured both by allegation, thus measuring the outcomes of cases in any state or the federal system making a similar allegation, and by state, thus measuring the impact on future filings of the outcome of other class actions in the state in the last four years. The specification,

$$cases_{ijt} = \beta_1 x_{ijt} + \beta_2 z_{ijt} + \beta_3 w_{ijt} + \beta_4 \; controls + \varepsilon_{ijt},$$

includes an error term clustered on the state-allegation cell.[6] We also estimate the model by using several different controls. In all specifications, we include the number of firms in our sample that offer insurance in the state in order to control for the impact of any differences in filings caused by market differences by state. We also include year fixed effects to control for the national trend (allowing for nonlinearities) and tort reforms.[7] In other specifications, we include fixed effects for state and allegation and then an interaction of the state-allegation fixed effects. The descriptive statistics are provided in Table 11.5.

The results are presented in Table 11.6. We estimate three basic models. Model 1 estimates the number of class actions of a particular allegation filed in a state in a given year, including all of the factors and several subsets of the factors but only controls for years. Model 2 includes controls for year, allegation, and state, while Model 3 adds a control for each state-allegation cell. The inclusion of state fixed effects necessitates the removal of state-level variables that do not vary though time. Thus Models 2 and 3 do not include the election variables. The difference between Models 2 and 3 is that in Model 2 we utilize the variation between states to estimate the allegation-specific variables and the variation between allegations to estimate the state-specific variables. In our Model 3 estimation, we use only the within-state allegation variation. This means

Table 11.5. Descriptive Statistics

Variable	Mean	SD	Min	Max
Number of cases	−0.040389	0.32458	0	17
Log market conduct exams	−4.36489	1.212156	−6.90776	−1.24321
Log market conduct examiners per firm	−5.84973	1.03248	−6.90776	−2.46308
Log budget per firm	15.94643	1.012368	13.0002	18.97122
Log fines per firm	−5.5933	0.930081	−6.90776	−2.30523
% of allegation with strong rank	0.274213	0.270612	0	1
% of allegation with modest rank	0.551745	0.300221	0	1
Agency officials elected	0.235294	0.424194	0	1
Judges chosen in election	0.470588	0.499148	0	1
Judges chosen in partisan election	0.235294	0.424194	0	1
Number of out-of-state companies in risk set	0.972525	0.063475	0	1
Proportion of cases moved to federal court by allegation, last 4 years	0.10179	0.165627	0	1
Proportion of cases moved to federal court by state, last 4 years	0.102579	0.223705	0	1
Proportion of cases with approved certification by allegation, last 4 years	0.090668	0.176659	0	1
Proportion of cases with approved certification by state, last 4 years	0.071095	0.169218	0	1
Proportion of multistate class actions by allegation, last 4 years	0.024949	0.09396	0	1
Proportion of multistate class actions by state, last 4 years	0.009881	0.058711	0	1
Proportion of nationwide class actions by allegation, last 4 years	0.022713	0.09262	0	1
Proportion of nationwide class actions by state, last 4 years	0.007485	0.056938	0	1
Regulators have filed briefs on behalf of the defendant in this line	0.028524	0.11737	0	1
Regulators have filed briefs on behalf of the defendant in this state	0.017489	0.088563	0	1

Table 11.6. Regression Results for the Number of Class Action Cases Filed by State, Allegation, and Year

Variable	Model		
	1	2	3
Log state population	0.02478*** (0.00680)	0.03385 (0.04760)	0.15069** (0.06563)
Log market conduct exams	−0.00224 (0.00267)	−0.00305 (0.00371)	−0.00180 (0.00336)
Log market conduct examiners per firm	0.00142 (0.00362)	0.01591** (0.00625)	0.00934* (0.00533)
Log budget per firm	0.01155* (0.00676)	−0.00721 (0.00735)	−0.00391 (0.00764)
Log fines per firm	0.01543* (0.00800)	0.01684** (0.00805)	0.01925** (0.00903)
% of allegation with strong rank	−0.02961** (0.01476)		
% of allegation with modest rank	−0.00596 (0.01688)		
Agency officials elected	0.02226 (0.01717)		
Judges chosen in election	−0.04595** (0.02032)		
Judges chosen in partisan election	0.05605*** (0.01307)		
Number of out-of-state companies in risk set	−0.07018 (0.04935)	−0.06066 (0.04333)	0.32209** (0.14169)
Proportion of cases moved to federal court by allegation, last 4 years	0.07224*** (0.01798)	0.03426** (0.01603)	0.03264* (0.01686)
Proportion of cases moved to federal court by state, last 4 years	−0.02610 (0.01627)	−0.01952 (0.01230)	−0.02055 (0.01298)
Proportion of cases with approved certification by allegation, last 4 years	0.06460*** (0.01525)	−0.02167 (0.02571)	−0.02230 (0.02800)
Proportion of cases with approved certification by state, last 4 years	0.00761 (0.01780)	−0.01291 (0.01741)	−0.01574 (0.01750)
Proportion of multistate class actions by allegation, last 4 years	1.22834*** (0.38047)	1.05796*** (0.39874)	1.06204** (0.42065)
Proportion of multistate class actions by state, last 4 years	0.38746 (0.27014)	0.05967 (0.26828)	0.11727 (0.24382)
Proportion of nationwide class actions by allegation, last 4 years	−1.36169*** (0.38250)	−1.12647*** (0.41455)	−1.12694** (0.43747)

	Model		
Variable	1	2	3
Proportion of nationwide class actions by state, last 4 years	−0.35764 (0.27234)	−0.03382 (0.27296)	−0.08870 (0.24735)
Regulators have filed briefs on behalf of the defendant in this line	0.02565 (0.01866)	0.01404 (0.02163)	0.01026 (0.02286)
Regulators have filed briefs on behalf of the defendant in this state	−0.03251 (0.02332)	0.01184 (0.02121)	0.01921 (0.02024)
Year controls	Yes	Yes	Yes
Tort reforms	Yes	Yes	Yes
Allegation controls	No	Yes	No
State controls	No	Yes	No
Allegation * state controls	No	No	Yes
Observations	14,145	16,605	16,605
R^2	0.03	0.08	0.28

Note: Robust standard errors are in parentheses.
*$p < .10$; **$p < .05$; $p < .01$.

that the state-specific variables such as state population, budget, market conduct examiners and exams, and fines will be the same in Models 2 and 3, while the variables capturing the state's or allegation's experience with class actions in the last four years will be different in the two corresponding columns.

Model 1 is the full model with all the factors. One common feature of all the models is that the log of population is significant and positive in all specifications. This suggests that potential class size is an important consideration in filing decisions. We also find that an increase in the log budget causes a statistically significant increase in the number of class actions filed in the state. The impact is relatively modest, as a one standard deviation increase in budget increases the number of alleged class actions filed in a state by 1.2 percent. The log of the number of fines per firm also has a positive and statistically significant impact on filings. We find that as a greater proportion of a specific allegation is ranked as being of strong interest to regulatory authorities in our survey, the number of alleged class actions filed in the state decreases. The effect is quite small, with a one standard deviation increase in the proportion of regulators ranking an allegation as having a strong connection to their regulatory mandate coincides with a decrease in the number of class actions by 0.2 percent.

Choosing judges in elections has an overall negative impact on the number of filings. However, choosing judges in a partisan election has a statistically significant and negative impact on filings. Electing a judge in a partisan election increases the number of class action filings in a state by 2 percent while overall states that use elections have about 1 percent fewer filings.

In Models 2 and 3, we include a more extensive set of controls. The addition of state controls does not alter the positive relationship between the log of fines per firm and the number of class actions. Although several of the state-level variables are no longer statistically significant, allegations that have more cases certified for multistate class status have more filings, while those with a nationwide certification have fewer filings.

One remaining issue is the impact of the outcome of previous cases on the decision as to where to file a case. In Table 11.7, we report the impact of the results of past cases on the likelihood of filing. We examine two dimensions of the filing decision: whether to file a case with a specific allegation and, if so, which state to file the case in.

Table 11.7. Marginal Effects

Factor	% change in the number of class actions resulting from a one standard deviation increase
Proportion of cases with a similar allegation moved to federal court	39
Proportion of cases filed in the state moved to federal court	−12.4
Proportion of cases with a similar allegation approved certification	34
Proportion of cases in the state in which the class was certified	12
Proportion of cases certified with multistate classes with a similar allegation	319
Proportion of cases certified with multistate classes in the state	58
Proportion of cases with a similar allegation certified for nationwide classes	−347
Proportion of cases in the state certified for nationwide classes	−54
Proportion of cases with similar allegation in which state regulators have filed briefs on behalf of the defendant	11
Proportion of cases in the state in which state regulators have filed briefs on behalf of the defendant	−13

Note: All factors are for the period covering the last four years.

There are a few surprises in the results. The proportion of cases making a similar allegation that were removed to federal court in the past four years actually increases the likelihood of future cases making similar allegations in state court. One explanation for this finding is that cases that are more important, either in terms of settlement value or the issues involved, are more likely to be removed to federal court.[8] By contrast, a one standard deviation increase in the proportion of cases from a particular state that are removed to federal court decreases the likelihood of future filings in that state by 12.8 percent.

Certification of cases making a similar allegation increases the likelihood that future cases making the same allegation will be filed, and the more cases of any allegation that are certified in a state, the more likely future cases are to be filed in state. The effect is most dramatic with cases certified for multistate litigation. A one standard deviation in the proportion of cases certified for a multistate class increases the likelihood of a future case making the same allegation by 35 percent. A one standard deviation in the proportion of the cases that a state's courts certify for multistate class actions increases the likelihood of future filings by 13.2 percent.

Certification of a nationwide class has the opposite effect. The impact is most dramatic for the proportion of cases making a similar allegation certified for nationwide class action status. This is likely a preemption effect. As more cases are certified for nationwide classes, the plaintiffs for future cases have already been included in ongoing cases. In fact, nationwide class actions are likely to be settlement classes, which suggest that this may well be the intent of the case (Cramton 1995: 811). Finally, removal of a case to federal court publicizes the line of action further, increasing the likelihood that other cases making similar allegations on behalf of plaintiffs in other states or against other defendants will be filed.[9] The negative impact on the proportion of a state's cases receiving nationwide class action status is contrary to our intuition. We would have expected a state allowing more nationwide classes to be certified to be a more attractive venue to file cases, but this appears not to be the case.[10]

Finally, the impact of regulatory intervention in other class actions in the state is consistent with our expectations. Because almost all briefs filed by regulators support the defense, we would expect more active regulators to discourage future filings.[11] Consistent with this theory, an increase in the proportion of class actions in the state in which the regulator filed a brief reduces the number of filings in the state.

The results suggest that plaintiffs' attorneys are determining where to file cases based on the outcome of previous cases rather than the other factors we have examined. Filings are generally more likely where states have been more willing to certify classes and particularly multistate classes. Future cases are less likely when regulators intervene on behalf of defendants and when nationwide classes preempt future filings of a particular allegation.

Conclusion

The evidence presented in this chapter suggests that class actions and regulation are parallel systems, at least in the context of insurance, and that this overlap does not appear to be generated by a desire to curb the effects of regulatory capture. Plaintiffs' filing decisions appear to be influenced by the success of previous plaintiffs both in the state and with a particular allegation. This success itself may be affected by a form of judicial capture whereby states with elected judges are more class-action friendly.

These results suggest that the standard economic models of the interplay between regulation and litigation do not usefully describe reality. Given that, the normative prescriptions of how to structure the dual system of regulation and litigation may well also be incorrect. More fruitful models will likely have to include a richer model of what drives litigation decisions. A deeper understanding of the regulation-liability dynamic may allow for sensible remedies to the problems identified by critics of the U.S. regulatory system, including the potential for overregulation and the creation of regulatory Catch-22s.

Notes

1. One complicating factor is that insurance agencies often differ in scope. The National Association of Insurance Commissioners notes that several agencies have multiple tasks. It is possible that regulators with a broader mission are more or less likely to be captured. We attempted to disaggregate insurance regulators by mission scope but found no differences in class action filings.

2. Nothing hinges on controlling for population, as similar results obtain using just the absolute number of filings.

3. For a discussion of the impact of judicial elections on tort awards, see Helland and Tabarrok (2000, 2002) and Tabarrok and Helland (1999:157).

4. Exactly which states "elect" judges is open to interpretation. We label a state as electing its judges if the state supreme court and appellate court judges are choose by election. We label states as having partisan elections if judges are chosen in partisan elections or if the parties choose which candidate to run in an election. For example, Ohio is a partisan state because although party affiliation is not listed on the ballot in the general election, the candidates are chosen in partisan primaries. We also list California as an unelected state although trial court judges are elected in California. For more detailed information, see the American Judicature Society's Judicial Selection Methods in the States website at www.judicialselection.us, as well as table 4 (Selection of Appellate Court Judges) and table 6 (Selection and Terms of Trial Court Judges) in Rottman et al. (2006).

5. Larger states elect their judges, which is why we show the results for filings per capita. Without adjusting for population, some of the solid-dot states in Figure 11.2 are hollow, and vice versa; however, more of above-average levels of filings are still in elected states (nine) rather than appointed states (three).

6. This allows for arbitrary nonindependence across observations for a given state.

7. These controls draw on the database produced by Avraham (2011), but we have also examined the relevant statutes in each state to ensure that the reforms are coded correctly as they apply to auto, bad faith, and product liability cases.

8. In general, all of our allegation measures, that is, proportion removed to federal court, proportion certified, and proportion certified for multistate classes, are likely to measure case importance.

9. These findings are consistent with previous research on forum choice. For example Hensler et al. (2000) found that plaintiffs' attorneys choose state courts because of a perception that state courts are more likely to certify a class. Willging and Wheatman (2005) found from a survey of attorneys that perceptions of how state versus federal judges would rule in the case, the source of law, and the residence of the preponderance of the class all influenced forum choice.

10. One possible explanation is that this variable is measuring the substantive law of class certification. States vary in how closely they follow federal Rule 23. Some states, such as Mississippi and Virginia, do not have a general class action rule (Rowe 2008).

11. Pace et al. (2007) found that only 7 percent of state class actions have a regulatory intervention in the case.

References

Avraham, Ronen (2011) "Database of State Tort Law Reforms (DSTLR 4th)." University of Texas Law School Law and Economics Research Paper No. 184, http://papers.ssrn.com/sol3/papers.cfm?abstract_id=902711.

Besley, Timothy, and Stephen Coate (2003) "Elected Versus Appointed Regulators: Theory and Evidence." *Journal of the European Economic Association* 1: 1176–206.

Cramton Roger C. (1995) "Individualized Justice, Mass Torts, and Settlement Class Actions: An Introduction." *Cornell Law Review* 80: 811–36.

Geyth, Charles G. (2003) "Why Judicial Elections Stink." *Ohio State Law Journal* 64: 43–63.

Government Accountability Office (2001) *Motor Vehicle Safety: NHTSA's Ability to Detect and Recall Defective Replacement Crash Parts Is Limited.* GAO-01-215. Washington, D.C.: Government Accountability Office.

Hall, Melina G., and Chris Bonneau (2006) "Does Quality Matter? Challengers in State Supreme Court Elections." *American Journal of Political Science* 50: 20–33.

——— (2008) "Mobilizing Interest: The Effects of Money on Citizen Participation in State Supreme Court Elections." *American Journal of Political Science* 52: 457–70.

Helland, Eric, and Jonathan Klick (2007) "The Tradeoffs Between Regulation and Litigation: Evidence From Insurance Class Actions." *Journal of Tort Law* 1 (3): article 2.

——— (forthcoming) "Regulation and Litigation: Complements or Substitutes?" In F. Buckley, ed., *The American Illness: Essays on the Rule of Law.* New Haven, Conn.: Yale University Press.

Helland, Eric, and Alexander Tabarrok (2000) "Exporting Tort Awards." *Regulation* 23(2): 21.

—— (2002) "The Effect of Electoral Institutions on Tort Awards." *American Law and Economics Review* 4 (2): 341–70.

Hensler, Deborah et al. (2000) *Class Action Dilemmas.* Santa Monica, Calif.: RAND Corporation.

Johnston, Jason, and Joel Wadfogel (2002) "Does Repeat Play Elicit Cooperation? Evidence from Federal Civil Litigation." *Journal of Legal Studies* 31: 39–60.

Pace, Nicholas M. et al. (2007) *Insurance Class Actions in the United States.* Santa Monica, Calif.: RAND Corporation.

Rottman, David B. et al. (2006) *State Court Organization, 2004.* Washington, D.C.: Bureau of Justice Statistics.

Rowe, Thomas D. (2008) "State and Foreign Class-Action Rules and Statutes: Difference From—and Lessons for?—Federal Rule 23." Duke Law School Faculty Scholarship Series Working Paper 108.

Schotland, Roy A. (1985) "Elective Judge's Campaign Financing: Are State Judges' Robes the Emperor's Clothes of American Democracy?" *Journal of Law and Politics* 2: 57–167.

Shavell, Steven (1984a) "Liability for Harm Versus Regulation of Safety." *Journal of Legal Studies* 13: 357–74.

—— (1984b) "A Model of the Optimal Use of Liability and Safety Regulation." *RAND Journal of Economics* 15: 271–80.

Stigler, George J. (1971) "The Theory of Economic Regulation." *Bell Journal of Economics and Management Science* 2: 3–21.

Tabarrok, Alexander, and Eric Helland (1999) "Court Politics: The Political Economy of Tort Awards." *Journal of of Law and Economics* 42: 157.

Willging, Thomas E., and Shannon R. Wheatman (2005) *An Empirical Examination of Attorney's Choice of Forum in Class Action Litigation.* Washington, D.C.: Federal Judicial Center.

Wright, John R. (1996) *Interest Groups and Congress: Lobbying, Contributions, and Influence.* New York: Longman Publishing.

Case Cited

Avery v. State Farm Mutual Auto Insurance, No. 97-L-114, Illinois Circuit Court Illinois (1999), 1999 WL 955543 and 1999 WL1022134.

Chapter 12

Failure by Obsolescence

Regulatory Challenges for the FDA in the Twenty-First Century

Theodore W. Ruger

The U.S. Food and Drug Administration (FDA) may seem a strange candidate for inclusion in a book on regulatory failure. For more than half a century, the FDA has been a high-status icon of the federal administrative state. Few agencies have been as successful at achieving their stated regulatory goals, and few have enjoyed the reputation for technocratic expertise that the FDA has long held among the press and the public (Carpenter 2010). The regulatory regime overseen by the FDA has produced sizeable public health gains over the past sixty years by virtue of ensuring safer food and therapeutic products for U.S. consumers. And in recent decades the FDA has done much to ameliorate a countervailing critique that it has been too careful, and too slow, in approving new therapeutic products: the "drug lag" in U.S. approval times relative to other nations' gatekeeping agencies has largely disappeared since the 1980s (FDA 2010). Even the rare instances of high-profile failure by the FDA in the past several years, when unsafe food or pharmaceuticals have slipped past the agency's scientific safety net, such as with Vioxx in 2004 or the *Salmonella* outbreak in peanut products in 2009, have been met by responsive and targeted congressional and administrative action, suggesting that relevant institutions are able to learn from, and swiftly correct, problematic gaps in the FDA's regulatory oversight (Herper 2007; FDA Food Safety Modernization Act 2011).

Taken together, the FDA's long track record of regulatory achievement has translated into significant reputational gains, and the FDA ranks highly among public opinion polls of the most trusted, effective, and independent federal agencies. According to Daniel Carpenter's compilation of copious survey data over the past several decades, the FDA has "consistently been named or identified as one of the most popular and well-respected agencies in government" (Carpenter 2010:12). Such reputational prestige even occasionally leads the nation's best attorneys to make elementary mistakes of administrative law, as when then White House counsel Lloyd Cutler told FDA commissioner David Kessler in the 1990s that he thought the FDA was an independent agency (Kessler 2001:107). It is not an independent agency but rather part of the U.S. Department of Health and Human Services. Its track record of regulatory success and reputation for scientific expertise and independence raises the question: what's not to like?

Despite the scant evidence of systemic failure looking retrospectively at the FDA's performance over the past half century, looking ahead into the next several decades suggests a different type of "failure" facing the FDA, one borne not of calamitous regulatory incompetence but rather of an increasing marginalization from the most pressing regulatory problems involving food and drugs in the United States. The food supply of the United States is statistically as safe as it has ever been, if safety is defined by an absence of pathogenic or chemical contamination. Yet illnesses relating to the consumption of food still represent the greatest preventable health problem the nation faces, attracting increasing institutional attention outside of the FDA. Likewise for pharmaceuticals and other therapeutic products: the greatest challenges going forward involve allocation, price, and cost-effectiveness, as opposed to abstracted "safety" and "efficacy." Yet the FDA is jurisdictionally limited and bureaucratically disinclined from addressing such issues. The end result going forward is an apparent mismatch between the FDA's core regulatory competencies and the most urgent policy issues in its broader domain. Although hardly an instance of abject "failure," this dynamic suggests that the FDA's long ascendency and reputational prestige in the area of food and drug regulation is destined to wane, as other institutions take up an increasing share of the new century's evolving regulatory challenges in this field.

To illuminate this dynamic of likely regulatory marginalization, I describe in the next section the twentieth-century development of the FDA as an agency with formidable authority over the nation's food and drug supply, but also as an agency with authority and institutional competence directed at the commodified products themselves, abstracted from behavioral concerns relating to production and consumption of those products. I then explain the current policy challenges relating to food and drugs, many of which relate to issues of end-stage pricing, allocation, and consumption as opposed to the intrinsic safety (or lack thereof) of the disembodied product. In the conclusion, I discuss the new shape of food and drug regulation in the twenty-first century and the diminished role the FDA can be expected to play in this new regime. The case of the FDA suggests the possibility of failure by obsolescence, a process by which even relatively successful agencies can fail at their broader missions over time if they are unable or unwilling to adapt in the face of new dynamics in regulatory problems.

The FDA Century

Federal regulation of food and drugs in the United States took shape in incremental form. The Pure Food and Drugs Act of 1906 established a predecessor office to the FDA housed within the U.S. Department of Agriculture, and then the Food, Drug, and Cosmetics Act (FDCA) of 1938 fully realized the federal regulatory framework. The latter statute is, according to one leading scholar, "one of the most important regulatory statutes in American and perhaps global history" (Carpenter 2010:73). Present in the FDCA were almost all of the key elements that would shape the FDA's regulatory posture and preeminence for the remainder of the century: the absolute gatekeeping authority over new drugs, the emphasis on technocratic assessment of product safety, and the regulatory focus on products rather than on firm or individual behavior.

Both the FDCA and its precursor 1906 Act reflected a regulatory concern for products rather than people, for things and words about things rather than primary conduct by producers and consumers. The FDCA's statutory language created a set of adjectival standards to be applied to products that are abstracted out of the stream of commerce: new drugs must be proven "safe" and, after amendments in 1962, "effective" before marketing, and foods must not be "adulterated" or "misbranded" or else face the prospect of government seizure (FDCA 2009:§§ 321, 355). Relatedly, the FDA's ample authority bears on the regulated products most heavily at temporally distinct moments in a particular product's life cycle: at the moment before initial marketing for new drugs and devices and at the period of retail sale for foods. More diffuse patterns of consumption and use, by individual physicians and consumers, have generally been beyond the FDA's jurisdictional ambit. And production of food and drugs is regulated by the FDA only to the extent that it impacts the composition of the finished product.

This product-specific focus of the FDA's jurisdiction was essential in the constitutional culture of its creation, and the agency's early power and prestige derived in part from its ability to enforce food and drug standards directly against offending products. Before the late New Deal "switch in time" in the Supreme Court's Commerce Clause jurisprudence, the federal government's authority over conditions of manufacturing and other features of firm behavior was extremely limited, even as applied to the largest companies (*Hammer v. Dagenhart* 1918). The 1906 Pure Food and Drugs Act and the FDCA avoided this problem for the FDA and its predecessor by giving the federal government authority to proceed directly against offending products in interstate commerce through *in rem* seizure and condemnation proceedings. Beyond generating a bevy of memorable case names, such as *United States v. Two Barrels Desiccated Eggs* (1911), this *in rem* authority lent the FDA ample power to enforce that was undiminished by the Supreme Court's crabbed and categorical reading of the "commerce" power in the 1920s and 1930s. It also helped foster a regulatory dynamic that would persist long after the Commerce Clause was broadened by the Court: the FDA through the twentieth century continued to regulate products more tightly than it did firm or consumer behavior.

Even from the earliest days of federal regulatory presence in the food and drug area, some observers recognized the limitations of the government's focus on product safety as opposed to broader intervention in the structures of production and consumption. *The Jungle*, Upton Sinclair's scandalous exposé of Chicago's meatpacking industry, was a crucial precursor to the 1906 Pure Food and Drugs Act, read and cited by Theodore Roosevelt and other sponsors of the act (Sinclair 1906a). Yet Sinclair himself was disappointed that the act addressed only product purity instead of also regulating labor and production in the food factories themselves, calling the actual policy impact of his book "all accidental" (Sinclair 1906b:49). In 1906, he wrote that in *The Jungle* he had "wished to frighten the country by a picture of what its industrial masters were doing to their victims; [but] entirely by chance I stumbled upon another discovery—what they were doing to the meat supply of the civilized world. In other words, I aimed at the public's heart, and by accident hit it in the stomach" (Sinclair 1906b:49).

Later in the century, other important observers of the FDA would notice, and lament, the incomplete and fragmented nature of the FDA's authority over food and pharmaceuticals. In the late 1950s and early 1960s, Senator Estes Kefauver of Tennessee was the most important federal legislator on FDA topics, chairing the Senate's Committee on Antitrust and Monopoly and authoring the key drug amendments of 1962. During this period, Kefauver recognized problems in the way drugs were sold and priced that went far beyond the FDCA's abstract standard of safety, and in 1961 he advocated amending federal law to reduce patent protection on "me-too" drugs with limited benefits relative to existing therapies and giving the FDA authority to create economic incentives to use cheaper generic alternatives (Carpenter 2010). These concerns about the pricing and relative cost-effectiveness of new drugs clearly resonate today, a half century after Kefauver raised them. But a major drug safety lapse in 1961—the thalidomide tragedy in Europe, which was recognized by acclaimed FDA reviewer Frances Kelsey—shifted congressional attention back to product safety and efficacy concerns, and the resulting drug amendments of 1962 changed the manner in which the FDA assessed safety and efficacy of new drugs without addressing Kefauver's broader concerns about high prices and comparative effectiveness (Carpenter 2010).

The result, then and now, is a drug regulatory regime administered by the FDA that is curiously dichotomous, with substantial gatekeeping authority over certain aspects of new therapies (safety and efficacy) and virtually no authority over other crucial variables, such as a drug's pricing or conditions of use. This dichotomy, and the resultant jurisdictional incapacity on the part of the FDA, is largely driven by statute. The terms of the FDCA as amended permit no direct consideration of a drug's cost by the agency in making its initial approval decision. But in important, if more nuanced, ways, the agency's own practices have extended and perpetuated the acontextual nature of its approval decisions. For instance, over a half century ago, Senator Kefauver and others recognized the perverse effect on overall prices of permitting approval and full patent protection of new drugs that offered only marginal gains, if at all, over existing therapies. But by continuing to adhere to placebo-controlled trials as the gold standard of safety and efficacy research, a choice not necessarily dictated by express statutory terminology, FDA has extended a regime where new compounds are tested abstractly against a placebo rather than comparatively against existing medicines.

This dichotomous regulatory uncoupling of safety and cost is mirrored in the FDA's hands-off approach to regulating the actual conditions of use of pharmaceuticals even as it exercises up-front gatekeeping authority over the ex ante safety and efficacy of those products. The FDA requires scientific proof of safety and efficacy of new drugs under specific conditions of use for treatment of a specified medical condition, but once approved physicians are free to use marketed drugs for treatment of other ailments, in dosages, durations, combination, and patient populations dramatically different from those of the controlled trials used for approval (*Washington Legal Foundation v. Henney* 1999). Early on, this agency disinterest in regulating "off label" use was a necessary compromise against physician resistance to regulation of the "practice of medicine," and it has persisted as a central limitation on FDA control of drug safety. In recent decades, the FDA has taken some steps to depart from this basic model and set conditions or warnings for actual use by physicians, but the basic terms of this regulatory compromise remain.

The FDA's regulation of food products during the twentieth century evinced a similar product-focused dynamic. Such a regulatory posture was exemplified by the FDA's ambitious midcentury effort to develop dozens of "standards of identity" for common foods, essentially commodifying large swaths of the American food supply (Merrill and Collier 1974:242). This effort was based on the premise that American consumers desired, and were best served by, a safe supply of uniform and fungible food products that were disconnected from the particulars of their production.

In sum, in its focus on technical scientific expertise, neutrally applied to products abstracted from the stream of commerce (and the related complexities of production, consumption, and price), the FDA was the quintessential twentieth-century agency, ideal for a world of unbounded consumerism and optimistic faith in the perfecting power of impartial science. The second half of the twentieth century witnessed the apogee of the "consumer's republic" (Cohen 2003), and the FDA was the ideal bureaucratic steward for a nation experiencing sustained growth in both purchasing power and scientific expertise. It is no accident that the agency's most triumphant moment of public acclaim—the 1961 ceremony honoring FDA pharmacologist Frances Kelsey for her role in preventing thalidomide's marketing in the United States—took place at the Kennedy White House also responsible for the Apollo space program. The National Aeronautics and Space Administration (NASA), like the FDA, reflected an optimistic faith in the virtues of scientific achievement to meet society's most urgent goals. But also like NASA, the FDA's fundamental role and its agency culture developed in a time relatively unconcerned with the harsh realities of resource constraints, allocative choices, and tradeoffs grounded in relative benefit assessments.

Today's Food and Drug Policy Problems

The FDA was instrumental in creating a safe and plentiful supply of food and drugs over the past century. Yet it has had little to say about allocating, constraining, or encouraging firm or individual behaviors along the way. The product-specific focus that was essential to the FDA's developing constitutionality and institutional prestige has become a hindrance in the twenty-first century, when the most pressing problems involve the end-stage use and price of the regulated products rather than their abstracted safety. In this changing world, the FDA's core competencies in abstract, acontextual assessment of product safety are increasingly anachronistic.

This point is illustrated by the paradox of the food "safety" situation in the United States today. By many statistical measures, the American food supply is as safe as it has been in history. The risk of severe pathogenic food poisoning is extraordinarily low, accounting for only a few thousand deaths per year in a nation of 300 million (Scallan 2011a, 2011b). And even this relatively low risk is expected to drop further with the enhanced FDA inspection and recall authority granted through the Food Safety Modernization Act of 2011, which implements changes designed to make the FDA more vigilant and responsive to food safety at the factory level. Relatedly, after a flurry of contestation in the 1950s and 1960s over new food additives and preservatives, careful FDA review has generally ameliorated consumer concern over the safety risks of new chemical components in food.

Yet on a different metric, food in the United States is far from "safe." It is actually the single biggest consumer product threat to population health in the nation today, exceeding even tobacco in its present effects on mortality and morbidity. Obesity, type 2 diabetes, coronary disease, and other health conditions related to the overconsumption of food are the single biggest source of preventable deaths in the nation today, accounting for over half a million deaths a year (Heron 2011). Many millions more suffer adverse health effects that impact their productivity and daily functioning. These food-related illnesses are a major driver of ever-increasing healthcare costs in the United States, by some measures accounting for almost a hundred billion dollars in additional medical expenditures each year (Finkelstein et al. 2009). For all of the evident urgency of addressing this obesity epidemic, the FDA's core regulatory paradigm is of only marginal utility: diseases of overconsumption arise from consuming products that are neither "adulterated" or "misbranded" by the FDCA's standards, leaving the FDA remains largely on the sidelines of this major public health crisis.

A similar story of mismatch between the FDA's traditional jurisdiction and core competence is apparent with respect to the most urgent problems in pharmaceutical policy today. Although occasional failures in the FDA-administered drug safety regime do periodically rise to great public salience (e.g., the Vioxx episode of 2004), the FDA continues to perform well in assessing the abstracted "safety" and "efficacy" of new drugs before they enter the market. Yet most current policy discourse about pharmaceuticals emphasizes drug pricing and comparative effectiveness as the key questions for public and private regulation, and these considerations are outside of the FDA's traditional regulatory ambit. Policy scholars, including some key architects of the 2010 Patient Protection and Affordable Care Act (PPACA), have identified variations in physician practice—including in the use of pharmaceuticals—as a major drag on healthcare quality and a major driver of increasing health costs. The FDA's historical inability (or unwillingness) to specify precise conditions of use for the drug products it approves has only encouraged the regime of diffuse individualized physician practice that gives rise to such suboptimal variation. To date, proposals for public or private regulation that would smooth out such variation in the delivery of healthcare look to institutions other than the FDA to fix this problematic authority structure.

The FDA is also jurisdictionally limited and culturally disinclined from considering the cost or cost-effectiveness of the new therapies it considers. This disinclination remains in place even as drug prices escalate to comprise an increasing share of national health expenditures every year and even as the federal government will subsidize increasing amounts of the nation's drug purchasing through Medicare Part D and through the Medicaid and state exchange provisions of the new PPACA. Although broad-based consideration of cost is beyond its statutory mandate, the FDA has made a consistent discretionary choice to avoid consideration of comparative effectiveness as well in its approval of new drugs, even as comparative effectiveness research has become the new holy grail of health economics. The FDA has stuck with the older (and industry-preferred) model of placebo-controlled studies as the gold standard by which to measure the efficacy of new products (FDA 2008), a decision that some have argued has escalated drug costs by facilitating the introduction of expensive "me-too" drugs, which offer only marginal efficacy gains, if any, over existing off-patent therapies.

Looking forward at the development of pharmaceutical regulatory policy over the next decade or more, one can discern a certain kind of subtle "failure" for the FDA. Even as the agency continues to perform its traditional function in assessing the abstract safety and efficacy of marketed products, it is operating in a world where such concerns, when abstracted from the realities of price, comparative effectiveness, and physician usage, will become progressively less important. Put in stark terms, ex ante FDA approval will cease to be the most important regulatory event in a new therapeutic product's life cycle: far more important will be the decision by public and private payors to include that product on their reimbursable formulary.

In sum, largely by statutory constraint and more slightly by its own regulatory choices, the FDA has been relegated to a minor role in addressing the most pressing issues of our time: adult and childhood obesity, rising drug costs, and comparative effectiveness and cost-effectiveness in an increasingly interconnected medical care system. Like NASA, the

FDA now exists as something of an anachronism, a modernist agency in a post-modern world of resource constraints, discretionary tradeoffs, and the imperatives of behavioral change that cannot be adequately addressed by the FDA's traditional, neutral application of scientific expertise.

New Directions in Food and Drug Regulation

In a world where patterns of consumption, pricing, and production of food and drugs have become imperatives, the FDA will continue to maintain a role, but a diminished one. Two policy responses are already emerging that reveal the FDA's diminished importance: multiplicitous regulation and regulation by payment

The first of these, the phenomenon of multiplicitous and multimodal regulation, involves numerous public and private entities at the state and federal levels that work in loose concert toward a given regulatory end. The progress made in reducing youth smoking rates over the past fifteen years illustrates the power of such a coordinated, multiplicitous approach—while also revealing the FDA's relative marginality on the issue. In the 1990s, smoking was identified as the leading preventable cause of death and disease in the United States. Under Commissioner David Kessler, the FDA famously took action to address this public health crisis, issuing new proposed regulations in 1995 that asserted agency jurisdiction over tobacco and ambitiously aimed to cut youth smoking in half in the seven years after promulgation of the new rules (FDA 1995). As is well known, the Supreme Court intervened in the landmark *Brown & Williamson* (2000) case, holding that the FDA lacked jurisdiction over tobacco entirely, thereby disabling the agency's efforts to regulate in the field. What is perhaps less well known is that even though the FDA was pushed to the side by the Court, the agency's stated goal of dramatically reducing youth smoking was almost fully realized. Youth smoking rates dropped from 36.4 percent in 1997 to 21.9 percent in 2003, close to the 50 percent reduction that the FDA had sought in its initial regulations (Centers for Disease Control 2008:689–91).

How did this happen? The answer lies in the range of institutional strategies and governmental interventions that emerged to fill the void created by the FDA's ultimate lack of jurisdiction. Aggressive counter-marketing campaigns by state governments, local bans on the sale or use of tobacco in public places and workplaces, employer disincentives for smoking, innovative state lawsuits, and continued Federal Trade Commission restriction of tobacco marketing all coalesced to achieve substantially the same goal that the FDA had sought in its assertion of regulation. Ultimately, the Supreme Court rebuke to the FDA was a setback for the agency's own jurisdiction and prestige, but less so for the broader policy struggle against tobacco.

This story has clear implications for the pressing policy battle in the decades ahead against obesity and its related health complications. The FDA is both jurisdictionally limited and bureaucratically disinclined to regulate the end-stage consumption of food, which is the greatest driver of population obesity. Yet already a multigovernmental, multiple set of institutions is beginning to address this problem. Although to date neither as coordinated nor as effective as the anti-tobacco efforts of a prior decade, this model of simultaneous and multiplicitous regulation offers the best prospect of achieving necessary behavioral changes in the American populace. Likewise, given the diffuse authority regime in American medicine, efforts to achieve standardization and cost-effectiveness in the use of prescription drugs will be achieved, if at all, only by a complex combination of multiple institutions, including public and private payors, hospitals, and integrated care organizations.

The second new direction in regulation that exacerbates the FDA's marginality is an emerging system of regulation by payment, in which rules for primary conduct are enforced not by traditional coercive regulation but rather by strings attached to government or private payment streams. This new trend accompanies and overlaps with this idea of multiple institutional involvement in achieving public health policy goals. Various public and private institutions are spending increasing amounts of money on food, pharmaceuticals, and medical care, and these institutional payors are becoming increasingly aggressive at attaching policy-related conditions to the funds they disburse. This model of regulation by payment stands in contradistinction to both the traditional model of command-and-control regulation and to the long-standing passivity of payors in the health insurance sector through much of the twentieth century.

Today in the healthcare field, particularly after the 2003 passage of Medicare Part D and the 2010 passage of the PPACA, the federal and state governments are major funders of medical purchasing of pharmaceuticals. Total U.S. expenditures on pharmaceuticals are about $250 billion, and government payors account for almost half of that amount (Kaiser Family Foundation 2009). Although the federal government remains (for now) reluctant to use its ample purchasing power to force price concessions from manufacturers or to encourage shifting to cheaper generics, state governments have already asserted authority through their Medicaid reimbursement policies to shift physician and patient behavior in the area of prescription drugs. Many states use multiple policy incentives and reimbursement criteria in their Medicaid programs to nudge or force prescribers to choose generic drugs over more expensive branded products, and such efforts have produced tangible policy payoff: from 2005 to 2009 the percentage of total prescriptions nationally that were filled with brand-name drugs fell from 40 percent to 25.6 percent (National Conference of State Legislatures 2010). Similar reimbursement incentives and restrictions have been implemented by private health insurance companies, and such targeted payment policies have stemmed the tide of pharmaceutical cost growth. From 2000 to 2005, pharmaceuticals were the most rapidly increasing component of national health costs (growing at about 11 percent per year), but since 2005 national drug expenses represent a rare systemic cost control success story, with increases of only about 3 percent per year.

In this world of restrictive and cost-conscious reimbursement policy, it is possible to imagine what would have been unthinkable only a few decades ago—namely, that within ten years the most important federal agency with jurisdiction over pharmaceuticals will not be the FDA but rather the Center for Medicare and Medicaid Services or some successor entity that decides which subset of approved drugs are cost-effective enough to include on the shrinking formulary for Medicare, Medicaid, and other publicly funded insurance plans. In the twenty-first century, the key question for patients, physicians, and pharmaceutical companies will increasingly be whether a drug is approved for reimbursement by public and private payors rather than whether it is "safe" and "effective" in the FDA's eyes. Products in the former group will be an increasingly small subset of the latter.

Although most individual food purchases are not directly subsidized by third-party payors, federal and state governments are actively involved in purchasing or subsidizing billions of dollars of food for segments of the population, and here too payors are beginning to exercise a more active, or directive, approach. By way of example, the U.S. Department of Agriculture (USDA) spends 3.5 times more annually on subsidized school lunches ($14 billion) than the entire yearly budget of the FDA ($4 billion), and with this huge funding stream comes the opportunity to compel healthier menus at tens of thousands of local schools. Under the Obama administration, the USDA has begun to require that recipient school districts offer a menu of healthy options for their students and remove those foods and beverages that increase public health risks. State and local governments are enacting similar policies for both school lunch and food stamp programs. Looking ahead on this dimension, the muscular funding discretion of the USDA, alongside a multi-faceted mix of state, local, and private actors, will likely perform more important functions relating to public health and food consumption in the years ahead than will the FDA.

Conclusion

Despite the increasing shift of policy relevance to institutions outside of the FDA, on some more incremental issues touching crucial food and drug policy questions the FDA retains significant discretionary authority, which it could use to remain an important player in addressing the major public health issues of the twenty-first century. To date, the agency interest in using its discretion has been inconsistent—occasionally taking account of new imperatives but more typically being slow to shift from its earlier model. The prime example of the agency's tone-deafness to new considerations on the effectiveness of drugs has been its refusal, in most cases, to require or encourage comparative effectiveness trials in the testing of new drugs. In its ongoing administrative practice, and in a recent rulemaking on foreign clinical trials, the FDA continues to adhere to placebo controls as the gold standard of efficacy research (FDA 2008), a view that is at odds with the emerging consensus among health policy scholars as well as other parts of the federal government itself, such as the National Institutes of Health and the 2009 economic stimulus law's funding of comparative effectiveness analysis.

However, in a recent case involving a treatment to lower the risk of premature birth, the FDA skillfully made use of its own procedural discretion to permit a cheaper unapproved therapy to remain accessible even after the agency had approved for the same condition a patented treatment that cost exponentially more. For years, physicians had written prescriptions for a particular progesterone gel to be compounded at individual pharmacies for their obstetric patients who were at risk for premature delivery. Yet by operation of FDA rule, approval of a new therapy through a formal New Drug Application (NDA) presumptively makes unlawful the continued compounding of that same substance in individual pharmacies. In early 2011, the FDA approved just such an NDA for a branded version of the progesterone gel called Makena. The effect of the normal trumping created by the NDA would have been disastrous from a cost perspective: the newly approved product was monopoly priced at \$30,000 per pregnancy, as compared with about \$400 per pregnancy for the pharmacy-compounded version (Armstrong 2011). Soon after becoming aware of these price implications, the FDA mooted the issue by using an ambiguity inherent in its own rules to exempt the pharmacists who made this particular substance from the ordinary application of the NDA trumping rule. This action had a doubly salutary cost effect—the low-cost pharmacy compounding option remained, accessible to those physicians and patients who preferred it, and the price of Makena itself (the branded product) was halved by the manufacturer (Armstrong 2011). Although the FDA never acknowledged any consideration of price in its decision to exempt pharmacy compounding in this case, such concerns unquestionably motivated the agency's swift action, and this nimble response by the agency is exactly the kind of incremental activity that the FDA can and ought to pursue in the future to increase its relevance and policy responsiveness

The FDA has long been a jewel of the federal administrative state, acclaimed for its notable regulatory successes and its culture of technocratic independence. Its continuing jurisdiction over developing technologies such as individualized and genetic medicine and other new innovations will assure it of some contemporary relevance in select areas. However, for the reasons I have presented in this chapter, the shifting imperatives of food and drug policy in the twenty-first century have created a policy world where the FDA will cede some of its traditional predominance. Today's most pressing food and drug problems arise from the way we use, consume, and pay for such products, and these are variables outside of FDA's traditional jurisdiction and core competency.

References

Armstrong, Joanne (2011) "Unintended Consequences—The Cost of Preventing Preterm Births After FDA Approval of a Branded Version of 170HP." *New England Journal of Medicine* 364: 1689–91.

Carpenter, Daniel (2010) *Reputation and Power: Organizational Image and Pharmaceutical Regulation at the FDA.* Princeton, N.J.: Princeton University Press.

Centers for Disease Control (2008) "Cigarette Use Among High School Students—United States, 1999–2007." *Morbidity and Mortality Weekly Report* 57 (June 27): 689–91.

Cohen, Lizabeth, (2003) *A Consumers' Republic: The Politics of Mass Consumption in Postwar America.* New York: Vintage Books.

Finkelstein, Eric et al. (2009) "Annual Medical Spending Attributable to Obesity: Payer- and Service-Specific Estimates." *Health Affairs* 28(5): w822–w831.

Heron, Melonie (2011) "Deaths: Leading Causes for 2007." *National Vital Statistics Report* 59 (August): 1–96.

Herper, Matthew (2007) "The Biggest FDA Reform in a Decade." *Forbes*, September 24. http://www.forbes.com/2007/09/21/drugs-safety-fda-biz-sci-cx_mh_0924fda.html, accessed November 28, 2011.

Kaiser Family Foundation (2009) *Report: Trends in Health Care Costs and Spending.* http://www.kff.org/insurance/index.cfm, accessed November 21, 2011.

Kessler, David (2001) *A Question of Intent: A Great American Battle with a Deadly Industry.* New York: Perseus Press.

Merrill, Richard A., and Earl M. Collier, Jr. (1974) "Like Mother Used to Make: An Analysis of FDA Food Standards of Identity." *Columbia Law Review* 74: 561–621.

National Conference of State Legislatures (2010) "Use of Generic Prescription Drugs and Brand-Name Discounts." *Health Cost Containment and Efficiencies: NCSL Briefs for State Legislators,* June, 1–6.

Scallan, Elaine et al. (2011a) "Foodborne Illness Acquired in the United States—Major Pathogens." *Emerging Infectious Diseases* 17 (January): 7–15.

———(2011b) "Foodborne Illness Acquired in the United States—Unspecified Agents." *Emerging Infectious Diseases* 17 (January): 16–22.

Sinclair, Upton (1906a) *The Jungle.* New York: Doubleday.

———(1906b) "What Life Means to Me." *Cosmopolitan* 41 (October): 594–96.

U.S. Food and Drug Administration (1995) "Proposed Rule: Regulations Restricting the Sale and Distribution of Cigarettes and Smokeless Tobacco Products." *Federal Register* 60 (August 11): 41314.

——— (2008) "Final Rule, Human Subject Protection; Foreign Clinical Studies Not Conducted Under an Investigational New Drug Application." *Federal Register* 73 (April 28): 22800.

——— (2010) *White Paper: Prescription Drug User Fee Act (PDUFA): Adding Resources and Improving Performance in FDA Review of New Drug Applications.* http://www.fda.gov/ForIndustry/UserFees/PrescriptionDrugUserFee /ucm119253.htm, accessed November 28, 2011.

Cases Cited

FDA v. Brown & Williamson Tobacco Corp., 529 U.S. 120 (2000).

Hammer v. Dagenhart, 247 U.S. 251 (1918).

United States v. Two Barrels Desiccated Eggs, 185 F. 302 (D. Minn. 1911).

Washington Legal Foundation v. Henney, 56 F. Supp.2d 81 (D.D.C. 1999).

Statutes Cited

Federal Food, Drug, and Cosmetic Act of 1938, 21 U.S.C. §§301–399 (1938 and subsequent amendments) (2006 & Supp. 2009).

FDA Food Safety Modernization Act, Pub. L. No. 111-353, 124 Stat. 3885 (2011).

Patient Protection and Affordable Care Act, Pub. L. No. 111-148, 124 Stat. 119 (2010).

Pure Foods and Drugs Act of 1906, 34 Stat. 768.

Contributors

Jonathan Baron

Jonathan Baron is Professor of Psychology at the University of Pennsylvania. He studies intuitions and judgment biases that impede maximization of utility. He is the editor of the journal *Judgment and Decision Making* and a consulting editor to the *Journal of Behavioral Decision Making* and the *Journal of Legal Analysis*. He holds a secondary appointment at the Wharton School and is a senior fellow at the Leonard Davis Institute and the Wharton Risk Center.

Matthew A. Baum

Matthew A. Baum is Marvin Kalb Professor of Global Communications and Professor of Public Policy at Harvard's John F. Kennedy School of Government. His research focuses on the domestic sources of foreign policy and the role of the mass media and public opinion in contemporary politics. He is the author of *Soft News Goes to War: Public Opinion and American Foreign Policy in the New Media Age* and *War Stories: The Causes and Consequences of Public Views of War*.

Lori S. Bennear

Lori S. Bennear is Assistant Professor of Environmental Economics and Policy at the Nicholas School of the Environment, Duke University. Her research focuses on evaluating the effectiveness of nontraditional environmental policies, including information disclosure regulations and management-based regulations. She received a Ph.D. in public policy from Harvard University in 2004, an M.A. in economics from Yale in 1996, and an A.B. in economics and environmental studies from Occidental College in 1995.

William W. Bratton

William W. Bratton is Nicholas F. Gallicchio Professor of Law at the University of Pennsylvania Law School. He writes on business law, bringing an interdisciplinary perspective to a wide range of subjects that encompass corporate governance, corporate finance, accounting, corporate legal history, and comparative corporate law. His book, *Corporate Finance: Cases and Materials*, is the leading law school text on the subject.

Christopher Carrigan

Christopher Carrigan is Assistant Professor of Public Policy and Public Administration at the George Washington University Trachtenberg School of Public Policy and Public Administration. Previously a Regulation Fellow with the Penn Program on Regulation at the University of Pennsylvania Law School, his research examines the impacts of organizational characteristics and political forces on the behavior of government regulatory agencies. He received a Ph.D. from the Harvard Kennedy School of Government and an M.B.A. from the University of Chicago.

Cary Coglianese

Cary Coglianese is Edward B. Shils Professor of Law and Professor of Political Science and Director of the Penn Program on Regulation at the University of Pennsylvania Law School. He specializes in the study of regulation and regulatory processes, with a particular emphasis on empirical evaluation of alternative regulatory strategies. He is the founder and faculty advisor to *RegBlog.org* and co-editor of *Import Safety: Regulatory Governance in the Global Economy*, also published by the University of Pennsylvania Press.

Eric Helland

Eric Helland is Robert J. Lowe Professor of Economics at Claremont McKenna College and a senior economist at the RAND Corporation. He has been senior economist at the Council of Economic Advisors, a visiting professor of economics at the Stigler Center for the Study of the Economy and the State at the University of Chicago, and a visiting professor of law at UCLA and USC.

Jonathan Klick

Jonathan Klick is Professor of Law at the University of Pennsylvania Law School. His work focuses on identifying the causal effects of laws and regulations on individual behavior using cutting-edge econometric tools. His research has addressed a host of issues, including the relationship between abortion access and risky sex, the health behaviors of diabetics, the effect of police on crime, addiction as rational choice, and how liability exposure affects the labor market for physicians.

Adam J. Levitin

Adam J. Levitin is Professor of Law at the Georgetown University Law Center. He specializes in bankruptcy, commercial law, and financial regulation, with recent research focusing on consumer and housing finance, payments, and debt restructuring.

William T. McEnroe

William T. McEnroe is an associate at Dechert LLP. He holds a B.A. from the University of Pennsylvania and a J.D. from the University of Pennsylvania Law School. He served as a law clerk with the U.S. District Court for the Eastern District of Pennsylvania and on the editorial board of the *University of Pennsylvania Law Review.*

Susan L. Moffitt

Susan L. Moffitt is Mary Tefft and John Hazen White Sr. Assistant Professor of Political Science and Public Policy at Brown University. Her research focuses on the development, distribution, and use of knowledge in government agencies, with particular emphasis on pharmaceutical regulation and on elementary and secondary education policy.

Christopher Poliquin

Christopher Poliquin is a research associate at the Harvard Business School. He holds a B.A. in philosophy, politics, and economics from the University of Pennsylvania.

Roberta Romano

Roberta Romano is Sterling Professor of Law and director of the Yale Law School Center for the Study of Corporate Law. Her research has focused on state competition for corporate charters, the political economy of takeover regulation, shareholder litigation, institutional investor activism, and financial market regulation. She is a fellow of the American Academy of Arts and Sciences and the European Corporate Governance Institute and a research associate of the National Bureau for Economic Research.

Theodore W. Ruger

Theodore W. Ruger is Professor of Law at the University of Pennsylvania Law School. He teaches and writes in the areas of constitutional law, health law, and pharmaceutical regulation. His scholarship brings fresh insight to the study of some of the oldest questions of American law—namely, the justifications for, and empirical contours of, the application of judicial authority. In exploring these issues, Ruger supplements traditional legal analysis with the methods of history and political science.

W. Kip Viscusi

W. Kip Viscusi is University Distinguished Professor of Law, Economics, and Management at Vanderbilt University and co-director of Vanderbilt's Ph.D. Program in Law and Economics. He has also been a professor at Harvard, Duke, and Northwestern Universities. Viscusi is the author of more than twenty books and three hundred articles, most of which focus on different aspects of health and safety risks. He is the founding editor of the *Journal of Risk and Uncertainty*.

Michael L. Wachter

Michael L. Wachter is William B. Johnson Professor of Law and Economics at the University of Pennsylvania Law School. He specializes in law and economics, with his current research focusing on topics of corporate law, corporate finance, and labor law and economics. Since 1984, he has served as a director of the Institute for Law and Economics, a nationally recognized center that focuses on cutting-edge issues in corporate governance and corporate finance.

Susan M. Wachter

Susan M. Wachter is Richard B. Worley Professor of Financial Management and Professor of Real Estate and Finance at the Wharton School of the University of Pennsylvania. She also is Professor of City and Regional Planning at Penn Design and co-director of the University of Pennsylvania's Institute of Urban Research. An expert in mortgage and real estate markets, she served as assistant secretary of policy development and research from 1998 to 2001 at the Department of Housing and Urban Development.

Jason Webb Yackee

Jason Webb Yackee is Assistant Professor of Law at the University of Wisconsin Law School. He works on issues of international investment law, international economic relations, foreign arbitration, and administrative law and politics. His latest article, "Breaking the Myth of Ossification," appears in the *George Washington Law Review*.

Susan Webb Yackee

Susan Webb Yackee is Associate Professor of Political Science and Public Affairs at the University of Wisconsin—Madison. Her research focuses on regulation, public management, and the politics of the policymaking process. Her most recent article, "Lobbying Coalitions and Government Policy Change: An Analysis of Federal Agency Rulemaking," appears in the *Journal of Politics.*

Richard Zeckhauser

Richard Zeckhauser is Frank P. Ramsey Professor of Political Economy at the Kennedy School of Government at Harvard University. Regulation and uncertainty have been themes of his work over many years. He examines humans' poor performance in dealing with uncertainty due to behavioral propensities, misestimated probabilities, and poorly structured incentives. Zeckhauser is an elected fellow of the Econometric Society, the Institute of Medicine (National Academy of Sciences), and the American Academy of Arts and Sciences.

Index

Acknowledgments

This book's scholarly addition to the dialogue about regulation in the United States could exist only due to the cooperation of many individuals. I am grateful first and foremost to the authors who have contributed chapters. Obviously any edited volume depends on its authors, but in this case they deserve special commendation for their timely responses to many demanding deadlines, allowing this volume to appear in print at a time of continued relevant debate over regulation.

I would also like to thank the commentators and other participants at the workshop the Penn Program on Regulation organized around the draft chapters of this book, especially Richard Berk, Adam Finkel, Jill Fisch, Robert A. Kagan, Howard Kunreuther, Jerry Mashaw, John Mendeloff, and David Zaring. I appreciate the insights Richard L. Revesz shared with us as the workshop's keynote speaker.

The collaboration that underpins this book reflects the distinctive, cross-disciplinary character of the institutions that have nurtured it: the Penn Program on Regulation, Penn Law, and the University of Pennsylvania.

Dean Michael A. Fitts's exceptional energy has been absolutely instrumental in fostering Penn Law's vibrant intellectual environment. His commitment to cross-disciplinary enterprises, including the school's law and public policy initiative of which this book project is a part, has been truly visionary.

This project was also made possible thanks to the generous and much-appreciated support of Allen J. Model and the Leo Model Foundation, as well as additional assistance provided by the University of Pennsylvania's Office of the Provost.

The Penn Program on Regulation's research fellow, Chris Carrigan, not only served as my co-author on the opening chapter but also played integral roles on the overall project, from start to finish. Among Penn Law's capable and dedicated staff, Anna Gavin stands out for her valued support in both organizing our workshop and processing the manuscript. Jennifer Evans also ably assisted with the manuscript.

I would like to express my appreciation for the keen interest and expert guidance of my editor at the University of Pennsylvania Press, Bill Finan, with whom it was again a delight to work. In addition to the team at the Press, Hope Steele provided solid and timely assistance with copyediting and proofreading.

Anyone who works on a book motivated by calamities and institutional breakdowns becomes acutely aware of human error. Thus, at the same time I express my sincere gratitude to all the organizations and individuals I have named here, I want to be clear that they should in no way be assumed to agree with everything in this book nor should they be held responsible for any errors—or should I say, breakdowns—contained herein.